A TIME OUT OF JOINT

A TIME OUT OF JOINT

A Journey from Nazi Germany to Post-War Britain

Roland Hill

The Radcliffe Press
LONDON • NEW YORK

Published in 2007 by The Radcliffe Press
6 Salem Road, London W2 4BU

In the United States and in Canada
distributed by Palgrave Macmillan, a division of St Martin's Press
175 Fifth Avenue, New York NY 10010

ISBN 978 1 84511 495 4

A full CIP record for this book is available from the British Library
A full CIP record for this book is available from the Library of Congress

Library of Congress Catalog card: available

Typeset in Sabon by Oxford Publishing Services, Oxford
Printed and bound in Great Britain by TJ International, Padstow

Contents

List of Illustrations

Preface

My life has been multinational, long and varied, but the Latin saying *ubi bene, ibi patria* (home is where I am doing well) was not meant for me, for the four countries I can call my own have become so through good and bad times. Although born in Hamburg, my formative years were spent in what was truly my *motherland*, Austria, which, after Hitler took over, we managed to exchange for Italy, to which I lost my heart, not just sentimentally, but lastingly by eventually marrying a Roman, my late and beloved Amelia. Great Britain came last when, aged nearly 18, I arrived alone at London's Victoria station on the last day of July 1939. My assets consisted of a white £5 note, which my mother had saved for me, and of course was then worth considerably more than it would be today. I managed not to touch it for a long time on my new and strange island.

However, I was a fairly bright teenager and streetwise long before that term came into use. As an only child, I was accustomed to a certain amount of independence and was insatiable in wanting to know the *pourquoi du pourquoi*. Picture books became my first companions and I had a strange craze for cutting bits and pieces out of newspapers, so perhaps I was meant to become a journalist, as I did. At any rate, in my teens I also had a bent for trying to connect disparate literary, religious, philosophical and historical thoughts. While I admit that my accumulated intellectual baggage was pretty chaotic, it was extensive. In Chamberlain's England I profited from the gentle initiation into the Second World War through its so-called 'phoney' phase, though it was not at all that for the poor Poles. Nevertheless, it enabled me to get to know my new surroundings, mainly behind stapled sandbags and in circumstances the stoic British grimly referred to as 'business as usual'. I had with me a few introductions from abroad, so I was hospitably invited to English homes and an official tribunal invested me with the nice-sounding status of 'friendly alien' and 'refugee from Nazi oppression', which made people agreeably sorry for me, meaning that I had not to be locked up for what they called 'the duration', but could get on with the intricacies of learning the English language. I paid a weekly visit to Bloomsbury House, then the headquarters of refugee organizations and a veritable warren of central Europeans, to collect a weekly assistance of one pound and five shillings. That actually, and incomprehensibly today, paid for my keep and even left two shilling and six pence over for wine, women and song.

This happy existence ended on 12 May 1940 when the Germans attacked the Low Countries and France, and there were rumours of dangerous 'fifth columnists'. The war was getting hot and the British, growing slightly worried, said: 'intern the lot'. Having spent that weekend with friends in Cambridge, where the police came on Sunday morning to arrest a German boy of my age, they said to me: 'You had better come along too.' There followed a train journey to Liverpool, where the streets from the station were lined with people angrily shouting 'bloody Germans' at our lot, which consisted mainly of harmless young and elderly Jews, German Catholic priests and members of various religious orders who had found refuge in this country. We were taken to Douglas on the Isle of Man and accommodated in former boarding houses along the sea promenade, though the high barbed wire fence and armed soldiers guarding it detracted from its holiday atmosphere. For me too the war had now begun in earnest.

Later that summer, at the time of the fall of France and the British evacuation from Dunkirk, some of us younger people were sent to Canada, where the concentration-camp-like watch towers were even higher, though the camp food was a definite improvement on the Isle of Man's. Nevertheless, we longed for freedom and a chance to choose this came quite soon for those of us prepared to 'volunteer' to take 'the King's shilling' and join the British army. I was among them. It entailed crossing the Atlantic again through the menace of German submarines to heavily blitzed 'Blighty'. However, we were keen to 'do our bit' and share the common burden, which the British as yet were carrying alone. In khaki, we certainly looked and were, as our English sergeant-major put it, 'a terrible shower', and some of the British civilian population, used to thinking of their soldiers in traditional national and patriotic ways, may even have

thought of us as a kind of Judas. We were advised to change our
German names in case we were taken prisoners of war, since
Nazi Germany would made short shrift of such traitors. But this
war was decidedly not of the traditional 'my country right or
wrong' sort and the noble British cause to free the world of
Hitler was very much our own.

After my stunt among the Pioneer Corps navvies, I was transferred to the Scots of the Highland Light Infantry, so donned a
Tam o'shanter or Glengarry cap to take part in the invasion of
Normandy and the subsequent Dutch and German campaigns. I
had reached the dizzy heights of staff-sergeant, helping to start
up the new democratic press in my native Germany. I never wore
a kilt, I am afraid. In wartime the Scots kept it jealously to
themselves and as not fit for scarcely even Anglicized soldiers,
but allowed us at least to cover our heads like temporary and
honorary members of the race.

Eventually, His Majesty released me into Civvy Street with the
parting gift of a double-breasted grey suit with soft felt hat. It
made me look, though unconvincingly, like Al Capone.
Moreover, HMG paid for me to complete my higher education,
which had been neglected in the sergeants' mess, and I enrolled
for a history degree at the University of London's King's College.
At this time I lived in digs in London's bed-sitter land and
cooked my meals on a gas ring. However, as a veteran
approaching my thirties, I felt rather too old for *Gaudeamus
igitur*. Still, I did my best to do what was expected, to
demonstrate in the streets for all kinds of good causes. I was glad
to have played a leading part in promoting our women students'
human rights by agreeing that they should be allowed to wear
the revolutionary long-skirted 'New Look'. The British sexual
revolution was happily far away, having been fixed rather
arbitrarily by Philip Larkin at 1963.

I was then offered an apprenticeship as a journalist on the
Catholic weekly, the *Tablet*, which I hope improved my written
English. Five years later, I embarked on my real professional
career as a London correspondent for leading newspapers and
publishers in the new Federal German Republic and Austria. My
job was to report on British political and cultural affairs, and at
a time when this country still carried great prestige for having
liberated Europe. The traditional ways, which even the British
liked to describe as 'second to none', were, however, becoming

noticeably jaded as the country slid from its former heights of Empire and Commonwealth down to a mere middle-ranking power. It was the wrong moment, in my view, to become inward-looking and to embark on the belated creation of a welfare state and National Health Service – yet another of those pretentious 'second to nones'. Instead, they should have learnt from the defeated Germans how not to do it. They, with characteristic Bismarckian and Prussian efficiency, had done that nearly 100 years earlier, with the then in mode obsession of the French Revolution for *liberté* and *égalité*, but noticeably less *fraternité*. It was organized from an all-powerful authoritarian state downwards, rather than from the individual upwards, unlike the way the English had developed their institutions in the past.

So an increasingly prosperous and united postwar Europe missed a great chance, for at first, at any rate, it was quite prepared to take lessons in practical democracy from their victorious British liberators. But the British had more important matters on their minds. Their course was to lead them from a society of freer opportunities in trade and enterprise, where excellence mattered rather than mediocrity in schools and higher education. And in the decades of the twentieth century they decided to discard what was good in their Westminster tradition and to replace it with their own kind of elected prime-ministerial dictatorship; not to speak of what they then achieved in breaking European records in crime, over-crowded prisons, the divorce rate and family breakdowns, as well as immigrants willing to do the jobs the British no longer wanted or were qualified to do.

The Christian virtue of loving your neighbour might not have been a particularly British one, but the British continued to be comparatively good at getting on with their neighbours, occasionally even smiling at them in the shops, the underground or during the rush hour, which is not how our continental neighbours were used to behaving. In Germany, Austria, France and Italy, people sit in much more comfortable modernized public conveyances and glare at those sitting opposite them. The British smile was so pleasantly neutral that it brightened your day. Was it not an Englishman, the great John Donne, who first told the world that 'No man is an island, entire of itself, but a part of the main'? Did the poor postwar British really have to become that insular? Instead, London indulged in allegedly and briefly 'swinging' in newly long-haired fashion. It was almost as though it had taken a leaf out of 'gay' Berlin after the First World War, attracting the Auden and Isherwood generation. Similarly, the British metropole became a magnet for a new breed of young continental au pairs and others rejoicing in their newfound sexual emancipation. As London correspondent I then received countless letters from anxious German and Austrian mothers asking me to find their lost daughters who were possibly nursing a coloured baby in one of the suburbs.

However, I remain thankful that not all that was good in the civilized values for which Great Britain was renowned in the past has been repudiated. It is still a relatively tolerant society that puts up with the most varied oddities, political and religious, that were once part of an honoured non-conformist tradition. It is still prepared to swim against the tide, but for how much longer? Naturally I am glad that it opened its doors to me at a time when no one else would and thereby saved my life. I also remain attached to all that was great and good, though disregarded, in the German, Austrian and Italian past. Nations like individuals clearly have their ups and downs, and never simultaneously. Every new generation finds good reasons to grieve over the alleged and real sins of their fathers, which, with passing time, seem to assume more forgiving aspects. By knowing so much more than our ancestors, we tend to shrink from appreciating what they did know, for human nature changes its bad ways very little through the ages.

In my case, I feel a primary debt to my musical Viennese mother for her firm belief that 'everybody can sing'. Behind that view was a professional's experience that voices are ruined by bad teachers, just as goodness is ruined by bad people. To both my parents I owe their respect for great ideals and all the arts, for keeping our house full of books and guiding me a little to roam among them. Among my memories there will always be that last sight, 70 years ago, of my old grandmother, my father's mother, leaning on her stick and tearfully waving to us on our Hamburg departure. She was destined for a very different 'journey into the distant world', as she humorously wrote in her last letter, quoting the German Romantic poet, Eichendorff whom she had learnt by heart in school. But she did not mean to be taken by an overcrowded Nazi cattle truck to Theresinstadt concentration camp and allowed on that journey hardly any belongings apart from her beloved duvet, under which, as we later unofficially learnt, she died peacefully of old age shortly after her arrival.

From my youth I have good reason to remember Fritz, my Austrian scout leader, who was instrumental in converting me, brought up as a Lutheran Protestant, to the Catholic faith, which I have gladly kept even though since finding out that man makes his religions in his own image, and that this also covers a divine institution like the Catholic Church, run with God's help by fallible men throughout the ages. That is why I regard myself as fortunate in having met, early on, a great man like Friedrich Wilhelm Foerster, the German educationist. He used to be compared with a man walking up and down outside a Catholic Church in the rain, showing generations of readers of his books the way in, though remaining outside. The reason was that the pre-Second Vatican Council Church had become too dogma-bound and Pharisaical for an intelligent man of his modern scientific outlook to remain a believer. In Milan there was another older friend, E. E. Baumbach, the poet who belonged to the Stefan George *Kreis*, the exclusive circle that great non-Nazi poet had gathered around himself, and sympathetically helped me over my own difficult teenage phase. Young people, I think, need such elderly friends to look up to and learn from if for some good reason their parents are not always there to play that role.

My journalistic career and remaining historical interests meant keeping in touch with like-minded friends in the diplomatic and scholarly world. These included Christoph Cornaro, Bernard Stillfried, Richard Sickinger and their families in Austria, Hermann Herder and Wolfgang Borgmann in Germany, not to mention my numerous godchildren in this country and abroad. Among English writers I feel a special regard for Ferdinand Mount, the former editor of the *Times Literary Supplement* who taught me what journalists rarely learn under the pressure of deadlines, 'to dwell more'. This was also what Goethe bid the fleeting moment by telling it – *Verweile doch, du bist so schön* (rest a while, you are so beautiful). Whether or not I have learnt that, I was pleased, after my retirement from professional journalism, to be able to return, as one might return to a first love, to historical research and writing books in German and English.

The granddaughter of the English Catholic and Liberal historian Lord Acton was the wife of Douglas Woodruff, the then editor of the *Tablet*. Both of them had befriended me on my first arrival in London. They also encouraged me to write Acton's biography, which I was able to do only in my retirement. He was a man after my own heart and mind, having famously coined the phrase: 'Power tends to corrupt and absolute power corrupts absolutely. Great men are almost always bad men,' but also because he was at home in four languages and countries. He ended his life as Cambridge Regius professor of modern history, having first begun his studies under the well-known Munich Catholic historian Ignaz von Döllinger and later marrying Marie-von Arco-Valley, the daughter of his mother's Italian cousin. For me this meant consulting the voluminous Acton papers preserved by Cambridge University Library on weekly visits and staying with dear Cambridge friends, Martin and Theresa Brett in typical but lovably professorial disorder, such as Acton had himself enjoyed in his time. A life's circle thus closed happily also for me at Cambridge. My biography, published by Yale University Press in 2000, was well received internationally and led also to me producing my own German version. This at least introduced the great 'Historian of Liberty', though too late unfortunately to be listened to in the country he always regarded as 'his'.

Fairly late in my life, when I was nearly fifty, I married Amelia whom I had known for many years in London. She was the granddaughter of a well-known Roman *sindaco* (mayor) Ernesto Nathan who had been a close protégé of Giuseppe Mazzini's. It was through my mother who had to spend the war years on her own in Italy, that I met Amelia, for she had been for a time Amelia's housekeeper in Rome. When she came to London my mother naturally gave her my address, but she did not immediately contact me. Then, sometime later, when I was laid up with a bad cold, my mother wrote to her, enclosing a pound note and asking her to buy and cook me a chicken. Amelia, well-off in Rome, had a hard life in London making ends meet, but the appeal to her good heart won her over. The chicken did it! However, she also happened to be beautiful, elegant, intelligent, bilingual and generally on my wave length.

She opened up some wholly new aspects of life to me. When eventually we were able to get married, our house in Wimbledon became a veritable haven for sick and healthy animals, cats, dogs, pigeons, squirrels and even a duck, all of which were eventually embalmed and kept on a high shelf in Amelia's office.

Her main claim to fame, however, the crowning achievement

of her life, was to have conquered the food and other allergies by which she had been plagued for years at a time when medical 'experts' used to pooh-pooh the mere idea that supposed allergies might have had some physical cause. She, however, was equally sure that these allergies came from her body rather than from a sick mind.

In 1987 she founded Action Against Allergy, as I helped her to call it, and it became a very successful organization with many branches at home and abroad. It became a registered charity and pressure group both for the conversion of 'unbelieving' doctors and to help thousands of allergy sufferers with advice on how to cope with their problems by themselves. Although the basic causes of these allergies to a range of foods and substances is still not fully understood, medical science is at least and at last taking the illness seriously. Before her own sad death from natural causes Amelia was fittingly honoured for her work both in her native Italy and in Great Britain. Her determination and stamina to pursue her aim to the end were undoubtedly among her finest and most admirable qualities.

1

The End of the Beginning

In mid-May 1945, a week after the war in Europe had ended, I returned to Hamburg, the city of my birth, which I had left only 12 years before. I came disguised as a so-called 'Tommy' in the khaki uniform of an Allied soldier. I had taken part in the Normandy landings and subsequent campaigns in France, Holland and Belgium. I was now a staff sergeant in the Highland Light Infantry, with a smart Glengarry cap worn somewhat jauntily with two black streamers down my back. I was 24 and a member of the press section of the British army of occupation. If my general demeanour was of a victor, it was a self-conscious one, causing some stares from passers-by, though not unfriendly ones. The British occupiers were by now a familiar sight in Germany's second largest city, and its inhabitants had remained what they had always been – open to the outside world. Linked through their port with the world's trade routes, they were used to odd-looking strangers. Moreover, familiar with the principle of 'live and let live', they paid no further attention to this particular alien, the more so because he did not behave like one and seemed to know his way about on that fine and peaceful spring morning.

Those German faces, many of them smiling and chatting, busy as in any big city, seemed more than anything else to reflect relief that the war had ended – Hitler's war, not theirs, as many of these survivors would probably feel by now, with some under-standable self-deception. Some weeks had passed since the Führer's Berlin bunker suicide with his mistress Eva Braun. What mattered more to Germans now that Hitler's promised millennium had failed to materialize, was that the air raid sirens were silent, and the destruction, death and suffering that invariably followed in their wake was over. No defeat was ever

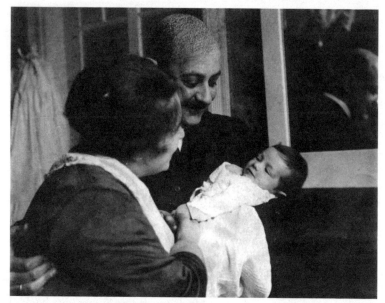

1. Admiring their one and only. December 1920.

more joyfully accepted, whether or not it was to be a lasting rest from arms.

I remembered my way about as though I had only been away briefly and took a tram to Eppendorf, the suburb where we had lived. While only 20 minutes' away from the centres of aerial destruction in the inner city and port areas, except for a mound of rubble here and there between tenement blocks, it was relatively undamaged. I soon passed familiar sights of my childhood and early teens, parks and playgrounds, as I seemed to have left them years ago. I found this return journey an unusually moving experience, though naturally I was careful to keep that to my soldierly inside.

Looking for my childhood
I reached the leafy little side street, Haynstrasse, where, at number seven, I was born nearly 25 years earlier. There was the blue number plate on the stone pillar of the tiny front garden and the four-storeyed apartment block rising behind it. We had lived, above the mezzanine, in the first-floor flat, with a small balcony outside what used to be our music room. For my mother, a pro-

fessional opera singer, it was the most important room, and her daily vocal practice, endlessly repeated, 'Do Re Mi Fa So La Si Do', remained imprinted on my inner ear, and almost caused those unsoldierly tears to well up in my eyes. The adjoining room, still part of the apartment block frontage, had been our sitting room with its deep leather chairs and bookcase. Behind it, connected by large folding double doors with glass panels, was our dining room, again bulkily furnished in the style of the German interwar years. This was accessible also from the entrance hall (with the guest toilets) and the long main passage leading to the kitchen and remainder of the flat, my parents bedroom, a bathroom, my own bedroom, playroom and study combined, and a smaller bedroom for our live-in domestic help. While the front of the apartment block was rather bleak, facing northwest, but just catching the afternoon and evening sun, the rear of the commodious flat had a roomy loggia attached to my parents bedroom and looking out over quiet gardens. This is where we had our meals on sunny days and warm summer evenings. I remember late Sunday breakfasts there, and my mother wearing a blue-green kimono dressing gown getting her suntan while enjoying fresh strawberries, which were then a rare and seasonal treat.

On the front balcony, our Christmas tree was kept fresh before being decorated. This was never done before the afternoon of 24 December, with Christmas Eve and Christmas Day as two days of the German festivities, kept more solemnly than the traditional British sort, given more to Dickensian merrymaking. That front balcony was my lookout for my father's, often weary, return from long office days. I would then excitedly alert the kitchen to be ready with his meal. The only visible change from that past in our street was that there was now a row of densely parked cars, the symbols of a new more mobile age.

As I was looking up at our former apartment block, a man with a dog on a lead passed by and, eyeing me suspiciously, asked 'Looking for something?' 'For my far away childhood,' I replied, whereupon he gave the enemy soldier an odd look and, puffing his pipe, left me to it.

The flat owners' names on the bell panel outside the main entrance were all new to me bar one, Soltau. He was the caretaker from our day and was evidently still living in the attic. I recalled his tattooed arms, blue dungarees and broad *Platt-*

deutsch slang of the Hamburg working class. The Soltaus'
younger son, Heini, had been my playmate, a secret one because
I was expressly forbidden to have anything to do with him, for
he was regarded as far too common. But the forbidden fruit
aspect added to his attraction, despite his bullying ways and
threats to have me beaten up by his bigger brother. I rang the
Soltaus' bell. Tears came to the old couple's eyes when I
explained who I was. Theirs was a typical German tragedy of the
time, with their eldest son killed in Russia, and Heini then still a
prisoner of war in France. Nevertheless, my British uniform was
no barrier to their welcome.

They made me sit down and share their frugal meal, an equivalent of high tea, but actually coffee or, rather, its German wartime substitute made from acorns and ominously known as
Muckefuck (pronounced mookefook) though with none of its
English connotation, the German slang word deriving from a
watered-down sort of mocha. This was accompanied by fresh
rolls on which, since butter was still scarce, unsweetened
applesauce was spread like jam. Their reception more than made
up for the food, which I had to force myself to swallow. There
was an unspoken but genuine sense of sorrow about the Hitlerite
past, including our own exile. I did not know the Soltaus'
politics. Like many Hamburg workers, they had probably been
communists who would then have come to support Hitler after
the successes of his early policies and war triumphs. Now, in the
catastrophe of Germany's defeat and collapse, they were
beginning to realize that the man they had trusted and wor-
shipped had in fact caused their ruin. He was then a convenient
scapegoat and, too bad, had taken the easy way out while
leaving them with his disastrous mess. At that time, few would
have been ready to admit that they too were responsible for what
had happened – though not for a long time yet.

By a strange coincidence, Soltau had only recently had cause
to remember us again. His job was to look after the coke-fired
boilers for the central heating in two apartment blocks and he
had only just used up, for occasional relighting, the heaps of
precious sheet music that my mother had been forced to leave
behind. The Soltaus remembered her as a singer, having been
given free tickets to see her in a Hamburg theatre starring in
Lehár's *Merry Widow*. That had forged a special bond between
them and us. Nor had Soltau forgotten my father, to whom he

2. Spruced up father and son.

used to proffer a polite 'Good morning' when leaving early for his office. Occasionally, this was rewarded by the gift of a good cigar. But my father had to be in the right mood for that, Soltau told me, and apparently he could tell this from the angle of his bowler. Worn straight, his morning temper was apparently less jovial, and a more formal salutation was indicated. It was a wholly new side to my father's character of which I had not been aware.

Leaving the Soltaus, I had time to look at some familiar childhood sights, for example, the paved stone entrance hall of our block with the lift, but now modernized, behind which dark stairs led to the basement and to my forbidden games with Heini. There was a box room where I kept my small wooden child's car, later my bicycle and winter sleigh. At Christmas this unlit passage always reminded me of *The Little Match Girl*, that saddest of Hans Andersen's tales. I always thought I saw her sitting there in the darkness, warming her frozen fingers by striking matches and dreaming of a roast goose in an imaginary oven.

When she had struck the last match, she died and I remember my sadness over that death. As to the imaginary roast goose, that might have been our Christmas dinner. Though it could not save the hungry match girl, at least we were not entirely to blame for her fate; my parents had a social conscience and annually used to invite some poor students in to have their Christmas dinner with us. This was admittedly served to them separately at a table in the entrance lobby. However, peeping from behind the drawn curtains and the passage leading to the kitchen, I remember watching them tucking in and myself becoming aware for the first time what it meant in those days for some people to be hungry.

Christmases in my early childhood were marked by the appearance of Father Christmas, alias St Nicolas. He rang our doorbell, and then came into the music room where our guests and we had assembled with an eager air of expectancy round the Christmas tree. My father read the passage from St Luke's Gospel on the birth of Jesus. After 'Peace on earth to all men of good will' I had to submit to some uncomfortable questions about my behaviour over the past year, after which the white-bearded personage left hurriedly, having a busy night ahead, and allowed us to get on with the serious business of unwrapping our presents. With my advancing years, there was less of Father Christmas. In a final, shameful denouement, his lisping speech revealed him as none other than Uncle Fritz. I was then considered grown up enough for St Luke's Gospel alone without the childish trimmings.

How wonderful it was to recall those past times on that return journey. I also revisited some familiar places, such as the old shoemaker who had always fascinated me in his basement, bent over his hammering work. Then there was the pastry shop round the corner, famous for its meringues with thick cream that remained favourites for life. The cinema next door was forever closed to me because 'UNDER 18 YEAR OLDS' were not admitted. There was the tobacconist where my father used to buy his cigars, and the hairdresser next door who dealt with me so roughly, I thought, when snipping my locks as I sat on a child's high chair.

Was there something providential for me in Hamburg's coat of arms, I wondered, with the medieval city gate opening up, as it were, to the wider world? This was suggested in my early child-hood by long, dreary Sunday walks with my parents. How I hated them! But then everybody seemed to enjoy going beyond the city's outskirts on the highway alongside Hamburg's River Elbe. Exhausted we used to end up at Jacobs, a famous garden restaurant where, sitting under old lime trees, cool ices and drinks helped us to recover and, simultaneously, to take in the magnificent view of the big river down below. Large passenger liners on their way to the open North Sea or others returning to the homeport occasionally passed, always surrounded by small sailing craft or motorboats. From the opposite river bank and Hamburg's largest wharf came the sound of constant hammering and knocking. Situated next to it was a quite different and very pretty region of old church spires and fertile fruit trees known as *Das alte Land*, the Old Land. It provided the venue for a popular annual outing in the spring and had the additional attraction of being the place from where, I was told, some of my favourite dishes came – thick white asparagus cooked deliciously soft and served with smoked ham and liquid butter. That one was allowed to eat the asparagus with one's fingertips remained imprinted on my mind. A delicious summer fruit jelly made from fresh raspberries and red currants served with cream always followed this dish. Its only off-putting part was its north German name, *rote Grütze* (red gruel), which dishonoured its delectable taste!

A Sunday outing like this was likely to show Hamburg's best side, opened again to the oceans and world trade after the First Great War, though it was not to remain so for long. Barely a decade later Germany startled herself and the world by the renewed bid for world domination. Early in that year, 1933, my father came home with a surprise for all of us, a large and colourful stamp in our passports, assuring us of a safe haven in Haiti, of all places. He had got it, anticipating world events, to make us feel safe, that come what may we would have somewhere secure to go to. While the land of Graham Greene's later Papa Doc was unlikely to provide a secure haven, it had discovered that money could be made by offering just such a haven to potential freedom and asylum seeking exiles.

My early memories are vivid, as though they had just happened. While this is not unusual, it was perhaps more marked in my case because I was an only child. I had the advantage (or disadvantage) of being or seeming to be the centre of attention and, of course, of being spoilt. I can see myself at play, staging, for example, an elaborate funeral rite in our flat, on the occasion of the death of

3. Hi, Hamburg sailor.

our beloved canary. I buried him in one of the flower boxes on our balcony where normally geraniums grew. I had secret feelings of guilt over his demise. As a special treat, he was always given a piece of sweet biscuit of which I was as fond as he was. My contrition may thus have added to the funeral solemnities, including a solo procession by myself through the flat. Onlookers like my mother may have wondered about the extent of my grief.

How to play the games
There were naturally favourite games, first among which was my railway, with a wind-up engine, later electrified. It led to many quarrels on the layout of the rails with my early friend, Rolf. He was all for daring ups and downs, which merely caused predictable derailments. I preferred safe and harmoniously wide rail loops, which bored him, though they assured accident-free travel. He eventually turned into a conservative-minded lawyer, noted for his over-careful attitudes. How far, I always wondered, is our character shaped by these youthful bents? Did I just have a more even temperament or was I simply afraid of taking risks? Whatever it was, it comforted me later to discover an evidently related

soul in the American poet Robert Frost (1874–1964) who, after having presumably passed his own railway-playing age, said: 'I never dared be radical when young, for fear it would make me conservative when old.'

I was able to demonstrate how comforting this philosophy could be at my twelfth birthday party, the last one I spent in Hamburg. I had invited several friends and we were sitting around our big dining-room table laden with all sorts of goodies. In the centre, my train made its rounds. By activating a lever each guest could stop it, help himself to sandwiches, cakes and sweets from its wagons, then send it on its way again, satisfying both our play instincts and appetites. That party was not only a great success but also proved my case for the politics of safe travel. I also had great fun with my knight's castle and its garrison of plastic and tin soldiers from a range of historical periods.

Some people of that age and generation puzzled about whether playing war games or 'Red Indians' ought to be stopped on the grounds that it led towards making war. I have never cared much for this way of making pacifism palatable and preferred the more basic approach of 'Ebenezer thought it wrong to fight/Roaring Bill who slew him thought it right.' Unforgettably for me, was an old lady, evidently of German origin, who used to go through London streets many years later attempting vainly to stop children's war games, and crying out to them in her stiff German accent: 'Stop those awful war games. Don't you know that the war is over?' The children used to look at her with open-mouthed amazement, as though she had come from another planet. Subconsciously, they seemed to have realized that playing war games or playing Red Indians was less likely to lead to war than appeasing bullies does, as had been forgotten in that old lady's own generation.

Intended probably to promote my non-existent commercial talent, so that I might follow my father's example, was a miniature grocer's shop, of a child's height, with drawers and shelves. As a sugar broker, my father proved useful in providing a constant supply of miniature sugar loaves, wrapped in blue paper, with which he used to regale his own clients. They were naturally in great demand among my contemporary customers. For payment, I used tin or chocolate money as well as bank notes to the value of 100,000 and even a million Reichsmark, which not long before had been real German inflationary currency.

Strangely, I have no recollection of that disastrous German postwar period. The protective care of me taken by my parents over my early years, being born in 1920, probably saw to it that my memory is blank for those hard times, which were to have their political repercussions much later. What I must admit to was an early bent for the very apolitical pastime of daydreaming. I remember how wonderful it felt to go on those long and dreary Sunday walks with my mother and father, holding onto their hands while walking between them. It enabled me to close my eyes and wholly to surrender to the play of my imagination, on the lines of Hilaire Belloc's counsel: 'Always keep a hold of nurse, for fear of finding something worse.' Naturally, rebukes followed: 'Open your eyes, or else there'll be tears before the day is out.' However, as the prediction invariably came true, it only made me wonder at the uncanny foresight of grown-ups.

Stamp collecting was a later teenage passion, producing predictable greed and the want to have more and more of those bits of coloured paper from all over the world. Aged 11, I pinched a particularly splendid specimen from my older cousin's collection.

The misdeed was discovered. Our mothers got together. I had to return the stamp with an appropriate apology. I have never forgotten that Canossa-like walk. My cousin's family lived in a fifth-floor flat. I had no key to the lift, but felt the stamp in my pocket getting heavier with every step up. Then there were tears, forgiveness, and the return walk back home, which was like walking on wings. Many years later, on my cousin's seventieth birthday, I recalled that incident, which he had forgotten, but the others there commiserated with me on the trauma they thought I must have suffered all those years ago. Unaware of any guilt or negative Freudian effects, I still regard that early act of shame as a salutary lesson from which I had benefited.

My father and mother each had brothers and sisters and I deeply deplored my 'only child' status. It seemed to add to the gulf between my parents and myself. They were unavailable as playmates, even though a Froebel-trained nanny from whom I learnt some skills, like making things, somewhat reduced my boredom and loneliness, but unfortunately she did not stay long enough for her teaching to have had a lasting effect. It was only with the beginning of school that there were friends like my railway mate, Rolf. He also had a younger sister, Gila, who was my first love. Once when playing Red Indians, I plucked up courage and kissed her on her heavily rouged mouth and face – she was playing the squaw. How I envied her brother that sister, and not least for the cool way in which he was able to say to her 'You old pig'; it seemed to express the height of that enviable fraternal intimacy of which I was forever deprived. Then there was a hospital visit to my mother who had suffered a miscarriage. It united all of us in sorrow over the little sister for whom I had longed but who was not to be any more.

Sunday afternoons when my parents used to rest and absolute quiet was ordained, was a particular trial before books became my companions. *Robinson Crusoe* was an early one to make a deep impression (my mother read it to me in bed when I had measles). When the passage came in which the shipwrecked Robinson called upon the Lord, I supposedly and precociously asked 'What is the Good Lord's number then?' A book in which I was strangely absorbed, probably because of the illustrations, but long before I had learnt to read English or had any notion that this country would one day become my adopted home, was H. E. Marshall's history book for children, called *The Story of the Sea*. Published as long ago as 1905, it gripped me with pride and delight, regardless of the fact that the British and Germans had been enemies in the First World War.

My north German father's inheritance from a faraway time when British and Germans, with their old Hanseatic bond, thought of one another as 'cousins' may have been a conciliating factor. Nevertheless, there was something that impressed me about the British Empire's story and the sense of self-confidence in the global role of the English-speaking peoples that seemed to be far from any war-mongering imperialism. I delighted in chapters called 'How Caligula Conquered Britain', 'Hengist's Treachery', 'Henry III', 'The Story of the Poisoned Dagger', 'Richard III', 'The Two Little Princes in The Tower', 'How England was Saved from the Spaniards', 'The Story of How the King was Brought to his Death', and so on up to the Boer War. Moreover, there were wonderful coloured illustrations, such as the longhaired bearded warrior scholar Alfred the Great, the battleaxe hung up on the wall next to his shield, perusing a huge scroll. 'Alfred found much pleasure in reading' was the caption, which I could understand. My delight in reading Rudyard Kipling's stories in translation later strengthened my introduction to English history.

I remain grateful to my parents for having responded to and guided my early reading mania. When I came to England, I felt sorry for English children who grew up without books at home or at best with cheap magazines. I remember my introduction to the world of learning when, nearly 11, I accompanied my father to meet the director of my future Hamburg grammar school, the renowned Johanneum. He was a forbidding-looking figure, wearing a long frock coat with high stiff collar and a pince-nez. While he and my father were exchanging formalities, I waited nervously near the door, knowing that I had to be on my best behaviour. So I did precisely the forbidden thing, perching on the very edge of a chair near the door, only to be hit by the stentorian rebuke: 'In this school one does not sit down before one is asked to do so.' He seemed to have been waiting for that moment to pounce.

Three years later, in the autumn of 1933, we left Hamburg for good. For me this meant leaving that school, and indeed my childhood. Our belongings were partly to be sold by auction, partly to be stored. For some reason, perhaps to deceive the Nazi authorities from whom we needed an exit permit, our departure was to look as though it was meant not to be final. My father was even prepared to pay high storage costs for some of our furniture.

Nobody could have known then that the warehouse, along with other parts of Germany's second-largest city and ten thousand of its inhabitants would, a little more than ten years later in the summer of 1943, go up in the flames of devastating nightly British bombing raids. My father did not want to cut all links, but having suffered badly in his business affairs in the 1930s decided to start up afresh abroad, in Prague, where, he hoped, my mother would find a position as a singer and I would attend a German school. Therefore, I had to play my part in preparing my possessions – my railway, the medieval castle and my soldiers – for the sale. My fervent hope was that these beloved things would find some kind father buying them for his son. Fortunately, we were spared having to be present at the auction to watch bargain-hunters knocking down the value of my mother's cherished grand piano, our comfortable armchairs, as well as our books and pictures. There was an embarrassing sequel to the sale when the heavy dining-room sideboard was moved away from the wall and a plate with the petrified remains of a rice pudding clattered to the floor. I had hidden it there, a particularly hated dessert, in the hope that it would never be found.

My father courts Adele

My farewell to the place of my birth may serve, if belatedly, to introduce my parents. Although we continued to remain together as a family for a few years, in Prague, Vienna and Milan, a major chapter of our life had come to an end. We were suddenly cut off from our roots to share the fate of tens of thousands of exiles. It meant a life of relative hardship in furnished accommodation, sometimes not knowing how to afford our next day's meals. Vienna was something of an exception in that as it was my mother's and grandfather's home and had always been a well loved place, except that we had to manage in furnished accommodation of two rooms for the three of us and generally rather cramped conditions. My father especially, who was accustomed to a fairly comfortable middle-class way of life, found it difficult to adjust.

My mother was better able to cope with the lack of money and having to make ends meet. She was quite free from any hankering after the comforts of the past and after what could not be recaptured. Our bleak times were marked by frequent rows with me somehow in the middle, going through my own teenage problems, inclined at first towards being my father's boy, but this was to change. In a sense, Goethe's famous lines somehow seemed to apply to me: 'From my father I have my stature, and life's earnest striving; from my mother a happy nature, and love of flights of the mind.' (*Vom Vater hab ich die Statur/des Lebens ernstes Führen/vom Mütterchen die Frohnatur und Lust zu fabulieren.*) However, I was actually rebelling against both of them for different and probably subconscious reasons.

On looking back, it seems difficult to believe quite how much the traditional bonds of family attachment and habit were capable of sustaining us. This was true even more so later, when the outbreak of the Second World War was to find all three of us dispersed over different countries, on different sides of the war, with only a receding memory of what life 'at home' was like. Inevitably, we were growing apart.

My father was born in 1888 at Celle, a small town near Hanover, whence his family (which ran a cigar import and export business) soon moved to Hamburg. He was 29, having established his economic independence in the sugar industry, when he met my mother. She was ten years younger than he was and, having completed her musical studies in Vienna during the First World War, was at the beginning of her career as a singer.

Her first public engagement was in touring German theatres after the war. One of these was at Bremen when she sang the soprano part of Adele, Rosalinda's maid, in a production of Johann Strauss's *Die Fledermaus* (The Bat), which became one of her favourite roles. Her voice was to change over the years to mezzo-soprano, which is not an unusual development. My father, though not particularly musical, happened to be on a business trip in Bremen, had a ticket for the front row stalls and the vivacious young singer evidently swept him off his feet. He went to every performance, always applauding wildly. It almost seemed that he might be one of the *claque*, as those given free tickets were called, for which they had to lead in the applause, as it were, *pour encourager les autres* and promote box office success. However, in that popular light opera, such outward stimulus was hardly necessary. My father, in his north German coolness and reserve was the very opposite of that young performer with her infectious outgoing personality and good looks. Afterwards, with other admirers, he beleaguered the stage door armed with a bunch of roses. Eventually, his 'siege' must have been successful, for she returned his love and they were married that same year in the spring of 1920.

Their meeting place, Bremen, was significant also for another reason. Not far from the theatre stood a more than life-size statue of Roland, Charlemagne's Palatine count, who inspired the choice of my name. My parents' generation still looked up to historical heroes and were far from suspecting their hidden blemishes, or at least tended to overlook them. For my light-hearted mother, the name of the valiant defender of the pass of Roncevalles was too much of a mouthful, too serious for daily usage – so for her, I am ashamed to say, I remained *Bubi*. This German term of endearment, I hasten to add, has nothing to do with the objectionable dull-witted, silly English booby, or indeed with equally obnoxious booby prizes or booby-traps. Etymologists believe that it was all Martin Luther's fault. His Old Testament translation *'Wenn dich die bösen Buben locken, söfolge nicht* (Proverbs of Salomon, 1.10) proved so popular that it may even have crossed the Channel. The English versions

4. My mother as opera *diva* with due autograph.

suggest a more refined equivalent, warning merely against 'the blandishments of seducers' in that passage: 'Listen, my son, to your father's instruction and do not forsake your mother's teaching' (Proverbs, 1.10, 11).

Even before my birth my mother was expected to make a more severe sacrifice, to forsake her professional career altogether. My father's family was still animated by an outdated prejudice against admitting 'someone from the stage', as being not quite proper, into their midst. The implied slight naturally outraged her, but, as a woman on her own, she found it difficult to go against the united front of her new in-laws. Besides, she was in love and so ultimately gave way. There was a last benefit performance in her honour of Puccini's *La Bohème* at Hamburg's Thalia Theatre in which she sang the role of Mimi.

The *Hamburger Fremdenblatt* music critic found it *hässlich* (monstrous) of her (by way of a German pun on my father's name Hess) to give up a promising career merely to get married. Her sacrifice, fortunately, remained limited to public appearances. She kept up her daily singing practice, lasting two to three hours, continued giving private recitals as a Lieder singer and returned to the stage eventually when I was seven or eight years old.

By then my father's family had long regretted their foolish objection. However, interrupting any artistic career imposes lasting damage and, though my mother took hers up again later and with great successes in the opera houses of Hamburg, Vienna and Milan, she was unable to make up those lost years. Nevertheless, it was ultimately a great satisfaction to her to be able to support the family as a singer and bel canto teacher, and indeed to find a self-fulfilling role in her later life in Italy and Canada.

Both my mother and father were of Jewish descent but had independently converted to Catholicism, my father shortly before his death in Brussels in 1945, my mother later when she spent some years living with relations in Canada. I was certainly instrumental in their change of religion, but only indirectly and in the long run. This occurred in Vienna, my mother's home, which spiritually, as it were, was to become my own as well. I grew up in Hamburg as an evangelical Lutheran and was about to be confirmed when we left Germany. My parents were wise enough not to exert any religious pressure on my development. An evening prayer and the Our Father were customary in our home. My early evangelical schooling corresponded to an innate religious inclination, with an Old Testament and Lutheran bent, which I have retained in an ecumenical sense. I was thus able to understand my Catholic conversion as a kind of fulfilment of what had gone before, a spiritual homecoming.

From early on I had a strong interest in religious and philosophical questions. Dabbling in our well-stocked library at home, I read, at first without much direction. In my later religious reading, I came across the age-old debate on the existence of a transcendental and personal God. I remember, aged not yet 13, holding forth on the subject at my mother's tea party for five or six lady friends who asked me to explain 'my' philosophical findings. The women listened attentively. In my mind's eye, I still see the little silver tray set with milk and sugar jugs, which served as a kind of mental aid in the recital of my arguments. They had, after all, preoccupied great minds like those of St Augustine and St Thomas Aquinas, though my tea table audience could hardly have corrected any howlers I might have made. My performance was rewarded with a handful of cakes, whereupon I returned to my room and school homework.

My father's name, somewhat ominously for our generation, was Rudolf Hess, the same as that of Hitler's deputy, though I am glad to say, they were not related and neither he nor I suffered any adverse effects from that coincidence. However, when in 1940/1, I joined the British army, it was thought advisable to effect a name change because of the unpleasant consequences if ever I had the misfortune to be taken prisoner of war by a possibly victorious German army. Impulsively I chose 'Roland Hill' because of my affection, as one-time stamp collector, for Rowland Hill, the amiable inventor of the penny postage and first English postmaster general. When, after the war, England became my adopted country and no chance of my returning to Germany or Austria arose, I saw no need to reverse the name change.

As far as my father was concerned, the name produced at least one brief moment of glory for him, as it had also for me after Austria's *Anschluss*. In his case, this happened when, before all of us went into exile, he had to make a business trip to Berlin. To his huge surprise, he found detachments of police and 'SA' storm troopers drawn up for his VIP reception. This was naturally and, to general embarrassment, speedily called off. In retrospect, it must have seemed like a scene from Charlie Chaplin's satirical film *The Great Dictator*, and confirmed how easy it was to make fun of the pompously strutting Nazis. On his return and understandably, my father regaled us with gleeful tales of having merely got what he thought due to him, as it were *se non è vero è ben trovato* (if not true, at least it

ought to have been). Tall and not to be overlooked in his
personal appearance, in his politics he was a conservative
democrat, proud of his record in the First World War, in which
he served with distinction in the ambulance corps. Though
embodying many of the German civic virtues, he was of course
deeply opposed to everything Hitler stood for. As for the
'other' Rudolf Hess, he received a life sentence at Nuremberg
and died at Berlin's Spandau prison in 1987. His mad flight to
Scotland had been undertaken in May 1941 in order to mediate
a peace deal whereby Britain would join Nazi Germany in a
war against Soviet Russia – a hare-brained misconstruction of
his alleged British Nazi contact, the Duke of Hamilton.

My father was a product of his north German environment; he
had a reserved manner, but was not really close to English ways.
His French was better than his English, in which he had learnt to
pronounce 'u' not as in 'but', but as in 'burglar' or 'world'. As a
businessman who dealt with imports and exports, he had an
affinity with a world and free trade outlook.

Anglophile sentiments were widespread in his German generation, but almost counter-balanced by German Anglophobia.
Both attitudes seemed, in retrospect, inspired by a considerable
amount of wishful thinking rather than any real knowledge of
the other nation. My father had built up his own business in the
sugar trade after completing an apprenticeship in which he had
shown his commercial talents, combined with almost pedantic
qualities of order, industry and punctuality. I always regarded
these as comparable to the perfectly sharpened pencils in the tray
on his office desk, and resented what they symbolized
accordingly. On the other hand, he probably hoped that I would
follow in his footsteps. From the outset, this was not to be,
whether or not due to typical father–son tensions in my teenage
years. However, these also extended to my mother, whose
influence on me I believe to have been the stronger one. I recall
distinctly an incident, typical for a teenager, when the three of us
were having dinner. I was nearly 15 and, under the table, had
involuntarily pushed against my father's long legs. He pushed
back, as though returning a threat and wanting to assert himself.
Insignificant as the little incident was, it was almost like an
unconscious sort of cockfight.

My father had his office or *Kontor*, as was the north German
term, in the Gröninger Strasse near the Hamburg port area. Its

special attraction for me as a boy was its open-door lift with
several cabins in constant slow motion, which people used to get
on and off at the required floors. If you missed your level, you
descended and came up again on the other side. The rotating
system was appropriately known as a *Paternoster,* derived from
the rosary's recital of Our Father. Children were of course not
allowed to use the lift on their own because of the evident danger
if you missed stepping on or off in time, which naturally added
to the fun and fear aspect of using it.

My father's office was near St Petri's, one of the finest
churches in Hamburg, with a slim pointed green-patinated spire,
which miraculously escaped the devastating air raids in the
Second World War. Occasionally on Saturdays, when my school
finished early, my mother and I used to collect father for lunch in
a nearby port tavern, the speciality of which was lobster soup
served on tables covered with lobster-coloured linen and there
was an enticing atmosphere of faraway places. St Petri was my
favourite church. It has remained deeply imbedded in my
memories, for there I sang Bach's St Matthew Passion as a
member of my school choir, trembling with excitement as well as
cold in the church's upper gallery. We boys were only wearing
short trousers, a white shirt and tie. Ever since the great chorale
'O sacred Head, surrounded crown of piercing thorn! O bleeding
Head so wounded, reviled and put to scorn' moves me to tears,
so also the bass recitative from the final act when Jesus has
expired and Pilate has allowed his body to be taken down from
the cross for burial. Bach's magnificent composition has
remained for me at the centre of my religious attitude, an
apotheosis of all that is greatest and finest in words and music.
Those resonances from the Old Testament's story from the
Garden of Eden and Noah's Ark, linked with the Gospel's
Crucifixion, and underlined by the pulsing basses, cellos, soft
violins and soloists' voices, proclaimed man's bond with God.
They were indeed, as Gerald Manley Hopkins has said, 'charged
with the grandeur of God' (*Poems* (1876–89) No.8).

Am Abend, da es kühler war
Ward Adams Fallen offenbar;
Am Abend drückt ihn der Heiland nieder;
Am Abend kommt die Taube wieder
Und trug ein Olblatt in dem Munde.

O schöne Zeit, O Abendstunde!
Der Freundesschluß ist nun mil Gott gemacht,
Denn Jesus hat sein Kreuz vollbracht.

(At evening was our Saviour now brought downward;
At evening did the dove fly homeward,
The leaf of olive gently bearing,
O beauteous time, O hour of evening!
The seal of peace is now with God ensured,
since Jesus has his cross endured.)

My mother's 'spark'

In stature the very opposite of her husband, my mother was small, with a well-proportioned rounded figure, a beautifully open facial expression, and long curly chestnut-brown hair. She had all the creative musical nature one associates with the Vienna of Mozart, Haydn and Strauss. But there was more to it, which I always think of as a divine spark as it marks particularly creatively gifted people. You felt that, as in the famous song from *My Fair Lady*, 'she had got it', be it the singer bringing out perfectly naturally the right tone, the musician playing his instrument as the composer probably intended it, or the artist getting things just right. In her case there was probably also an innate musicality inherited from her father, Isidor Löwit, a well-known cantor and choral director of the Vienna Sephardic community. He had fully encouraged and supported her voice training at the Vienna Music Academy, knowing how easily bad teachers can ruin it. She was fortunate in having in that respect the famous Polish singer Jean De Reszke (1850–1935), a baritone at first who developed into one of the finest nineteenth-century tenors. And, as often happens, she too changed from soprano with a special talent at first for the soubrette parts in operas and musicals, to an alto voice later on.

For me she remains identified with the conviction she came to hold in later years as a renowned singer and singing teacher: 'Everybody can sing.' It seemed a startling, even naïve, observation when you think of the many people who, when merely opening their mouths, produce only wrong notes, but she meant it not only in her own special way, as one who has 'got it'. She reached out for a deeper wisdom, of which she was herself perhaps only vaguely aware. That was well expressed, as I

discovered, by the English mystic and divine, William Law
(1686–1761) who wrote:

> Every one, at some time or other, finds himself able to sing
> in some degree; there are some times and occasions of joy,
> that make some people ready to express their sense of it in
> some sort of harmony. The joy they feel forces them to let
> their voice have a part in it. ...
> Singing, indeed, as it is improved into an art, as it
> signifies the running of the voice through such and such a
> compass of notes, and keeping time with a studied variety
> of changes, is not natural, not the effect of any state of
> mind; so in this sense, it is not common to all people, any
> more than those antic and invented motions which make
> fine dancing common to all people.
> But singing, as it signifies a motion of the voice suitable
> to motions of the heart, and the changing of its tone
> according to the meaning of the words we utter, is as
> natural and common to all men, as it is to speak high
> when they are in anger, to speak low, when they are
> dejected and ask for pardon.
> All men therefore are singers, in the same manner as all
> men think, speak, laugh, and lament. For singing is no
> more an invention, than grief or joy are inventions.

I grew up from early childhood with the sound of music in my
ears, the classical Lieder of Schubert, Brahms and Hugo Wolf,
knowing all about the operettas, the musicals of that day, by
Franz Lehár, Emmerich Kàlmàn and Robert Stolz. My mother
unfailingly did her singing exercises every day, beginning with
the monotonously repeated vocal scales that bored everybody in
the house, accompanying herself on the piano. I was put through
the obligatory piano lessons early on, but spoilt as I was, refused
to practise. Proud of their liberal attitude, my parents
unfortunately gave in to my laziness. They said, 'Let him if he
doesn't want to,' to my later and eternal regret. More than likely,
I would have given in eventually, especially when I realized what
I was missing. Therefore, I came to lament such parental *laissez-
faire*, except of course if there had been serious grounds for such
childish resistance.

There was much music in our home. My mother had a good

stock of Schubert, Hugo Wolf and Joseph Marx Lieder, all those non-Austrian geniuses who made Austrian musicality their own like Beethoven, Richard Strauss and Brahms, and she was of course *au fait* with most of the Mozart, Puccini and Verdi opera roles. She needed little encouragement to come out with anything on the spur of the moment, according to her mood, particularly as far as her easily embarrassed silly son was concerned. Like all teenagers, I could not bear my mother to make a public spectacle of herself, which of course was not what she was doing; she was simply being herself and allowing the occasion to inspire her. Her audience, be it at a private party or at a restaurant with musical accompaniment, would inevitably respond to her. My embarrassment was very childish, though inside me I was immensely proud of her. But did she really have to let all those strange men on the stage kiss her! Moreover, in the darkened theatre I imagined that those sitting around were nudging one another, whispering: 'That's his mother, up there on stage.'

No doubt, I absorbed from my mother's family and occasional childhood visits to Vienna many impulses from my grandfather's religious world. Being the youngest present at the family table on high Jewish holidays, it fell to me to recite the famous daily 'Schma Israel' prayer: 'Hear, O Israel: the Lord our God is one Lord, and you shall love the Lord your God with all your heart, and with all your might' (Deuteronomy 6:4–5).

It did not occur to me as yet that I was soon to accept with my new Catholic faith a completely new direction and life-giving horizon, but indirectly linked with that prayer. The Old Testament, my grandfather's beliefs, with its laws, command-ments, emphasis on everything that was strict, dutiful, severe, including an apparently avenging God, was presented to me in that way. Aged ten, I remember on the Easter feast of Pesach how my imagination was stirred when a cup of wine was poured for the prophet Elias to enter and drink from it. Gazing fixedly at the cup, I watched to see what really happened. It was the sort of religious magic that would fascinate a child. It was only much later that I became seriously aware of the uniting bond of love for God and love for your neighbour being really grounded in the Old Testament, 'You shall love your neighbour as thyself' (Leviticus 19:18) but summed up by Jesus into more than a mere 'command', indeed a key to all Scripture: 'God is love and he who abides in love abides in God, and God abides in him' (1

5. My Viennese grandparents, two aunts, mother and self.

John 4–16). Pope Benedict XVI reminded the world of this in his first Encyclical. Here he attempted to rescue human love (of family, work, neighbour and God, but especially the love between man and woman) from that age-old, one-sided sexual over emphasis on despising the body, for which modern atheism and Christianity have been equally responsible through the ages.

I also recall the traditional pious Jewish toast and wish – 'Next year in Jerusalem'. My grandfather, who felt at home with traditional old 'anti' or rather 'supranational' Austrian thinking, understood that wish as it had been understood by Jews throughout the ages since their 'diaspora' or dispersal among the heathens, not in any nationalist sense but as a timeless, religious promise and fulfilment. Although this was many years before the creation of the State of Israel, he would have been opposed to Zionism.

In postwar democratic Austria, a discussion arose about

whether to regard Holocaust survivors who returned as 'Austrians' or 'Jews'. Behind it was the old debate about whether people like Sigmund Freud, Franz Werfel, Gustav Mahler (who became a Catholic to qualify as director of the Vienna State Opera) should be regarded as proselytizing Austrians or Jews, namely in the racist sense in which first Catholic Austria and then the Nazis had considered them. After Hitler the problem was complicated by the creation of the State of Israel and the status of Jews living outside Israel's borders. Were they to be considered racially as Jews, even though this was no longer meant in its former Germanic legalistic and derogatory sense?

In 1996, the issue was taken up in London by Sir Ernest Gombrich, the art historian, who expressed resentment at the continuing slight upon Jews like himself who were not Jews by religious conviction but as part of a humanist tradition. All they wanted to be and remain was culturally Austrian. There was a parallel with my Viennese grandfather who, albeit religiously orthodox, was deeply attached to Austria and felt a strong religious and cultural bond. My grandfather tragically died in the Nazi concentration camp, Theresienstadt, but Gombrich survived the Holocaust and made his secular protest heard. In the new democratic Austria, he felt as though he was still being denied his Austrian cultural attachment. 'Sorry, old chap', the post-Hitler generation seemed to say to him, whom it had honoured in many ways, 'we like you, but we can't help seeing you other than racially as a Jew, whether you want to be one by religion or not.' In other words, the old legalistic Nazi discrimination was still being applied. Being a Jew, in the State of Israel, could similarly only be understood in a racist, nationalist sense and thus excluded oddly the cultural and non-religious status of assimilated Jews.

There was the comparable case of Heinrich Heine. Was he, should he be considered as a German poet, which he wanted to be and was *par excellence*, or as a Jewish poet? Nazi racism was thus unfairly perpetuated even after its official demise.

My childhood years were happily spent in Hamburg. We were used to its well-functioning public transport system, trams, buses and the elevated suburban line, which held out to me, as a small boy, the most desirable of occupations. What a life, I dreamed, to be a train guard with a whistle, the only one allowed to get on or off the moving train while all the other doors had already closed. How I envied his apparently carefree existence! Though money was short, a German middle-class way of life, even then, in the 1920s or 1930s, seemed considerably in advance of neighbouring countries like Austria, certainly with respect to health, dental care, vaccinations, and the latest bathroom, toilet and kitchen equipment. We even had a washing machine in 1929, albeit it one that looked like a spacecraft, was unbearably noisy, turned violently on its axis and forever flooded the kitchen floor. Social conditions in Prague, Vienna and Milan, as I came to know them later, were worse than in Germany, just as German social legislation was more advanced, going back to the late nineteenth century and Bismarck's social insurance policies.

We spent many of our Hamburg summer holidays in Baltic seaside resorts like Travemünde, Timmendorf, Scharbeutz, or on the fine beaches of the North Sea islands Sylt and Westerland. Once or twice, when my parents went alone on more distant holidays, I was sent to a boarding school on the North Sea island of Wyk auf Föhr, an experience I did not care for at all, mainly because of the bullies in our dormitory. It left me with much sympathy for all those not suited to the boarding school system, which was so much more prevalent in Britain. I felt particularly sorry for young Winston Churchill who, though not particularly a 'mother's boy', suffered deeply from his parents' apparent neglect, with English public schools like Harrow seeming to require a particularly tough skin (which I also lacked). Heart-rending are Churchill's letters home, imploring his mother to come and visit him. No wonder it used to be said that boarding schools were invented for the convenience of parents, whatever other advantages of learning early independence they offered. I, however, felt fortunate in my own experience of the continental state schools of the 1930s, which were excellent models of social equality.

Other summer holidays were spent in the Silesian mountains, the Riesengebirge, where we used to rent a cottage near the beautiful hilly parts of Hirschberg and the Czech border, now Polish territory. It was wonderful hiking country, which we combined with blueberry picking, the evidence showing afterwards on our dyed mouths and faces. Sometimes we went across the border and enjoyed the excellent Czech food. However, I was always frightened of having to sleep in the old cottage attic with its ghostly creaking beams and floorboards. These Silesian holidays concluded with a visit to my favourite aunt, Rosel, my mother's sister, formerly also a professional singer, and Fritz, the famous lisping Father Christmas who, being childless, passed on to me a passion for chess and collecting stamps. They lived in Breslau, where he practised as a dentist. It is now called Wroclaw and is part of the annexed southwest Polish province of Wojewodztwo. Their street address, too, was a symbol of the historical changes within barely a quarter of century, from 'Kaiser Wilhelm Strasse' to 'Strasse der SA' (Storm Troopers Street) and a new Polish name. They, too, in 1938, went into exile, to Shanghai. Barred from taking any capital with them, they had a luxurious 'last fling' by way of a first-class sea passage. When their liner called at Genoa, which was when my mother and I were staying in Milan, we went so see them for lunch on board and afterwards waved them on their way. World travel thus became an unexpected pattern for my generation.

Our life in Hamburg in the early 1930s seemed to pass within the limits of home, school, office and family. A particular focus were our traditional Sunday midday visits to my grandmother, my father's widowed mother. She was called the *Olle, die Alte,* endearingly so in Hamburg's local idiom, and enjoyed the specially revered status of a matriarch of a large family, all of whom were soon to be dispersed worldwide, as had never been anticipated. She always wore a widow's long black dress with a black ribbon round her neck on which hung the medallion portrait of her husband who had died many years earlier. Her distinguishing mark was a big red wart on her nose, which fascinated me as a child, though it did not detract from her radiant beauty and kindness, with her long soft grey hair piled high on her head. Her dark eyes gleamed with fun and intelligence. She used to hold court, sitting in her armchair by a window, her feet resting on a little velvet-covered stool, and was forever busy with her crochet needles, while talking animatedly and separately with everyone.

She had a lively mind and was keen to know everything about our lives; she asked me many questions and took my childish concerns seriously. There was nothing phoney about her interest. She seemed to live our lives with us; she cared deeply about her beloved daughter Martchen, her eldest son, my father and his younger brother and about her numerous grandchildren.

Refreshments were always provided – special fruit juices and

6. Beloved 'Olle', my Hamburg grandmother.

biscuits for the children, and sherry, sweet liqueurs and Vermouth for the grown-ups.

A good deal of smoking went on, with cigars for the men and cigarettes for the ladies who sported little silver cases and long holders, apart from my mother who, ahead of her generation, took care of her voice and throat. We children crawled about on an ancient rocking chair with a straw-plaited seat that stood in a corner. I was very attached to my grandmother, as she was to me. My father caused her special concern in his mid-life years when he found it difficult to adapt to his changed economic circumstances, but she could do little except show him her deep maternal compassion. All those dear to her were soon to be

separated from her. Martchen went with her family to the
Argentine where her husband died early on and, though having
the support of three children, she was inconsolable and killed
herself. Her old mother was at least spared that tragic news.

The coming of Hitler

Then happened what was to affect all our lives. On Monday 30
January 1933, Hitler came to power as the result of a democratic
general election. Earlier, on 6 November, his National Socialist
Party had polled 33.1 per cent of the votes, evidently because of
a general fear of civil unrest and 'red revolution'. While the
Hitlerite votes had then actually been reduced by as much as 6
per cent compared with a previous poll held only in July 1932,
the communist vote had actually increased its share of the votes
by 600,000, topping their magical limit of 100 seats and ending
up a narrow third behind the Social Democrats' nearly 17 per
cent.

My parents were not very political, but the uncertainty cast
over our lives from one day to the next did shake them. I was not
yet 13, but the event of that January night remained as clear as
though I had personally witnessed every moment of it. This was
long before television, but radio, cinema newsreels and illustrated magazines made much of the historical torchlight procession in Berlin and of the jubilant crowds hailing Hindenburg,
the old Pétain-like head of state, venerated field marshal and
victor over the Russians in the First World War. With his
wooden face and doddery military bearing, he was said to have
only contempt for Hitler, a former First World War corporal. It
was hoped, vainly, that the old soldier would keep him from
abusing his newly won power.

On that January night, the new Führer stood at the window of
the Berlin Chancellery in Wilhelmstrasse acknowledging the
cheers of the crowds below. He seemed to show an unusually
modest side of himself, as though humbled by the event, wanting
to convey how unworthy he was, which indeed he was, of that
totally unforeseen and democratic triumph. Behind him stood the
vile and treacherous Franz von Papen, vice-chancellor, Catholic,
'kingmaker' and old political 'fixer', the man of straw supposedly picked to guarantee Hitler's best behaviour. The people
guessed that Hitler, the real victor of that night, would have the
last laugh.

The following day big rallies were held all over Germany to celebrate that victory. In Hamburg, on the vast square in front of the neo-Gothic City Hall, a large crowd had assembled, with my school class among it. Afterwards we had to write an essay about it, which I have kept, but not because I was proud of having witnessed Armageddon or indeed because I had done literary justice to that historic occasion. My essay no doubt reflected my teenage political naivety and the mental gymnastics involved in confronting the dawn of a new era. It boiled down to what I had gleaned from general comments in the press and radio. This was a hope that the 'good elements in society', by which at that time were meant the conservative middle classes, the top men in German heavy industry and the Prussian landowners, all of them close to Hindenburg, could manage to prevent the new Chancellor of the German *Reich* from abusing his powers. In that, I was probably typical of my age and generation. I took the safe, cowardly, neutral line on the Hitlerite future, giving it the terrible and costly benefit of the doubt. How easy it was to hide behind pious hopes, talk about Hitler's promised *Arbeit und Brot* (employment and an end to famine) so easily and wrongly exploited as stemming from the defeat of 1918 and the Treaty of Versailles, as safety from the threat of revolutionary chaos and civil war.

I felt safe enough in those early days to voice some criticism and ironical comment of that bragging superior kind characteristic of those who always pretend to know everything. I allowed myself some harmless fun at the expense of those who had been singing the German national anthem and the Nazi's 'Horst Wessel' hymn in the wrong tune, and gave a factual account of the events with a patriotic bow to old Hindenburg and a non-committal reference to Hitler. Even though my essay earned the distinction of being read out in class and earning some titters of approval, I secretly felt ashamed of the dishonesty of my allegedly 'objective' account. It allowed me of course to miss the political point of those decisive days and hours in the history of my century and generation. But so had, of course, most of the German millions and the rest of the world missed it, except for the few who saw what was coming and had the guts to speak out. If only this minority had prevailed over the cowardly majority early on, when this was still possible.

In the following days, weeks and months began that slide into totalitarianism, which we have since learnt to understand rightly as Big Brother taking over Animal Farm. We were, of course, not aware of his existence all those tragic years before George Orwell had the genius to show up the Soviet situation, which in a similar sense was Hitler's too. In my time, we were far from regarding it as a subject for political satire. In the early phase of Hitler's German honeymoon, ominous new laws were passed to create the terrible equality of all 'animals' and to strengthen the centralized powers of the ruling pigs over the stupid horses. One merely heard of a suicide here and there, of people fleeing the country, taking with them only the barest necessities. The police came knocking at doors in the early morning; their shouts to open up took on a new and fearful symbolism. Some people disappeared, not to be heard of again, others into concentration camps, for the 're-education' of society's 'shady' characters, one was told – communists, homosexuals, Jews and gypsies. Were not the concentration camps, after all, a tried British invention from the Boer War? 'Decent, ordinary citizens', it was forever repeated, had nothing to fear. Powerful trades unions and other political parties were gradually dissolved on the grounds that in the new Third Reich one party, one people, one Führer sufficed to take care of all that democratic stuff.

Christian churches were not openly molested at first, mainly because their bishops, Protestant and quite a few Catholic ones, could be relied on to lend their moral support in welcoming Hitler as 'a bulwark against Bolshevism' and the moral ally of all decent, hard-working citizens. Some Jewish shops were boycotted, others had to close down, Jewish-owned stores were expropriated and the books of Nazi opponents were publicly burnt, but as yet, it was all done in the nicest of ways. Only much later, in June 1934, were leftist, opposition elements within Hitler's storm troopers openly eliminated in the famous 'Night of the Long Knives'. Then, in August 1934, Hindenburg died, leaving the Führer in sole command. One of Hitler's cleverest, most diabolical innovations was his ability to rally those behind him who, without agreeing with him, shared bits of his ideology. These were the patriots and German nationalists, the Jew haters in the Christian churches, and the Liberals, intellectuals and academics who felt that Hitler was completing the work of the French Revolution as far as *fraternité* and *égalité* were concerned. Thus, his particular mix of national socialism proved most effective in adding a leftist element to Nazism, and turning it into a much more powerful weapon than mere fascist or right-wing extremism could have been.

A few months later in the first year of Hitler's *Machtergreifung* (seizure of power), as it came euphemistically to be called to conceal the shameful fact that it was all happening democratically, the day came for our own departure from Hamburg. I can still see my old grandmother standing at the end of the Dammtor railway station platform, supporting herself on her black ebony walking stick and trying bravely to wave to us, my mother and me, as though it were not a terrible parting for 'good' or forever. My father had left earlier to prepare accommodation for us in Prague. All my grandmother's children and grandchildren had by then left. She remained behind, writing to us frequently. It did not seem to have occurred to us, or perhaps we would not admit it openly to ourselves, that she too would be, as yet unthinkably, among Hitler's ultimate victims.

My grandmama's big journey
However, this was not to happen at once, but almost ten years later. She then wrote what was her last letter from Hamburg dated 8 June 1943. Even before that, her life had been changed in ways of which we knew only the barest details, such as her enforced removal to ghetto-like accommodation with other old people. Her actual last letter was addressed to a friend in neutral Sweden who by previous arrangement passed the information on to other of her relations. Numbered '163', in her orderly way, she merely wrote that she had just heard the news that she was about 'to go on her big journey'. This was an ironic allusion to the famous poem 'The Happy Wanderer' by Eichendorff, a Romantic poet that all German children learnt by heart in school, however inappropriate its meaning in the Nazi context: 'God sends those into the far distant world to whom he wants to show his special favour.' Aged 85, mentally alert, though badly weakened physically by arthritis, my poor grandmother wrote that for her, too, this long journey was about to begin. She did not mention her destination. However, everybody guessed that it would be Theresienstadt or Terezin, the concentration camp euphemistically also known as the 'old people's ghetto', in remote northern Bohemia by the River Eger. Founded by Austrian Emperor Joseph II in the second half of the eighteenth century, it was a 12-turreted garrison town of neat two-storeyed

houses with basements and lofts along straight roads, covering an area of 1200 by 920 metres, with six fortified gateways. It was intended for three regiments and 2000 civilians with all amenities such as bakeries, halls and shops. Gavrilo Princip, who shot the Archduke Franz Ferdinand and the Archduchess in 1914, died in its hospital. Under Hitler, it was under SS control, but administered by a council of Jewish elders. It was euphemistically not regarded as a concentration camp but as a kind of intermediate stop for the extermination camps of the final solution like Auschwitz in Poland, a kind of 'second best', or 'lesser evil', in the Nazi scale of inhumanity, but unimaginable in its full reality to a present generation.

The 60,000 people who were there at any one time had misleadingly been told to take only light clothes because they would be staying at a 'spa' in the Bohemian mountains. Of the 135,000 people deported there, only 7 per cent survived, for 35,000 died of famine or old age. Between 1941 and 1945 some 41,900 German and 15,266 Austrian Jews were 'evacuated' there, the term 'deported' was forbidden to be used, according to H. G. Adler's monumental documented study of that hell, which he subtitled euphemistically *Profile of an Enforced Community*.

My grandmother was evidently aware of what the 'journey into the big wide world' in overcrowded cattle trucks involved. She went prepared for the ordeal as best she could, taking no more than a carrier basket with a change of clothing and the precious soft duvet under which she was used to sleeping at night. On the one hand, as she put it, she was glad that at least the 'great fear' over what was to happen was over. Once that was behind one, she wrote, everything else mattered less. There was even a chance she might meet relatives, friends or people she knew.

She faced the journey with tremendous resolve: 'What must be must be, and what so many are able to bear, I want to bear, too. Do not worry at all on my account. My greatest pain will be to be deprived of news from all of you. My prayers will ever be with all of you. May everything turn out well for all of you. I embrace you with all my love and affection. Yours, Anna Hess.'

From another source it was eventually confirmed that the beloved 'old one', equipped as she was with so many admirable, indeed, heroic virtues of mind, heart and spirit had been fortunate to live in that human hell for only three months after arriving at Theresienstadt. She died of old age and, one hoped, was spared the ultimate indignity of being deprived of her last link with civilization and everything that was dear to her, namely her beloved feather duvet.

2

Viennese Emancipation

My father's hope of starting up a viable new existence in Prague was to be disappointed. So soon after Hitler's rise, nobody in Czechoslovakia wanted to have any dealings with someone bearing the name of his deputy and apparently representing the commercial interests of the Third Reich. Moving to Prague seemed to have been a harebrained idea. Still, neither he nor the Czechs could be blamed for not anticipating what Hitlerism held in store for the world. Aged 47 and used to a comfortable middle-class way of life, my father lacked an émigré's knack for turning his mind and hands to anything remunerative that came his way. While the stage engagements for which my mother had hoped were not forthcoming, as a woman and being more adaptable, she was ungrudgingly able to make the best of things. I, as an immature teenager, was probably a growing nuisance to both of them.

One advantage for us in Czechoslovakia, little more than a decade after the independent Czechoslovakian republic had been carved out of the Habsburg Empire by Thomas Masaryk, was that the older generation was brought up learning to speak German, so one could get along quite well in that language. Considering how much the people in that part of central Europe suffered, first under Hitler, then under the iron curtain countries, it is not surprising that there has since been a wholesale linguistic shift. English/American, even Russian has replaced German as central Europe's lingua franca, and that applies to cultural changes as well. The Habsburgs have finally had their day.

In Prague, we lived on practically no income in a small, furnished, two-room flat, and later in a cheap hotel-pension. The cramped conditions made for frequent rows. I was beginning to feel closer to my mother and, at 13, wanted to protect her. Lying in bed at night behind a drawn curtain, I would overhear my parents quarreling. My mother had apparently found out about my father's penchant for pretty Czech women, while for her, as a good looking Austrian with a lively temperament, she felt at home in Mozart's Prague and was not averse to being found attractive by chivalrous Czech gentlemen. One day, when my father was out, the fairly young manager of our hotel came to have tea with us. I could not help noticing how he picked up my mother's paper napkin, which she had dropped accidentally. It bore the imprint of her lipstick and, with an admiring look, he pocketed it as a souvenir. It was the sort of thing at which any central European charmer would excel, causing her an embarrassed smile but I, a puritanical teenager, was shocked.

I went to a German secondary school in Prague, Stefan's gymnasium, and had to prepare for an examination in rudimentary Czech, which was not too difficult and which I passed. I was also beginning to be interested in girls. In Hamburg, there had been a sad parting from Eva, my first real girlfriend. My feelings for her were, however, complicated because the real object of my infatuation happened to be her beautiful mother, which of course remained secret. When, many years later, I came to write the biography of Lord Acton, the nineteenth-century English historian, I was not least attracted to him because of his similar experience. Aged 16, he was sent to Munich for higher studies where he became devoted to a beautiful Italian cousin, ten years his senior and the mother of several children. She cared for the young man and was the first woman to take an interest in his ideas. Later he married one of her daughters, expecting to recapture what he had felt for her mother and hoping that she would become like her. The daughter resented his secret attachment and naturally wanted to be loved for her own sake. Happily, no similar complication existed in my case, but it gave me, I think, some empathy for such complicated teenage involvements.

Lovely Prague seemed fertile ground for romantic attachments. Its coeducational school system, which was new to me, provided a distraction. On Saturdays, when school finished early, some of us boys would combine a longer stroll home through the inner city streets in pursuit of four or five girls from our class. They always stayed ahead, with much giggling and turning round to see if we were still there. We usually ended up in a café renowned for its delicious poppy seed cakes on Wencelas Square. I do not think we had much conversation with the girls. The point of the innocent flirting was the relaxing pursuit rather than the catching up, an early form of *nachsteigen* (literally going after the girls), which was a well-known central European pastime. There might have been for us an unconscious link with the fable of the fox and the sour grapes, in which a fox secretly practises jumping over the wall until he is successful, only to discover that the grapes really are sour. How innocent we were compared with the teenagers of a later generation! Nevertheless, being in Prague seemed to bring me happiness then, and I have always remained greatly attached to that lovely city with its special Central European atmosphere. Along with countless others, I felt helpless anger when, a few years later, Neville Chamberlain referred to it in terms of 'a quarrel in a faraway country between people of whom we know nothing' and, as British prime minister, encouraged Hitler to help himself to it.

The killing of Chancellor Dollfuss

After little more than a year in Prague, my parents decided to move to Vienna, which, though offering us little economic improvement, was at least where my mother was at home. It also became my intellectual, emotional and spiritual home at an important phase of my development. However, soon after our arrival we had a bitter foretaste of things to come. While listening to the one o'clock radio news during lunch in my grand-father's home on 25 July 1934, there was a strange silence followed by a shuffling noise. Then, unexpectedly the newsreader announced that the Austrian federal government had resigned, that Anton Rintelen had taken over from Chancellor Dr Engelbert Dollfuss and that people were to abide by the new government's ordinances. Then, equally abruptly, the broadcast stopped and German marching songs followed. We looked at one another alarmed. Rintelen was known to be a politician with Nazi sympathies. Apparently, we had witnessed a startling political development.

Soon it emerged that a detachment of German SS troops, dis-guised as Austrian soldiers, had stormed RAVAG (the Vienna broadcasting headquarters) and forced the newsreaders to make that announcement. However, the coup failed because Austrian security forces overpowered the attackers. We then heard that a similar gang had forced its way into the federal chancellor's office when Dr Dollfuss was alone, his other ministers having already left for lunch. Little Dollfuss, known as the 'pocket-size' chancellor, tried to resist his attackers, but was overpowered, shot and left to die without medical aid or priestly assistance, for which he had asked. These attackers were later overpowered and arrested, as was another batch of armed men who tried to occupy the federal president's residence.

The attack on the Vienna broadcasting station was to have been the signal for uprisings in the Austrian provincial capitals. However, the Nazi plotters reckoned neither on the Austrian army's loyalty to the elected government, nor on the Austrians rejecting their old dream of becoming part of a greater German Reich. Therefore, nothing came of the planned invasion by exiled Austrian Nazis from across the Bavarian frontier, assisted by German troops under Hitler's command. The affair was a dismal failure, indeed Hitler's first international defeat.

But it was also a rehearsal for what was to happen, more successfully, four years later when Austria ceased to be an independent country. After Dollfuss's funeral, I was selected to join a delegation of Austrian boy scouts to present condolences and flowers to his widow, Mrs Alwine Dollfuss, and her orphaned children. It was a sad occasion and added to my resolve to support a free Austria for which Dollfuss had died. Germany, my 'fatherland' had lost its freedom to Hitler. Perhaps I could help my 'mother's land' prevail against him. Kurt von Schuschnigg, who succeeded Dollfuss as chancellor, told the German ambassador in Vienna that he would 'not allow Austria to be turned into a colony or province of the German Reich', words he had to swallow when that came about but that the whole world's revulsion at Dollfuss's callous murder enabled him to use at the time. But Austria won only a brief respite. There was a wave of support for Schuschnigg's 'Patriotic Front' government, which I joined with fervour. But the Socialists, whom the right-wing Austrian government had heavily defeated in the earlier February 1934 rising, would never allow themselves to be reconciled to it. Four years later, on the night of 10 March 1938 and of the real German invasion, I was travelling home in the underground when a workman, a little high on beer, proclaimed to all the passengers: 'If they hadn't shot at us in 1934, we would be fighting for *them* at this moment.' That wretched drunk was expressing the old division between 'them' and 'us', but failed to see that by reviling the Austrian establishment, he was punishing himself too.

Meanwhile, in Prague, I had developed a facility for essay writing, producing stories and articles, which, though I was not yet 14, I managed to get published in the Sunday youth supplement of *Prager Tagblatt,* the leading German newspaper in Czechoslovakia. In Vienna I later found similar outlets in the *Tagerl,* the children's supplement of a prominent Viennese paper. I even got into the *Kronen Zeitung,* then and still the tabloid with the largest circulation, a sort of Austrian *Daily Mirror.* These freelance activities became my private cottage industry, at the cost, I must admit, of my progress at school, though the occasional fees I received provided welcome pocket money. Still wearing short trousers, I must have been an unusual sight in the Vienna editorial offices on Friday evenings when I made occasional deliveries of copy before the Sunday supplements went to press. I had learnt to produce my copy as required, typed in double-space on only one side of the paper. I used a self-invented 'four or five finger-typing system', which has lasted me into the computer age. I then had the satisfaction of appearing in print on Sunday and basking in some early glory on Monday from my schoolmate-readers' reactions – 'Read your article yesterday, jolly good.'

In June 1937, not yet 17, I won first prize in the *7-Tage Blatt,* competition for 'Tell us the biggest adventure of your life'. My contribution was a story, told in the first person, of a workman in a factory that produced super phosphates, or artificial fertilizer. His, 'my' job was to look after several huge vats of sulphuric acid at near boiling point. There was a short-circuit over one of the vats, the lamp had to be replaced, a dangerous exercise high up over the whirling liquid. For the repair 'I' stood on a plank over the vat, which, however, suddenly slipped away. I thus had only a rope to hang onto over the poisonous liquid. For the thrill and benefit of the reader I added: 'One drop of that liquid in my eyes and I would go blind for ever. And to swallow only a minute drop would make it impossible for any doctor to pump out my stomach, since no stomach would be left after the stuff had passed through my guts like molten lead! No use calling for help. The motor noise was such that I didn't even try.'

Eventually 'I' made it to safety. I described how I managed to

7. Teenager as budding journalist.

swing my body to and fro and thereby fall just over the vat's
edge. I forget from where I got the idea, probably from a
newspaper report about just such a happening, which I then
embroidered. I must have described the hair-raising incident
fairly accurately, for it evoked no angry rejoinders. My parents
merely shook their heads in disbelief at my 'imaginative' skills.
Personal vanity, above all, an eagerness to see my name in print,
undoubtedly inspired these early journalistic ventures. When,
later on, I became a full blooded journalist and discovered what
a vain calling it was, I could hope that my unusually early start
might at least have reduced any disposition on my part in that
respect.

I was a teenager with a good intellectual grasp and quick wit,
evidently based on my wide reading and passion for sitting on

the floor to cut out newspaper articles and collect interesting bits. I was also inclined not to think before I leapt. I evidently had need for Prudence's golden rule – 'When in doubt, leave out', though a British environment was needed for that to bear fruit. Moreover, my lack of discretion and argumentative nature led to religious tensions with my Viennese Orthodox Jewish grandfather. He was never told that I had been baptized in Hamburg and brought up as an evangelical Lutheran, which he would not have tolerated.

When, through my boy-scout activities in my teens, I came increasingly under another, Catholic, religious influence this added to the difficulties in my grandfather's house. Outwardly of course I knew that I had to respect his outlook and attend his customary religious ceremonies. But this was clearly not my world and he would neither have allowed an apostate under his roof, which racially I was in his eyes, nor made allowances for a genuine and conscientious change of religious conviction. I resented that racist attitude almost as much as I did the Nazi variety.

In my changing religious ideas, the Old Testament acquired a new meaning, expressed by the prophet Isaiah:

> Thus says the, Lord, he who formed you, O Israel: 'Fear not, for I have redeemed you; I have called you by name, you are mine. When you pass through the waters I will be with you; and through the rivers, they shall not overwhelm you; and when you walk through fire you shall not be burned, and the flame shall not consume you. For I am the Lord your God, the Holy One of Israel, your Saviour.'
>
> (Isaiah 43)

And what for me was about to harden into more than mere promise, indeed convinced me as a truth was St Paul's message:

> For through faith you are all sons of God in Christ Jesus. Baptized into union with him, you have put on Christ as a garment. There is no such thing as Jew or Greek, slave and freeman, male and female; for you are all one person in Jesus Christ. But if you thus belong, you are the 'issue' of Abraham, and so heirs by promise.
>
> (Gal. 3, 28)

Intellectually, I was entering upon a new relationship with my inherited religious Old Testament origins, which were neither racial nor national and in which I came to hold that Christ the Messiah had already come.

Austria, my mother's cultural world, was becoming for me a new sort of political home in which I felt close to what were to be the last years of an independent Austria and I steeped myself in its history. Austria had attracted many people who had not been Austrians by birth; it was rather like ancient Rome insofar as it was the homeland rather than the race that became the focus of these people's loyalty and patriotism. My native Hamburg, for example, always assumed more importance in my affections than Germany, which I had always been loath to accept in the narrowly nationalist nineteenth-century sense forged by Bismarck. As the Austrian writer Heimito von Doderer described it, 'To be Austrian is a condition, a state of mind rather than a nationality.' And many others thought likewise, including Prince Eugene who came from Savoy, Beethoven, Metternich, Brahms, and the surgeon Billroth, who all came from Germany but became Austrian 'mentally' or by predilection.

Tu, felix Austria

The Habsburgs, who ruled Austria for 650 years, were originally Swabian and they turned it into a supra-national empire at the crossroads of Europe, or, to a lesser extent, a melting pot for its various conquerors – the Romans, Huns, Lombards, Avars, Slavs and Magyars. The Habsburgs taught them how to live together, how to consolidate power through marriage alliances according to the motto *Tu, felix Austria, nube* (You, happy Austria, marry). The Vienna telephone directory is still full of the foreign names of those who had settled there – Bohemian shoemakers and tailors, as well as others from Bulgaria, Romania, Poland, Russia, Serbia, Spain, Portugal, along with the Jews who mainly became victims of the Holocaust. Early twentieth-century Catholic Austria produced a particularly virulent mix of nationalist xenophobia and anti-Semitism under politicians like Karl Lueger, the famous mayor of Vienna (1844–1910), or Karl Georg von Schönerer (1842–1921). In his formative Viennese years, Adolf Hitler was to become their acolyte.

Hitler was the grandson of Maria Anna Schickelgruber, who was seduced by a Jewish lawyer called Frankenberger who paid

her alimony for 14 years. This is how the rumour started of
Hitler's alleged Jewish descent. With the help of his later party
ally, the Bavarian minister of justice Hans Frank, hanged after
1945, Hitler combated these rumours and created the more
familiar version of his background given in *Mein Kampf*. But the
story of a frail Aryan blonde innocently victimized by a crafty
Jew links convincingly with his anti-alcoholism, vegetarianism
and hatred of Jews. Hitler's version of his antecedents includes a
severe, authoritarian but respectable father, Alois Hitler, an
official in the imperial Austrian customs service (who died in
1903), and descent from peasant stock in the lower Austrian
forests. Friedrich Heer, a well-known Austrian Catholic historian
(1916–83) dealt in great and well-researched detail with Hitler's
ancestry in his *Der Glaube des Adolf Hitler* (The Faith of Adolf
Hitler), aptly subtitled 'The anatomy of a political religiosity'
(published by Bechtle, Munich 1968), before the wave of Hitler
biographies. Perhaps on that account and because Heer was able
knowledgeably to deal with religious ideas, which were at that
time taken less seriously by other historians, his book never
received the notice it deserved and was neglected by later Hitler
biographers.

Vienna was naturally added to my historical interests. There
was something special about the way the past was looked upon
in this part of old Europe; there was an acceptance of the
transience of man's life on earth, of the inevitable passing of
things, as well as of empires, indeed of the mystery of time, as
symbolized in Dürer's and Schubert's *Death of the Maiden*. I had
a friend who was a passionate collector of clocks, which is a
peculiarly Austrian hobby that is no doubt linked to time and its
passing. 'What a delightful, seductive time it was,' says a
character in Albert Lortzing's comic opera *Der Waffenschmied*
(1848). The Austrian poet Anastasius Grün (Count Anton von
Auersperg) wrote: 'Do not mock time, it is pure! Mocking time is
to mock yourself! For time is like the clean white page, not yet
written upon: the paper is without blemish, but it is you who are
the writing! And if the writing fails to edify, why blame the
paper?' If one strolls through the inner city streets and alleys of
Vienna in the heart of the old imperial royal city, one can hear
whispering, plaintive sounds, as if a multiple-voiced choir is
evoking the passing generations – or is it the wind sweeping into
Vienna from the Pannonian Plain?

Where else could one have been made more aware of the tragedy of Austria's past than through the *force majeure* of German unity being forged by Prussian arms so long before any thought of a united Europe? The little Austrian republic of the 1930s had seen the decline and fall of other empires and few Austrians believed in the economic viability of their country. Being part of a larger Germany caused a fatal blindness to reality, especially after the ex-Austrian Hitler appeared across the border to be the restorer of new German nationalist greatness. Their common language and cultural unity, many then felt, should naturally lead to a common nationality, but nobody believes that any more. It took the loss of independence and of relative democratic freedom, not to mention untold Austrian lives in Hiler's war, for the reborn postwar Austria to gain a new faith in itself. Practically nothing has changed in its actual economic or geographical viability between 1938 and now that Austria is part of the bigger European Union. However, since the nineteenth century Germany had been embarking on a German–Prussian solution and the German nationalist path seemed to be a desirable option for Austrians too. Defeated by Prussia in 1864, Austria was excluded from its historically German concerns. *1866* The whirlpool of nationalities in the heart of Europe was bound to prove an explosive mixture once Austria was pushed to the edge and towards its old Italian and southeast European interests, until it became blocked there too by nationalist stirrings.

However, in the political climate of the late nineteenth century the dual Austro–Hungarian monarchy would have been no better than the Hohenzollerns at promoting German unification, for the sense of German and Hungarian nationalist supremacy was already far too advanced. There was no option other than to bury once and for all any hope of a multinational society. When a Serbian nationalist assassinated Archduke Franz Ferdinand and his wife in Sarajevo on 28 June 1914, the arrogant Germans in Vienna were able to insist on punitive measures against Serbia, but only in the certainty of Berlin's staunchest support, which took the world into the First World War.

Among my childhood memories I recall holding onto a grown-up's hand while walking on the elevated balustrade of the former Vienna Ministry of War building. '*Si vis pacem, para bellum*' (If you want peace, prepare for war) was inscribed on its roof in large gold letters and that old message derived from the Roman writer Vegetius became imprinted on my mind, perhaps because of its arrogant truth. Only later did I come to realize that the twelve million German Austrians and ten million Magyars had usurped their numerical dominance over all the other nationalities that formed the old empire.

Significantly, Joseph Roth (1894–1939) from Brady in eastern Galicia, one of the despised *Ostjuden* or *Ashkenazim*, wrote the classic tribute to the Habsburg tradition. In *Radetzkymarsch* (1932) he describes old Austria as embodied in three generations of a family of officers and officials who served Emperor Franz Josef between 1859 and 1914. It was symbolic of the history of that tragic century that Roth should then die in Paris as Hitler's exile.

Living in Vienna acquainted one with two mythical figures of fun – Count Bobby and Count Rudy, who were counts of course because, among the Viennese, flattery would always get you far. In Vienna people were easily elevated to a 'Herr Doktor' or 'Herr Baron' because they felt pleased to be thus recognized, were duly flattered and would often respond with a generous tip. Counts Bobby and Rudi belonged to 'the good old days' of feeling at home with *noblesse oblige*. That they were not particularly bright only added to their charm, and they serve as fitting illustrations of the Austrian character.

For example, Bobby gets into a tram on which his former corporal from the First World War is the conductor. They celebrate their unexpected meeting. 'How are you, Schmidt?' Bobby asks with customary concern. 'Not well at all, Herr Major, I have a wife, three children, we are quite hard up.' Bobby feels sorry for him. 'You know what, Schmidt? Sell me another of your tickets.'

When Bobby has to go on a business trip, he asks Rudi to keep an eye on things in his absence. On returning, he asks for a report. 'Everything went fine', says Rudi, 'except one evening when your wife went out with another man. I went secretly after them.' 'And then what happened?' 'Well, they went to a restaurant and while they were there they held hands all the time. Then back they go to your house.' 'And then?' 'Well, I follow them, they go to your bedroom, with me watching from outside. They get undressed. Then the lights were turned out.' 'How terrible', Bobby groans, 'Being left with such uncertainty!'

Then Bobby happens to meet Rudi riding on a lady's bicycle. 'How did you get that?' he asks. 'Well, quite simple, you know. I was walking in the Vienna woods when I met this pretty girl riding a bike. I talk to her. She gets off. We walk together, then suddenly, she leans the bike against a tree, throws herself into the grass and says to me: "Take what you like." So I took the bicycle.' Of course, Austrian literary humour has comparable treasures – Grillparzer's definition of the Bavarians, for example, as 'marking the transition from Prussia to humanity', or Johann Nestroy's very Viennese maxim: 'I always think the worst of every man, myself included, and have rarely been mistaken.' Or the poet Ferdinand Raimund pronouncing his own obituary: 'Oh, forever to be regretted me.' Summing up, as it were, all the scourges of life as well as the fact that nothing can be done about it, is the regretful and nostalgic musical exclamation from Johann Strauss's *Die Fledermaus*: 'Happy is he who forgets what cannot be changed.'

Meeting a great contemporary

In Vienna I was introduced to the writings of a famous German exile, Friedrich Wilhelm Foerster (1869–1966), widely known for his educational books and, in particular, for the graphic and practical manner in which he dealt with the sometimes difficult moral problems of young people. I had written to him first. He answered cordially without condescension and from this a correspondence developed, indeed a friendship over his last years. What attracted me to him at first was his rejection of woolly-headed idealism, which had become the bane of all German thinking from the nineteenth to the twentieth century.

Philosophers like Hegel and Schelling were the originators of this idealism, which had a profound influence on the politics of the time, with national unification achieved in 1870 under Prussia's military leadership. Significantly, Hegel, a south German, hailed Prussian statecraft as Germany's redemptive feature.

Prussian discipline, authority and order henceforth exercised a strong attraction for non-Prussian Germans. No greater contrast of opposites was then thinkable than between Bismarck, the statesman of *Realpolitik,* and the great Hölderlin, a Swabian man of sentiment, visionary poet and prophet, yet the two types were only united much later after long and mutual rejection. It was almost a psychological problem.

Foerster, a Prussian by birth, illustrated it by referring to Plato's definition of Eros as an attraction of opposites: 'poverty's desire for riches', but also in the opposite sense, in which men or women of great intellect sometimes choose bores or dullards as partners because they need a hold on life that is quite different from their own. With respect to German history Foerster suggested that after Luther's Reformation the Prussian masculine and military virtues came to be accepted as a substitute for the Christian element then uprooted from its Roman origins and left, as it were, to the abundance of Germanic feeling.

Another fitting comparison was between the soft, sensitive snail that grows its shell from its own secretions, like the Germans of the south and west, the men of feeling and sentiment, and the hardened masculinity of Prussia's historical apartheid, based on the legendary model of Siegfried putting on his dragon's skin.

Such a mentality produced, after Bismarck, all that far-off noisy emphasis on 'the Iron Chancellor' and the symbols of 'steel-hardened reality'. Against that, and being a good teacher, Foerster articulated another notion of strength and masculinity based on character rather than outward show. Quoting the memoirs of clever German women he pointed to the lack of 'iron-like' qualities among their noisily strutting jackbooted and steel-helmeted men. After Bismarck that mentality was taken over by the Nazis, as Göring tellingly put it in 1933: 'Henceforth the pace of goose-stepping Potsdam grenadiers has become the pace of the German people.' To counter that German nationalist madness and aware that nothing was worse than 'Prussianized' south Germans, indeed Austrians (like Hitler), Foerster half-seriously tried to persuade the German educational establishment to ban all idealism, recommending teaching the ancient 'Persian arts', as they were called, as a substitute.

These were riding, archery and telling the truth, for they aimed precisely and metaphorically at what German idealism had neglected to promote and what ought to be the basis of all education, namely instilling a sense of reality as an attribute of character. Riding would achieve that through learning to control one's animal instincts. Those who dream or hesitate are likely to be thrown off their horse. Archery was useful in training eyes and hands to hit a target's centre, as darts or throwing a cricket ball accurately had shown in the English-speaking countries. Finally, learning to tell the truth is its own reward. Unfortunately, Foerster failed to have his ideas adopted.

8. Professor Friedrich Wilhelm Foerster (1869–1966), my German mentor and friend.

His own long life had a German historical relevance. A 'good' Prussian, he was born in Berlin shortly before it became the capital of the united German Reich. His mother was a close relative of Field Marshal von Moltke, victor in the Franco–Prussian war of 1870. While their home was a centre for the new

Prussian military elite, the liberal-humanist influence of
Foerster's father was more decisive. He was an astronomer, the
director of the Berlin planetarium and a friend of Alexander von
Humboldt, one of the great early natural scientists in Europe. In
his memoirs Foerster recalls how as a teenager in his school choir
he had refused to sing the new German national anthem
'Deutschland, Deutschland über alles' because his father had
questioned its sentiment: 'Really above everything else in the
world! Perhaps also above honour, right and conscience?' The
teacher punished him by sending him home, saying 'Foerster, we
two shall never get along.'

It was a foretaste of his life, for Foerster became a leading
opponent of that generation's new German militarist nationalism. Evoking Prussia's martial spirit as the salvation of the
nation on the 25th anniversary of the battle of Sedan, young
Kaiser Wilhelm II delivered a speech denouncing German Social
Democrats as 'unpatriotic fellows'. Foerster, then aged 26,
criticized the emperor in an article that closed with the words:
'You, William II, are leading the German people into war. You,
William II, King of Prussia, are spreading the poison of Prussian-
ism over Europe.' This led to a charge of *lèse-majesté* (high
treason) and a sentence of three months' confinement in a
fortress, which temporarily excluded Foerster from a German
academic career.

He then went abroad and in London studied the early development of the English working-class movement and the work of
social reformers like Arnold Toynbee. After that he became a
university lecturer in Zurich. In his first and immediately successful book *Jugendlehre* (Teaching the Young, 1912) he
approached the problems of the young from the viewpoint of a
realist and inductive thinker opposed as much to the abstract
intellectualism of the time as to its authoritarian methods.
'Cathedrals', he wrote, 'are planned from above and built up
from below.' The metaphor was relevant, for he soon discovered
that it was impossible to deal with human nature realistically
without a religious foundation. Eventually, he felt compelled to
admit to the failure of Auguste Comte's positivist 'reconstruction
sans Dieu' (Reconstruction without God) to which he had originally been committed.

Studying Plato's *The Republic* taught him that individuals
were ill suited to discovering on their own the supreme ideas of

their lives. This rather was the task of Plato's 'class of guardians', equipped for such leadership through appropriate preparation and suitability. The concept was of course dangerously exploited by right-wingers, of whom Foerster remained no less critical than he was of the extreme left. Gradually he came to see the problems of the supreme authority of the Church in the same way. Studying the great Christian authors, especially the works of St Augustine, showed him that he had, unwittingly, strayed into Christianity. And I followed Foerster along that path.

However, conscious that the mystery the Church presented to the world had little to do with its basic truths or supreme purpose, which he felt ready to accept, he stopped on that road. Like many of his contemporaries, he drew the line over its man-made customs, ceremonies and structures. He would have sympathized with Simone Weil (1909–43), the French philosopher whose *Gravity and Grace* and *Waiting for God* showed her restless search for the absolute. She was drawn to Christ and the Church through her sense of the secret of suffering, yet, because of her solidarity with the unbaptized, she never fully accepted either and died in England among the 'Free French'. Similarly, the French writer André Gide (1869–1951), wavered throughout his life between the denominations of his Huguenot father and Catholic mother. The Catholic poet Paul Claudel tried to encourage him to return to the Church, but his communism and homosexuality thwarted him. Foerster believed that the Church had in the course of the nineteenth century arrived at a Vatican-centred materialization of its dogma.

By way of an explanatory comparison he used to refer to the customary notice at the entrance of concert halls: 'Hats, coats and umbrellas are to be left in the cloakroom and not taken into the auditorium.' Applied to the Church, this meant that the immortal soul, too, had been endowed, so to speak, with an earthly home and shield in the form of skin, bones, nose, ears, teeth and intestines. The immortal soul, too, had to leave such human aids in the heavenly 'cloakroom'.

In his memoirs, *Erlebte Weltgeschichte* (Experienced World History, 1954), Foerster describes how as a student he once, in disgust, left a lecture given by the Darwinian scholar Weismann because he wanted to subject man's conscience to the principle of selection. After that, Foerster entered the cathedral of Freiburg and there, suddenly amid its Gothic splendours, found his true spiritual home. Aged 30, he had become a convinced Christian, but he never entered the Catholic Church, comparing himself humorously with a man holding an umbrella walking outside 'in the rain' while past him flocked the faithful, many of them, myself included, having been shown the way there through his books. His decision to 'wait outside' was not dictated by facile motives like intellectual pride. He regarded himself in a higher service, recommending Catholics to adopt more freedom and Protestants more authority. He quoted St Thomas, who said there might be circumstances when, for reasons of conscience, a man should accept even excommunication. Was it justifiable, Foerster wondered, under particular circumstances to delay one's entry?

One of his many reasons was undoubtedly that his understanding of the truths and mission of the Catholic Church had, as it were, outrun the capacity for belief of one brought up in the categories of modern scientific thinking. A German contemporary, Wilhelm Busch (1832–1908), the famous comic writer and caricaturist, something of a German Edward Lear, expressed this feeling on behalf of his whole generation: 'Over there, on the other shore, St Augustine seemed to be waiting, beckoning to me in all seriousness: Here is the ship of faith, the bark of Peter and divine grace, with its ferryman calling out: Come over to us. But I am incapable of responding, having lost my spiritual voice, philosophically speaking; my soul having caught a chill.' The close alliance between throne and altar had been particularly obnoxious for German Protestants no less than Catholics, surrendering to Caesar what was God's and causing the 'Babylonian Exile'.

Like many others Foerster humbly remained outside the threshold. 'If the Church were only a Sacrament, it would be easy enough to accept, but it is so much more and that is where the difficulties of belief come in,' he wrote in a private letter to me who, as a fresh convert, naively thought I could encourage someone much older than I was to take the step I had taken. But there was a consoling truth in what a Catholic friend of his, the Hungarian Bishop Ottokar Proházka (1859–1927), said of him: 'God knows what grounds Providence has for putting these obstacles in his way. Perhaps he is meant to say things that as yet you cannot say within the Catholic Church today.' And he added that he ought to be called 'a bishop of the invisible Church'.

Foerster's educational and religious ideas found expression in more than thirty books. He had a profound influence on the German youth movement before and after the First World War and on generations of Christian teachers throughout Europe. He tried to reconcile apparent opposites, as indicated in the titles of his books – *The Cultural Problem of the Church*, *Technology and Morality*, *Christianity and the Class Struggle* and, in 1937, *Europe and the German Question*, a prophetic work that was happily realized 70 years later. I was partly responsible for getting it translated by E. I. Watkin and published by Sheed & Ward in London in 1943. However, it was publicly burned in Nazi Germany in 1937, along with books by Thomas Mann and others in one of the *autos-da-fé* that Hitler had taken over from the Inquisition.

In Vienna I became aware of what German nationalism, in which Foerster had played an important though little known historical role, had meant in its past imperial days. He told me about it and, since it was an integral part of his and the century's struggle against one of its worst evils, it is worth recording. Early in 1914, while he was a professor at the university of Vienna, the main hall of the university, crowded to the rafters, was the scene of a noisy demonstration, which was symptomatic of the political climate at the time of the outbreak of the First World War. The event, a cultural celebration in honour of Richard Wagner, was before an audience drawn from all the nationalities of the dual monarchy. It consisted of an aggressive panegyric and glorification of German culure that culminated in the students singing the aggressively nationalistic German *Wacht am Rhein*.

Foerster and others were struck by the significance of that event happening in Vienna, at the university of a supranational state that depended for its existence on relegating national sentiment to the background and remaining conscious of the many different foreign traditions, including Slavonic and Hungarian, in its political community. He regarded such national boasting as primitive and barbaric. People of normal intelligence and feeling know the worth of their national culture and leave it to others to recognize and express it. But when the race at the centre of Europe ceases to act as a bulwark against nationalism and power politics and stoops to glorify it, intending to make its victims tremble, Europe must, as we saw, be cleft asunder and a world catastrophe ensue.

The Danubian monarchy was the surviving relic of the medieval supernational German empire. Had the Austrians preserved the old German tradition of international organization, they could have brought in these young nations, whose sons came to the capital to study, and be confirmed as part of a great enterprise in international and supposedly fraternal relations, rather than one in which dominance of one national group over the others should have been decisive.

The murderous shots at Sarajevo in June 1914 and their repercussions were to drown that possibility, though not before a last attempt to solve the central European problem of nationalities had been made by creating a Slav and German community that was to transform the dual monarchy into a genuine confederation, including the Czechs. Foerster developed these ideas in a pamphlet entitled *Das Österreichische Problem* (published in 1916) in which he sought to demonstrate the political as well as religious and moral regeneration of the whole world. But the idea of harmonizing races of opposing characteristics in a single community then seemed laughable; that 'ramshackle' monarchy appeared to have no place in history. But, as Foerster showed, anyone knowing how much organizing ability and constructive political education was required to negotiate all the arrangements great and small between the nationalities under Austrian rule, would perhaps understand that those other states with their comparably simple domestic problems would fail miserably if confronted with Austria's task.

Arising from all this was an audience granted to Foerster in early July 1917 by the Emperor Karl who had succeeded Franz Josef to the throne. The meeting, which took place in the park of the emperor's palace at Reichenau, was almost overshadowed by the dramatic and disastrous defeat soon to threaten the central powers. The emperor, aged 30, strode at Foerster's side through the twilight, having thrown his cloak onto the stump of a tree. He told Foerster about a recent visit by Hindenburg and Ludendorff at which the two German generals assured him that the Americans would never come to Europe and that the prospects of victory were excellent.

The emperor's view was different. He feared that the blind effort to force a military decision would lead to catastrophe. He maintained that the war aims of the entente should be met by a completely new southeast European federal organization; he saw this as the only chance of a speedy conclusion of a separate peace treaty, and the only possibility of securing the domestic peace of the nationalities under his rule. Verbatim, as afterwards confirmed by a protocol, Karl said to Foerster:

> It has long been my firm conviction that the hopeless situation of the peoples demands a radical change of policy. And that can only be confirmed and guaranteed by the dynasty which has for centuries symbolized the unity of the Austrian peoples and whose moral authority over its subject nations depends entirely on the sublimity of its supernational mission.
>
> I am well aware that thousands of every nationality in the Monarchy have long been eager for such a fresh start, but in the Empire no one understands the purpose for which Providence has united us in South-eastern Europe. Austria is neither a German nor a Slavonic state. The Germans, it is true, founded the Danubian Monarchy. But today they are a minority surrounded and penetrated by peoples striving to realize their own nationality. They can remain leaders of these young cultures only if they set an example of very high culture and meet these aspirants with love, respect and patience, Sin has been committed on all sides. The harm done must be made good. Therefore the past must be obliterated. Unless it is applied to the realities of Austria in an academic fashion, I have no fear of 'national self-determination'.
>
> If we generously grant each national group the utmost possible scope to develop its characteristic way of living, to develop its culture and to enjoy the use of its native language, they will be united in the Empire in a novel form more intimately than before and discard any impracticable excesses. In Austria even less than elsewhere can a political union be forcibly imposed on its nationalities from without. It must proceed from a moral union of the peoples. This spirit must be instilled into the young. In place of textbooks inflaming each side against the other, textbooks must be written, which will acquaint German children with the great endowments and virtues of the Slavs and inform Slavonic children of the German contribution to the world's culture and in particular to the

culture of the young Slavonic peoples of Southern Europe.
If we settle our domestic problems in this new spirit of
responsibility towards Europe we shall certainly regain the
trust of Europe and set an example of a universal league of
nations in the cause of peace.

Foerster was astonished by the emperor's freedom from the
prejudices and nationalist slogans that then imbued even
Austrians and from the German conviction that the hostile
powers were bent on Germany's complete destruction. He felt
that he was able to talk to the emperor about the war and its
foreseeable end as with a brother brought up in the same
intellectual atmosphere, and that he was as opposed as he, the
Prussian, was to the European nationalist evils. But the audience
also left him with the gloomy foreboding that the emperor's ideal
was far ahead of his time and that it had no chance of being
realized.

It was only some seven or eight decades later, long after
another destructive world war, that another united Europe was
to bear some resemblance to what Emperor Karl had envisaged
and seemed, at any rate, politically to justify (*if that were
possible, which of course it wasn't*), namely that beatification of
the Emperor Karl by the Catholic Church was to take place
nearly a century later in May 2004. 'A likeable Austrian
lieutenant', was how a university colleague described Karl to
Foerster. That indeed was what he appeared to be on the surface,
but to Foerster then he combined two distinct personalities. As
Foerster noted:

> The man who spoke to me was a young officer, but an
> independent thinker, a ruler deeply conscious of his
> responsibilities and enlightened by a tradition centuries
> old, who had achieved an original reinterpretation of that
> tradition in which he was rooted and which was then
> confronted with its most severe trial. He was, therefore,
> not understood by his entourage. Certainly he was no
> intellectual; but he was, all the same, head and shoulders
> above the highly intellectual experts and experienced
> advisers who thought themselves vastly superior to him.
> Nor was this surprising. For a man whose ideas had been
> derived from steeping himself in an age-long tradition was

by that very fact rendered far superior to all those self-conceited intellectuals and mandarins. He was, perhaps, the most intelligent and clear-sighted of the Habsburgs. In him that mighty imperial tree came to a late blossoming and revealed all the hidden possibilities of genuine political far-sightedness. He was prepared to draw the full consequences of his imperial tradition, to translate it into contemporary terms, and to sacrifice completely the German hegemony of his time.

Like Franz Josef over the Bohemian question, Karl was frustrated by the incomprehension of public opinion at that time. Its outlook had for decades been radically distorted by the German and Hungarian domination of old imperial Vienna, which was to continue until after 1938 when, one after the other, Hitler put an end to small, independent Austria and its neighbours.

An amnesty followed Foerster's audience, particularly of Czechs who were then still part of Austria–Hungary. It infuriated the army, but Karl knew what he was doing and why. 'There are symbolic gestures whose seed-plot is eternity,' Foerster noted at the time, 'which proceed from recognition of essential truth and, therefore, yield their blessing in due time, even if from the standpoint of practical politics they seem foolish.' The plan involved reforming the cabinet that Heinrich Lammasch, a member of the upper house was about to form as prime minister with, on Foerster's suggestion, all nationalities in the Austro–Hungarian state representated. Foerster then suggested that the emperor's views should be seen in the context of the amnesty for the Czechs and should be conveyed even to the hostile powers abroad. The emperor consented, with the proviso that he must first submit the text to Count Czernin, the foreign minister. That proved fatal, for Czernin said: 'If this is published, the Prussians will invade Bohemia tomorrow.'

Obviously, Austria's German allies would not have dreamt of taking such a step, but Czernin was a short-sighted politician and his compromises caused Austria–Hungary's doom. Even at that point in the war, publication of the emperor's plan would have made a powerful impression on the Austrian Empire and abroad and would have opened the road to European reconciliation. But Vienna's German and Hungarian ruling circles were not ripe for such a move. The emperor felt completely isolated and because of the German nationalist opposition in Vienna had to withdraw his intention to offer the premiership to Lammasch.

Before that happened a conference of all the nationalities was called at which the delegates were asked to pledge their loyalty to an Austria remodelled according to the plan described above. All were prepared to do so except the German representatives. The Slovene representative, Dr Krek, then made an impassioned speech in which he quoted Schiller: 'Your strife achieves great things, your alliance achieves greater still.'

It was extraordinary so near the end of the First World War to note, despite everything that had happened, how deeply rooted the attachment of the southeastern peoples still was to their Austrian connection. Addressing that Vienna meeting, Foerster pointed out that the application of the Christian leaven to politics was shown this time by the rulers being the ones to embrace new ideals. In the conscience of the oppressor the victim stood up and took from him his old conviction of his right to rule. Those who opposed the demand for the revision of antiquated claims based on force would be crushed beneath the chariot wheels of omnipotent time. In this context Foerster quoted the passage in which Macbeth, confronted by Banquo's ghost, exclaims:

Murders have been performed
Too terrible for the ear: the times have been,
That, when the brains were out, the man would die,
And there an end: but now, they rise again,
With twenty mortal murders on their crowns,
And push us from our stools: and this is more strange
Than such a murder is.

This evocation of Banquo's ghost was too much for the German representatives. In protest they left the hall, led by Prince Auersperg, howling down Lammasch who would have brought them to reason, and shouting: 'We want war and victory.' Their nationalist fervour went so far as to accuse the supporters of the emperor's policy of being 'treacherous pleaders for the entente' and 'Whom God will destroy He blinds.' Thus, the last chance of concluding a separate peace with the Western allies was lost.

After this fruitless effort Foerster returned to Zurich where he was visited by the Swedish ambassador who told him that, if the Emperor Karl's plan were carried through, influential Western circles were keen to enlarge the new southeastern confederation. In their view, Serbia and Romania might be prepared, on the conclusion of peace, to enter a Danubian confederation as independent states, provided that the Croats joined with Serbia and that the Hungarian Romanians with their territory joined with Romania. Foerster submitted the suggestion to the emperor, having no hope that anything could be done even with this prospect in view. But he was answered by the head of the cabinet sadly: '*Lasciate ogni speranza, voi ch'entrate*' (the last verse of the inscription above the gates of hell in Dante's *Divina Commedia*, Inferno, 3,9).

Foerster returned to Switzerland where in 1919, as Bavarian ambassador, he had a memorable meeting with the then papal nuncio in Munich, Eugenio Pacelli, later Pope Pius XII, who wanted to hear Foerster's views on Germany. They had an hour's conversation in a convent at Rohrschach. Recalling the encounter in a private letter to me in 1946, Foerster wrote how amazed he had been by 'the dangerous one-sidedness' of Monsignor Pacelli's pro-German and, correspondingly, anti-communist outlook. According to Foerster, the nuncio saw Germany as the medieval church had seen the ancient Catholic empire, as a major secular support and shield. The nuncio had not realized how much times had changed and that no such comparison could be made with the modern German nation-state with which he was dealing; he was clearly just reflecting the views of right-wing German officers to whom he was close.

Foerster's recollection of that meeting was important, given the role that the later cardinal and Vatican secretary of state played as the key figure behind the *Reichskonkordat*, concluded by Pius XI in 1934. This was Hitler's first treaty with a foreign power, and he derived huge international prestige from it, even though four years later Pius XI was forced to publish his encyclical *Mit brennender Sorge* (With burning anxiety). This document registered Hitler's breaches of that concordat and justified complaints over his treatment of the German Catholic Church, but without acknowledging that it was the Vatican and Monsignor Pacelli's diplomacy that had delivered to Hitler the once flourishing German Catholic structures. Behind that was

also the Vatican's reliance on concordats for the purely legal
status of the Church as derived from its temporal power.

In this connection Foerster wrote me a personal letter on 10
May 1946:

> No exception can be made of the German bishops like
> Galen and Faulhaber who protested against Hitler's treat-
> ment of the Church but never against his foreign policy.
> Just like the Pope himself! I was deeply shocked that
> neither during the war nor afterwards did the Pope find
> any word of solemn condemnation for the immense crimes
> committed by the German people in uniform. To me this
> illustrates the tremendous crisis of the Universal Church.
> Rome's dealing with Germany is very near to heresy,
> evidence of the monstrous power of evil in our time,
> capable of masking itself and hiding and intimidating the
> whole world. All this is foreseen in the Apocalypse.
> Nothing is more interesting than to observe the part played
> by the devil in our time: he bears the mask of a monsignor.

And Foerster added in the margin of his letter the quotation from
W. B. Yeats 'Things fall apart, the centre cannot hold; mere
anarchy is loosed upon the world. ... The best lack all conviction, while the worst are full of passionate intensity.' I shall
deal with this severe criticism by an eminent scholar in connection with the fundamental changes in the Church's outlook
nearer the time of the second Vatican council.

Foerster spent the years between the two world wars living in
Switzerland and France, managing to evade expulsion or even the
possibility of being handed over to Hitler's Germany by the
Swiss accustomed to cooperating with Hitler, their powerful
neighbour, as long as he was victorious. President Salazar personally intervened to help Foerster eventually to escape to
neutral Portugal and thence to the United States.

To have known a man of such intellectual and moral stature
and to have been in regular correspondence with him, was of
course quite unusual for one not yet 18 years old, and I basked
in my discipleship. He knew most of his generation's distinguished
contemporaries, including Albert Einstein who recommended
him for the Nobel Peace Prize but drew a blank. It is nevertheless
significant, I think, that even the new Germany, which has done so

much by way of restitution for the crimes of its past and honour-
ing its victims, has neglected to give him his due for spending his
long life trying to get across one single message, namely that:
'The German people will not be reconciled with Europe without
previously reconciling themselves with the truth.' The reason was
probably the old one given in St Matthew's Gospel: 'A prophet is
not without honour, save in his own country, and in his own
house' (Matthew 13, 57). Foerster's warning, which was earlier,
clearer and less ambiguous than, for example, Thomas Mann's,
can be compared with that of Gaius Coriolanus, the patriot/traitor
of the early Roman legend whom Shakespeare immortalized.

After 1945 Foerster had some modest recognition when an
association of friends enabled him to return to Switzerland and
to live there modestly until his death in 1966, aged 96 and
having seen many of his books republished. He was always
shown great consideration in Rome, where St Pius X, Pius XII,
John XXIII and John Paul II sent him their personal blessings.
The teaching staff of the University of Jerusalem, as indeed Jews
all over the world, expressed their admiration for Foerster's
lifelong fight against anti-Semitism and for his efforts towards
ecumenical and especially Christian–Jewish understanding.

God writes straight with crooked lines

'Live and let live' suits the relaxed ways of life in Vienna. For me
as a teenager, at a time of rapid physical and intellectual development, it expressed my longing for freedom from parental control
and authority. I wanted 'to belong to' something that absorbed
me more than the routines of home and school, to be taken out
of myself by something big and worthy of admiration and
devotion. I had no taste for the political substitute religions then
on offer, like communism, Marxism, fascism or Nazism, but was
vaguely groping for something that could satisfy my mind, heart
and soul, but had no idea what that might be. The evangelism of
my Hamburg childhood and schools had given me a desire for
truth and an interest in moral questions, probably also some
Lutheran critical sense, but with my inadequate understanding of
the Old and New Testaments, I felt intellectually immature. The
Sephardic Jewish tradition, which I encountered in my Viennese
grandfather's home, was impressive in its solemn ceremony, but
too full of apparently meaningless rules and customs.

A Gospel passage that early on rather impressed me concerned

Jesus's visit to the house of two sisters, Martha and Mary. The situation is familiar, as are the types, the active and the contemplative one. Martha busies herself about the house and fusses about the honoured guest. Someone has to do the chores, she says, with a meaningful glance at Mary, but probably secretly enjoying her part, while Mary, who leaves all the work to her sister, sits at the visitor's feet and listens to his words. She is even rewarded for having chosen 'the best role', for according to the divine admonition *unum necessarium est*, 'only one thing is necessary'. Ever since then this has been incomprehensible to people with Martha's nature – just like a man, they would say, sitting there and doing nothing!

Many years later I came across a similar distinction, quoted by the Oxford scholar, Isaiah Berlin who, apparently unaware of St Luke, had derived it from the fragments on the Greek poet Archilochus who said: 'The fox knows many things, but the hedgehog knows one big thing.' Berlin quotes it to illustrate this discussion of Tolstoy's view of history in *The Hedgehog and the Fox* (1953) but also relating it to a major distinction among human beings in general: those inclined to a single central vision and others pursuing many, possibly unrelated or even contradictory, ends. To the first category, according to Berlin, belong Dante, to the second Shakespeare. Hedgehogs in varying degrees are also Plato, Pascal, Hegel, Dostoevsky, Nietzsche and Proust. Foxes are Herodotus, Aristotle, Montaigne, Erasmus, Molière, Goethe, Pushkin, Balzac and Joyce. Of course, like all such classifications, this one, too, becomes, if pressed too far, ultimately artificial and absurd. But it is helpful as a starting point for further investigation, within or without the religious field.

In my Austrian teenage years I should have liked to have been patriotic and proud of my country's achievements, but I had no sympathy for the more recent nineteenth-century German history with its emphasis on Prussian militarism and strident German nationalism. I obviously looked to the faiths on offer, but found what I encountered in people and books inadequate. It was only much later that I heard of that great Englishman, Dr Samuel Johnson, and his wise definition of 'a last refuge for a scoundrel'. What was evidently quite ahistorical were the slogans of the First, Second and Third Reich; the Holy Roman Empire was supranational in its conception, but the notion of a 'German nation' referred precisely to the German parts only.

Little Austria, as it now was, was never far from accommodating ethnic and historical mixes in the heart of Europe where the assertion of any one nationalism could only have been destructive and explosive. But dreams of former national greatness corrupted post-1919 Austrians who wanted to belong to the greater German Reich, which was now led by a fellow countryman. From beyond the German border skilful Nazi propaganda remained a powerful weapon. As I remember from Austrian cinema audiences, the devil has not only the best tunes but also the best films. For instance, at Leni Riefenstahl's evocation of the 1936 Nuremberg rally, called *Triumph of the Will*, people sat spellbound under the sheer artistic impact of what was not even intended as a glorification of Hitler, but all the more effective for that. The title made everybody forget that Hitler's real triumph of the will had actually occurred two years earlier when he crashed the leftist Roehm rebellion and assumed full dictatorial powers.

Another film stunt, a tear-jerker with an emotionally effective appeal, was *Hitlerjunge Quex*, in which an endearing young, blond Nazi teenager suffered martyrdom for his ghastly cause. It appealed, as the film makers intended, to the characteristic mix of that younger generation's witless idealism and puritanism: the young people around me were visibly shocked by the lewd behaviour of a group of young communists and their screeching girls on a Sunday outing, in contrast to a doomed Hitler youth troop behaving with bourgeois propriety. That cinema audience was completely gripped by the black-and-white propaganda cliché.

What my generation meant by wanting to belong to a religious or political whole, or *Weltanschauung*, was very different from the emphasis on individual development prevalent in the Anglo-Saxon world. Ever since the French Revolution and the Napoleonic occupations that followed it, we had adhered to a continental tradition in which the state, society or social whole was dominant. This was not necessarily a bad thing. The state schools I attended in Germany, Czechoslovakia and Austria certainly fulfilled their objectives well, for they tacitly promoted social equality without any hang-ups and irrespective of parental background, class or income.

One difference between our search for truth and that of later generations was that we seemed to aim more at an 'orthodox' rather than a 'sectarian' entity, whatever that might be. Religious or political splinter groups like the 'Moonies' or 'Trotskyites' seemed not to exert a similar attraction then. Perhaps we were naïve to think that such wholeness of religious, political and social truth is humanly attainable at all, or was 'better', and that restricting one's ideals to a narrower field may suggest greater realism or modesty. Whatever the case, the Gospel warned against that form of emancipation: 'If any one comes to me and does hate his father and mother, wife and children, brothers and sisters, even his own life, he cannot be a disciple of mine' (Luke, 26–7).

I was less attracted than other boys to sports and games, but was not a bad swimmer, rower, hockey player, skater or mountain walker in my teens and later. The jazz age, which fascinated so many of my generation, passed me by. I had clearly inherited my mother's musical ear and preferred classical music either in the concert hall or on the wireless in our pre-TV age. I was enthusiastic about Tchaikovsky, Bach, Beethoven, Schubert, Mahler, and Mozart, whom my mother venerated and whose roles and *Lieder* were part of her repertoire, as also were Verdi's and Brahms's. Our family was used to listening in silence to opera broadcasts from Salzburg or Beirut, especially in my very musical grandfather's house. One relaxed only at intervals. Vienna was naturally the home of the golden tunes of Johann Strauss, and of his followers' silvery *Singspiele*, operettas and musicals. I collected autographs, calling by bicycle on the private residences of famous composers like Franz Lehár, and waiting outside until the maid came back with my little book and the precious new signature.

The scout troop I had joined chose the trumpet solo from Tchaikovsky's Italian Capriccio as our signature tune, which our trumpeter blew in shattering abandon, I am sure, and inconsiderately on our early Sunday morning marches out of Vienna. Baden Powell's international movement enjoyed great popularity in Austria, as elsewhere on the continent, except of course in Nazi Germany, which had the Hitler Youth instead. Even there some of the older romantic, idealist anti-bourgeois enthusiasm of the old German youth movement survived, as many non-Nazis, like the young Ratzinger who later became Pope Benedict XVI would have known. Some of the *Wanderlust* survived, with unspoilt nature beckoning and the uniting bond of singing songs around a blazing camp fire. That was very much part of

Germany's idealist pre- and post-First World War national culture, on which my mentor Friedrich Wilhelm Foerster had exerted an important influence before it disintegrated into party-political factions. From Austria I remember attending the international scout jamboree at Gödöllö, in neighbouring Hungary, and feeling uplifted by the impressive internationalism of the gathering.

Undoubtedly, the Boy Scouts owed much to the then widespread popularity of British ways in the 1930s, which was hardly justified when one recalls how they appeased the dictators. The then Prince of Wales, before becoming Edward VIII, played his part in it as did George VI, father of Queen Elizabeth II, by promoting Baden Powell's contribution to peace and international goodwill. It remained a very English thing and on that account perhaps fell short of realizing 'human brotherhood'. The reputation of the Austrian scouts was high, probably due to the selfless devotion of their leaders to Scouting ideals. There was none of that sniggering sexual innuendo with which the more salacious of the British Sunday newspapers treated just another scout leader's misbehaviour. Not unsurprisingly, the memory of the hero of Mafeking came ultimately to be suspected and besmirched, but I do not recall any such scandal in my Austrian days.

To convey some of the liberating effect that joining the scouts had on me, let me quote extracts from a holiday journal I found among my papers. I do not recall who wrote it. It describes our camping in the Austrian Tyrol in the summer of 1937 when I was nearly 17, lucky to be allowed to stay away from home for more than four weeks. About 30 of us were in the advance party, departing from Vienna's Westbahnhof. Some anxious parents had come to see us off and to impart last-minute advice to Tommy, who was in charge:

'You'll see to it, won't you, that my boy cleans his teeth regularly, twice a day, as he is used to, please.' Tommy, aged 19, nods and promises to do his best. Then the last farewells, the train moves off, some mothers have moist eyes, waving their handkerchiefs. It was nearly 10 p.m., too dark to see much of the passing countryside. Some of us get our sandwiches out; others stretch out to sleep on benches or suitcases; the tallest one, Paul, even climbs into one of the luggage racks. The journey would take all night.

The indefatigable Alfons, known as Ali, unpacks the latest game he has brought along called Monopoly. That was to dominate our lives in the next few days and weeks, though needing the wheeler-dealer skills, which Ali had.

At 2 a.m. we get to Salzburg, at 7 Innsbruck, where we have to change to a local train. We pass though the lovely Tyrolean countryside, new for some of us who had never seen such high mountains on both sides of the track. At half past nine we get to Imst, our final stop. Ali and Roland stay behind with the luggage, waiting for a later train with the wooden boxes and equipment for building the camp. The others go ahead by bus, some 25 minutes, to the campsite at Fernstein, below an old castle ruin.

But the chests with tents and tools were late in arriving. So we are also late in starting work. By the evening of our first day we have at least got up four wooden hut walls. The lovely mountain air made us quite hungry. Tommy distributes salami sandwiches. We go to bed early, as we have to be up early, to get the camp up for the others, it has to be ready in five days.

Our first camping night was all but comfortable. Some of us felt homesick, thought as yet little of the joys of camping. But our mood was to change. The next few days passed more or less alike. Getting up at 5.30 a.m., when Tommy blows his whistle, calling 'Good morning, all.' Then a quick wash at the brook outside the camp and starting work, then breakfast, a break at 10. At 12 we walk up to Angerer. That is the name of the nearby innkeeper – Herr Angerer, soon to become our friend, who sold stamps and postcards. We always have our midday and evening meals on his sheltered dining veranda with its grand views of the mountains. The food was always good and plentiful. Then [we have] an hour's rest, passed with playing chess or Monopoly or going for a swim in icy cold mountain waters – impossible to stay in longer than a few minutes Then [it is] back to work in the afternoon and a walk up again for the evening meal. Four days later the hut walls were completed, then we had to make the frames for the beds, four for each hut, and the gable ends, over which afterwards tents were stretched Some thirty steps away, a latrine ditch was dug, according to Tommy's artistic design, with partitions for four occupants and a simple semaphore system, an arrow pointing down, meaning 'engaged' or up when free. Every cabin had a little spade for some earth to be dropped. One clot had already dropped his spade as well into the depths and failed to retrieve it.

Then a professional bricklayer came to build the kitchen stove and a lockable food shed. In the meantime the others had arrived led by our chief, Dr Schopf, and moved in. Everybody made his hut as comfortable as possible, with shelves and lanterns. Then the palliasses had to be filled with straw, which needed a special knack.

At last normal camping life could start: the whistle at 6 or 6.30, depending on the weather, ten minutes for a quick wash, then morning parade in front of the flag mast, some warming-up exercises, a run down to the playground for 15 minutes of PT and a more thorough wash in the 'Blue Danube', as we called our pretty cold mountain brook. Then [it was] time for getting dressed, making beds, breakfast at 8, consisting of cocoa, bread and butter, followed by morning activities such as a course in signalling or camp cookery and perhaps a ball game. Lunch at 12.30, usually soup, meat on Wednesdays and Sundays, and a starchy sweet. Then an hour's compulsory rest, followed by another quiet hour, when the post, letters, newspapers are distributed by our postmaster, Roland. After the midday break, usually in fine weather, a swim, followed by tea and bread and butter at four, then a game of hand- or football. At 8 we have our evening meal, after that assembly at the flag pole, some singing, led and accompanied on his guitar by Baczi, another of our leaders, an engineer by profession and liked by everybody. Between 9.30 and 10 bedtime.

Our days passed quickly, too soon the time came for dismantling the camp again. The planks used for the hut walls had to be loaded onto a farm cart, which we then pushed to one of our innkeeper's barns for storage till next year. Pots and pans were put into wooden crates for the rail transport back to Vienna. The straw from our palliasses had to be burned. The August weather had been pretty awful, torrents of rain, a terrible storm one night. It turned the whole camp into a vast lake, with everybody getting drenched. But nothing diminished our high spirits. We passed our last night in an empty villa nearby, getting dry and warm again. Then back to Innsbruck by train, where we had breakfast in the station restaurant, coffee and cake, and got on the train for the last stretch of our return journey. Goodbye, wonderful Tyrol, or rather *Auf Wiedersehen*, we hoped, for all of us were keen to go back next year. We got into Vienna half an hour late, at 11 p.m. Many parents had come to meet us. Then home again with memories of what, with all its ups and downs had been a great experience.

Our hope of returning the following year was to be disappointed. Independent Austria, and with it our scouts, ceased to exist in March 1938 and was replaced by the Hitler Youth, though without most of us.

I have already mentioned Fritz among my scout leaders, who played an important role in my life. He was in his mid-thirties and in command of one of our higher echelons, a *Kolonne*, covering 12 scout groups with about 30 boys each. This was Dr Fritz Schopf, a civil servant by profession with a doctorate in Roman Law, a typical public employee of that generation, an 'obedient servant' in the literal sense of combining brains, honesty and general culture and enjoying a certain social prestige, being a *Herr Doktor*, which made up for their meagre salary. According to a Viennese jingle, he was a *Fixangestellter* (a permanent employee). *Der hat am Ersten nix, der hat am Zweiten nix, doch was er hat, das hot er fix.*' (He has nought on the first of the month, nought on the second, but what he has, he has forever.)

Fritz was neither particularly good-looking nor a sportsman, as his English equivalent could have been expected to be. He was a typical Austrian intellectual with a good brain and rational outlook, who would have conceded, if pressed, that the heart was important, though it came rather low down in his scale of values. He had a good sense of irony, but was basically of a serious disposition.

When I saw him again after the Second World War he had reached the rank of *Obersenatsrat*, and was responsible for Vienna's traffic system, which functioned perfectly on the logical

9. Dr Fritz Schopf (1912–1987) Austrian civil servant, the man with the powerful motorcycle who, as Boy Scout leader, was instrumental in my becoming a Catholic.

basis of Roman law. This meant, I always thought, that unless you were on the same wave length, you could easily get lost in the intricacies of the oneway system he had devised.

Politically, in the 1930s Fritz was a Catholic right-winger, as then were most members of the Vienna city administration. Mussolini was his romantic hero, though admired for his Italian panache rather than as a fascist. There has always been considerable misunderstanding, especially in later generations, over what these political clichés meant and what ignorant people wanted them to mean. Fritz had a theologically-trained mind, was a devout Catholic and went to mass daily. He was an Austrian patriot who, being unfit for German military service, continued to work underground for the Austrian cause during the war by boycotting the German occupation as best he could. After the war he changed politically. He left the 'Christian Socialists', his

Catholic soul mates, to join the party of his new socialist political masters in the Vienna city administration. The latter had dropped their previous Marxism and now, as 'model socialists' under their clever Jewish premier Bruno Kreisky, supported the coalition government that ruled postwar Austria for many years.

Since Fritz was instrumental in my Catholic conversion, I must say a little more about him. As yet unmarried, he lived alone with his aged father in an admittedly odd male ménage, in which no one else, certainly no woman, was ever allowed into the kitchen because of its chaotic state. Later in the war he married an Austrian war widow on the mere compassionate grounds that her orphaned son needed a father. Nowadays, given his friendships with so many teenage scouts who became Catholics under his influence, one might suspect his motives. His friendships were undoubtedly sincere and whatever homosexual inclinations he may have had, they were clearly sublimated by his devout faith. Having known most of these protegés, I can vouch that there was never a single case that might have caused the slightest concern. A well-known French distinction became customary for differentiating degrees of homosexuality, namely *croyant* (vaguely so disposed), *fidèle* (pursuing more of a neutral stance) and *pratiquant*, which would apply to 'regulars'. In this respect Fritz could probably have been classified as a *croyant*.

My parents, suspicious of the hold Fritz seemed to have gained over me, disapproved of the friendship. In a letter my mother had written to my father, which by chance I discovered many years later, she voiced her anxiety:

> The boy is firmly resolved on it, and nice man though Fritz is, I did not feel up to his Jesuitical tricks. You know what these people are like once they have got hold of a young person's soul. So I had to give it my blessing. My only concern is that my own father should hear of it and turn the rebellious boy out of his house. Yet the boy is still only a big dreamer, so unstable in character, with no practical sense at all, hopeless in money matters.

It seemed significant that, when it came to religious matters, the liberal-mindedness of my parents had definite limits. For their part, neither my mother nor my father could have realized then that, years later, they would both quite independently of each other and of me, follow in my first despised footsteps.

But there was something else about my relationship with Fritz: he had a powerful Puch 250 motorcycle, which added to his general intellectual–religious attraction; indeed, it caused great jealousies in the large circle proud to be befriended by him. What teenager can resist the noisy arrival of a begoggled leather-coated grown-up man on his doorstep, to say nothing of the neighbours' reaction when they learn that the gentleman in question is also a respectable *Herr Doktor*? The procedure was always the same. Fritz would arrive sometime in the late afternoon after work and the eagerly waiting boy would climb up behind him, hold onto his back and be taken at lightning speed to a beauty spot in the *Wienerwald*, the capital's enchanting green and hilly outskirts. There they would walk around and talk about God and the world. You cannot imagine how grand it felt to be able to do this at all, quite seriously, with no holds barred. No one's parents could have done that. After about two hours of heart-to-heart exchanges, they would return and the boy, full of his unique experience, would be delivered back – unmolested – in time for tea, Fritz having departed with a wave and the loudest of engine rumbles.

Was his influence 'Jesuitical or 'Machiavellian'? At most the old Spanish proverb 'God writes straight with crooked lines' seemed to apply. His motorbike undoubtedly exerted a magic spell, with Fritz in the role of a good rather than evil winged spirit. His bond with his friends was clearly a voluntary one, freely offered and accepted. These friends were unbelievers or agnostics of vaguely Jewish or Christian adherence; all of them were seekers, as most young people are, after some Holy Grail, though no one would have been able to specify it. We yearned for something more than our boring selves, something more satisfying and more all-embracing spiritually and intellectually. Fritz was ready to provide this new *Weltanschauung*, present it in an attractive and cogent way, and argue about it convincingly.

Certainly no force or deception was involved. It was up to us to listen, accept or reject. What mattered most was that, immature as we were, we were for the first time in our lives being taken seriously by somebody we could respect. In a way we were fortunate that Fritz was the purveyor of an orthodox faith, centuries old and tested by greater minds, for this was also a time of political and religious half-truths, which took those in who allowed themselves to be deceived, sometimes with disastrous effects, as the isms of that generation (communism, fascism and national-socialism) showed, to say nothing of the various sects out to capture the gullible. I do not want to suggest that we were less gullible. Many of us fell by the wayside in later life, praising ourselves lucky to have escaped Fritz's 'clutches'.

As for myself I cannot claim any greater foresight or wisdom, nor indeed was I aware at the time of what such a trans-formation of mind and soul involved. It was more a vague groping for a new philosophy of life, for which Fritz merely supplied the data, rather like a new compass in a desert, which, I am happy to say, has lasted me for more than six decades. What at the beginning amounted to a vague notion of having found 'it', took shape only after much time and growing accustomed to unfamiliar surroundings. They revealed, not surprisingly, that 'in my Father's house are many mansions' (St John 14, 2).

Eamon Duffy, the Cambridge historian, has compared the complexities of Catholic tradition with an ancient basilica, San Clemente, near the Roman Coliseum. It is famous for its magnifi-cently carved and gilded ceiling, inserted by an eighteenth-century pope, and a glorious medieval pavement. For centuries, people thought that what they could see of the church above ground was all there was. Then some nineteenth-century Irish Domini-cans dug down to discover another complete basilica dating from the sixth century and, deeper still, a first-century Roman street with a house thought to have belonged to St Clement, one of the earliest popes, as well as a complete Mithraic temple.

Recent excavations have uncovered other hitherto unknown sites, such as the grave of St Cyril from the time when the popes were engaged in bitter conflicts with the patriarchs of Constan-tinople for control of the church in the Balkans. The present basilica was built because the old church was burnt to the ground by Norman bandits summoned to rescue the reforming but overbearing Pope Gregory VII from the German King Henry IV who had seized the city and appointed an anti-pope. Thus, according to Duffy, this Roman basilica comes to represent the very meaning of Catholic tradition, some of it half burnt and forgotten, 'layer upon layer of shared prayer, thought and sufferings and sin' (Cardinal Hume Memorial Lecture, 17 November 2003).

What attracted me first to Christianity was a childish Christmas notion of the birth in the manger of someone cherished and secure in the love of his parents, regardless of the smelly surroundings. Only later did I identify it with something called 'the Word-made-Flesh', the Incarnation. For me, this has remained the heart of Christianity, almost more important than the divine child's later fulfilment in his much more significant death on the cross and resurrection. In my faith I had no difficulty accepting that if A why not B and C? The idea and mystery of the Incarnation made sense to me later also historically and in European culture in the 'vertical' God–man relationship of the Gothic age. I always think of Heinrich Heine, a non-believing Jew, exclaiming at his first sight of the magnificent and massive Strasbourg Minster: 'Only dogmas could produce such a building; we have only opinions, but with opinions you cannot build cathedrals.'

In Austria and southern Germany, I came to discover another way of seeing a link between God and his creation. This was in baroque architecture, which is as triumphant as the Gothic, but 'horizontal' rather than vertical. Renaissance man had meanwhile come into his own with all the arts and achievements of that age, including the forlorn one of reconquering in the Counter-Reformation what Martin Luther had earlier destroyed in his break with Rome.

In Vienna, I was received into the Catholic Church early in July 1937, with my Lutheran christening considered sufficiently valid not to require Catholic renewal. The priest conducting the ceremony was a good friend and Fritz assisted him. It was a fine summer's day – *Kaiserwetter*, as it is still called in republican Austria. Afterwards we celebrated with coffee and *Schlagobers*, delicious whipped cream, and *Guglhupf*, a dry raisin cake and Austrian speciality for joyous occasions. I still have my present from Fritz, which was the 'Schott' edition of the traditional missal text in Latin and German, now out of date since the introduction of a vernacular liturgy. I learnt to find my way about it by means of variously coloured ribbons, as in a railway timetable. Many of us converts – Fritz had nearly a hundred – became altar servers, then natural for boys, not girls, in a Catholic country. It took some time to master that art.

We were warned against the sin of becoming a know-all, which converts have a tendency to be. There was the off-putting lesson John Henry Newman had to impart, when, long before his own conversion he witnessed, in a Naples church, the incredible routine dexterity of a local altar server. He seemed to do everything with speed and finesse, handing the celebrant the cruets with wine and water, making the required responses, ringing the altar bell and passing the collection purse round among the faithful, and he never failed to genuflect when passing the Sacrament altar. The man's eyes were everywhere, Newman related, spotting even the handbag a woman had left behind and slipping it, unseen, into the wide folds of his cassock when following the priest on his way out after Mass.

'Out of these convertites there is much matter to be heard and learned,' says a courtier in Shakespeare's *As You Like It*. How much of a convert Catholic England's greatest poet was, having also to live in an age when it was dangerous to be one, is a question that has always intrigued me. Converts often have the advantage of receiving or renewing their faith at a more mature age. I steeped myself in learning about the great converts. There was St Paul with his blinding challenge on the road to Damascus, and St Augustine who, on listening to a sermon of St Ambrose in Milan, decided to change his life, become a monk and write his *Confessions* with that memorable beginning: 'Thou hast created us for Thyself, and our heart is not quiet, until it rests in Thee.'

What attracted me to St Augustine was less his stern absolutism than his loving capacity and understanding of human nature that seemed to anticipate so much that was to happen in divided Christendom. How strange it was, for instance, that Luther was an Augustinian monk, so the great St Augustine cannot be absolved entirely from responsibility for the Reformation. When it came to that other modern heresy, Freud's psychoanalysis, St Augustine clearly saw deeper into the hidden springs of man.

One wished that the great Viennese doctor had been without that religious block that stopped him seeing Augustine's insight into human nature. Freud certainly displayed a humorous wisdom when the Gestapo came to search his office in the Berghofgasse. He is said to have certified them having proceeded in orderly fashion, adding 'And I can only recommend the Gestapo to the best of my capacity to anyone in need of it.'

A conversion closer to our time, which came to mean much more to me after the British Isles became my adopted home, was Newman's. His long life, from 1801 to 1890, divided exactly into two religious halves. I came to find especially appealing his distinction between 'notional' and 'real' assent to religious truth, namely with Catholics and Russian Orthodox really assenting to Christian belief because of their numinous liturgies and religious imagery. Miracles would not surprise them. They felt surrounded by God, the Virgin Mary and the saints. To the early Newman the Protestants of his Low Church seemed coldly 'notional'. Then there was Newman, the supreme master among the greatest English writers whose letters, *Apologia pro Vita sua: Idea of a Catholic University* became for me great models of the best English style.

Newman, the Oxford don, remains for outsiders much more difficult to understand, for he was so immensely sensitive and charitable, yet psychologically suppressed, 'nuts'. One remembered a telling description of Newman by Sir John Acton, the liberal Catholic historian, himself half German, who worked with him closely to edit some outstanding Catholic reviews. Once, when Newman felt that the much younger Acton needed to be taught greater care in the treatment of the Catholic Church dignitaries of the day, 'Newman hummed and hawed, rocking to and fro in front of the fire like an old woman with a toothache.' Why? Because he was so anxious not to hurt, but felt that he had to tell a blunt truth that he could not suppress.

Then there were the trials that Newman's new fellow Catholics seemed to enjoy heaping on him because of their lack of understanding of him intellectually, emotionally and humanly, making his life as a Catholic a misery. He bore it with equanimity, which, however, is not among the qualities required for sanctity and thus has so far eluded that great Englishman.

Here we touch on the old problem of the Catholic Church in an often all too human form when it tries to denigrate those who are especially close to it. Repeatedly, it heaps the trials of Jesus on them and, like the grand inquisitor in Dostoevsky's *Brothers Karamasov*, hands Jesus over to be crucified again. One could not after all have him interfering in what the Church saw as its own task! Perhaps Christ's real charity is easily lost in the human apparatus that the Church he founded was bound to become during the course of history. As far as Newman is concerned, we may indeed wonder whether he would 'have come over' in 1845 had he known then that his beloved vicar of Christ, Pius IX, would, barely three decades later, proclaim papal infallibility, which Newman, like many of his Catholic contemporaries, regarded as 'inopportune', a dogma of the Church. The great convert actually provided a theological justification for it, which helped to earn him the deserved Red Hat belatedly, by saying that 'of course we should always drink to the Pope's health, but to conscience first.' It sounded much like a lame excuse.

As a Catholic by birth, Sir Thomas More (1478–1535) does not strictly belong in my gallery of great converts, but indirectly he does because of the stark choice he was forced to make between Caesar and God. By way of extenuation, it is often said that the Church thinks only in centuries. Four of these had after all passed before Thomas More was thought worthy of being raised to the altars. The delays may possibly have had something to do with the Church's desire not to give diplomatic offence to the now even mightier British Empire, or, St Joan's France, which was after all the Church's eldest daughter. Whether or not this was the true explanation, both were certainly cases of better late than never. Not long before him, Jeanne de Pucelle, as Joan of Arc called herself, had been canonized (1920) after a similarly 'late' beatification in 1909.

Sub speciae aeternitatis, the year 1935, the four-hundredth anniversary of St Thomas's martyrdom, was timely. It was only two years since Hitler had come to power and, though the Tudor king's problems with his wives and heirs seemed small compared with what was to come, they were not in their long-term effect. The coveted title of 'Defender of the Faith', which More had procured for his king in their younger and happier relations, had come via a sovereign Parliament in the British constitution, though for a theologically somewhat changed Church of England. Thus, the honour remained proudly preserved in human history, giving the new saint–martyr the last laugh over the follies of humankind down below. His humanist sense of humour was surely a welcome new quality among God's saints that made his life and personality lovable for me among the newer converts. It is worth noting that even so soon after that canonization quite a few churches in Germany and Austria chose to be dedicated to the memory of the new English saint, even though this might have made them suspect in the modern totalitarian context. Fortunately, the Nazis were less interested in the parallels between Hitler's Reich and Tudor religious history than in the fact that modern Great Britain was all for appeasing present-day dictators.

In that similarly rich English vein of laughter and paradox, I came to discover G. K. Chesterton (1874–1936). In his chivalrous way, he delayed his own reception into the Catholic Church until he was already 48 out of consideration for his Anglo-Catholic wife. By then he had waged his many polemical battles with the *Heretics* (1905) of his time, as he wrongly called Rudyard Kipling and George Bernard Shaw, who gloried in rationalist non-belief; against them he defended his romantic vision of *Orthodoxy* (1908). From the Francophone right-winger, Hilaire Belloc, Chesterton unfortunately absorbed some of the anti-Semitic notions that dominated Catholic thinking in the 1930s, but he was a master of the fantastic novel *The Man who was Thursday* (1907), a gifted poet and outstanding biographer, whose *St Thomas Aquinas* made scholars like Etienne Gilson despair over GKC's intuitive genius for understanding him.

He was a true original of his generation in his intellectual and bodily dimensions. Wearing a huge cloak and wide-brimmed artist's hat, he carried a swordstick should he need to come to the aid of the weaker sex or fearlessly fight the wicked. The weaker sex, though, repeatedly saved him from himself, absent-minded as he was. 'Am in Market-Harborough, where ought I to be?' he famously cabled home while on a lecture tour. His wife merely cabled back 'HOME' in order to dispatch him again to his proper destination. He spouted aphorisms. For instance, of an 'amateur', one who literally loves doing things, he said 'If a thing is worth doing, it is worth doing badly.' Or, 'The Christian ideal, it is said, has not been tried and found wanting. It has been found difficult, and left untried.' 'My country, right or wrong, is a thing no patriot would think of saying, it is like saying my mother, drunk or sober.' 'When people stop believing in God, they do not believe in nothing but in anything.'

I was inspired by two French philosophers, Jacques and Raïssa Maritain (she was a convert from Judaism), who did much to make Catholic thought intellectually respectable again after its long right-wing domination by Charles Maurras and 'Action française'. In the preface to *Redeeming the Time* (1943) Maritain defined his aims well.

This is not a book of philosophy separated from concrete life. I believe, on the contrary, that philosophy attains its aims, particularly in practical matters, only when vitally

united with every source of light and experience in the
human mind. Thus it becomes able, in its own domain, to
ransom the time, and to redeem the human search after
truth, however it wanders, in manifold, even opposite
ways.

One can vividly imagine the two young Maritains, long
before, with such thoughts germinating, climbing the everlasting
stairs leading to the Paris Sacré Coeur, two typical products of
modern intellectual despair hungering for the truth and knocking
on the door of a strange man who, disdaining all philosophy,
was nevertheless shouting the divine truth from the rooftops. As
a believing Catholic he condemned his times, saying there is but
one sadness – not to be a saint. He was Léon Bloy (1846–1917)
who did not want to be a journalist, writer, thinker or artist, but
someone who adored. To the young couple he appeared 'almost
shy, speaking little, almost inaudibly, and yet, trying to tell them
something weighty that would not disappoint'. Many other visits
followed and, a year later, the Maritains were received into the
Catholic Church in the nearby St John the Evangelist church.
    When Jacques Maritain was French ambassador to the Holy
See after the Second World War, I visited him in Rome, for we
had our friendship with my mentor, Friedrich Wilhelm Foerster,
in common. Another mentor, on Maritain's side, was Henri
Bergson (1859–1941) who had helped the Maritains 'to cleanse
our minds from the scientific superstitions, with which the
Sorbonne had fed us.' Bergson had postponed his own Catholic
baptism because of the pain it would cause his Jewish brethren at
a time of their greatest trials and persecutions.
    Among the French Catholic writers I most admired was
Georges Bernanos (1888–1948), author of the unique *Diary of a
Country Priest*. His great theme is the essential Catholic faith
rather than the traditional French Jansenist version that so often
serves as a substitute. Grace, the spirit of the old Christendom,
shines through his certainty that its death has come. From
Bernanos I learnt 'how the worst of evil in man can yet allow for
the proclamation of Christian hope, and that what the Church
needs above all is not so much reformers but saints'. This
conviction has often helped me never to despair when confronted
by the all too human aspects of the Church.
    There was a special tragedy about the inevitability of Edith

Stein's death under her name in religion, Sister Teresa Benedict of the Cross (1891–1941). For me her life as a German Jewess finding Christ and her anonymous end as part of the Holocaust remain living symbols of our age. She was the youngest of a large and loving family and lost her Jewish faith in the intellectual climate of the early twentieth century. Christianity first came to her when in the course of her Germanic studies she read the Lord's Prayer in Gothic and then heard it spoken on a mountain farm by the head of a family setting out for a day's haymaking. She first encountered Catholic ideas when attending lectures by the convert philosopher Max Scheler at Göttingen in 1921. More decisive for her, however, was to read the autobiography of St Theresa of Avila, which made her exclaim 'This is the truth', and she went out to buy a missal. She then attended her first Mass in her local church and was baptized on 1 January 1922.

Hitler's rise to power in January 1933 caused her dismissal as a public employee and philosophy lecturer and, in October of that year, she entered the Cologne Convent of Discalced Carmelites. She was then sent to Holland and, after the German invasion of 1940, was called to the Gestapo to register – hardly improving matters when entering by saying provocatively 'Praised be to the Lord Jesus Christ'. When the Dutch bishops issued their fatal protest against the deportations of Jews, this was followed by way of retaliation by the arrest of all those of Jewish descent, Sister Teresa among them. She managed to send three brief messages, posted for her by kind stangers, 'Greetings, I am on my way to Poland.' She was probably gassed at Auschwitz on 9 August 1942 or 1943, the vigil of St Lawrence, when the Church recalls the words of Christ: 'if any man will follow me, let him deny himself, and take up the cross and follow me' (Matthew, 16.24).

Edith Stein is among the *Seven Jewish Philosophers Discover Christ* (1952) whose author, Monsignor John M. Oesterreicher (1904–93), was a friend and fellow convert in Vienna where his reception into the Church had deeply shocked his own devout Jewish family. A worse blow for them was his decision to enter the priesthood in 1977. Some orthodox Jews feared that a priest able to consecrate wine and bread would be able to do so surreptitiously when opening a bottle of wine at a meal, which is an unspeakable blasphemy.

10. Symbolizing the victims of the Holocaust. Blessed Teresa of the Cross (Edith Stein, 1891–1942), a memorial window in Freiburg Cathedral.

In Austria Father Oesterreicher founded the Opus St Pauli, an organization to help converts, which also published the journal *Die Erfüllung* (Fulfilment). He escaped to Paris after the *Anschluss*, then in 1940 went on to New York where he became a well-known Catholic writer. He later played an important part at the Second Vatican Council in the commission that revised the Catholic Church's relations towards Judaism.

As a Catholic convert I owe much to the ideas of two Russian philosophers – Nicolai Berdyaev (1874–1948), who had come to accept an Eastern type of existentialist Christianity and was a notable writer on the problems of our time, and Vladimir Solov'ev (1853–1900). Solov'ev's religious journey had led him from the Russian Orthodox Church to atheism and materialism, then back to a spiritualist Gnostic form of Christianity. Being close to Catholicism, he was responsible for a famous declaration that recognized the pope as supreme judge in matters of religion on behalf of 100 million Russian Christians (1889). He became widely known for his imaginative and ironic *Story of the Antichrist*, in which, at an end of time and with the help of Jews, an emperor superman who believes only in himself is elected president of the United States of Europe. A few true believers oppose the Antichrist. They are Pope Peter II, long since expelled from Rome who reduced his faith to a minimum of its former liturgy, the German Evangelical Professor Ernest Pauli, and the Russian Orthodox monk John. When the Jews discover that the Antichrist's claim to be their circumcised Messiah is false, they rebel against him. He kills many of them, but those who remain, together with the Christian rest, overpower him and reign with Christ for 1000 years.

Both Berdyaev and Solov'ev were followers of Dostoevsky who, for me, too, is of course the greatest of them in that, wanting neither to teach nor preach, succeeds in raising his creations to the supreme achievements of any writer's mind.

Farewell free Austria

As March 1938 approached, independent Austria's existence became increasingly vulnerable. Deep in their own appeasement of the dictators, London and Paris had written Austria off as unlikely to make a fighting stand. This emboldened Mussolini, no longer interested in a friendly sovereign Austria guaranteeing the safety of his northern border, to adopt a more aggressive foreign policy. Eventually, this was to produce Hitler's grateful telegram when, on the night of Friday 11 March 1938, he ordered the Wehrmacht to invade Austria: 'Duce, I'll never forget you for that.' Mussolini's non-intervention sealed Austria's fate. Hitler's second, successful gamble was to forestall the democratic elections the Austrian chancellor, Kurt von Schuschnigg, had called for after Hitler had put him under grave pressure at their Berchtesgaden encounter. Only four years earlier an Austrian majority had voted against Hitler, so he, unable to afford a repetition of that failure, had to risk superior force.

Meanwhile, things had changed inside Austria as well as abroad. Everybody was getting cold feet under the threat of

Germany's superior military might. Schuschnigg had called for 'a free and German Austria, independent, social and united.' His proffered slogan was *Rot-Weiss-Rot bis in den Tod* (red-white-red, independent Austria's colours until death). However, a German Austria, available 'freely' on Hitler's terms, seemed preferable then and suggested the half-heartenedness of Austria's rulers. It needed another world war and untold sacrifices to convince present-day little Austria that its language does not dictate its nationality.

So, on a warm spring night in March 1938, I stood with all the family on my grandfather's little third-floor balcony watching joyful groups of shouting people making their way to some central Vienna rally. Some wore knitted white stockings and leather pants, long known as 'Nazi-rig', but then it seemed as though, like packs of rats, they had swarmed out of their sewers while a silent majority looked on helplessly with hushed or real tears for their fallen country.

Four days later Hitler took possession of the land of his birth. A vast crowd had gathered outside the famous Ringstrasse Hotel Imperial, where he was staying. I was there with some ex-school friends, evidently drawn by the irresistible pull of the herd instinct, though we did not join in the cheerful rhyming chorus: '*Lieber Führer, sei so nett, und zeige Dich am Fensterbrett*' (Dear Führer be so nice and show yourself at the window sill). Craning our necks, we saw the VIPs arriving to make their obeisance to the new head of state. Among the first was the Austrian primate, Cardinal Innitzer and, as a recent convert, I found it unpleasant to witness his appearance. Being of Sudeten-German origin, his Hitlerite sympathies were well known, but then, whatever their country, Catholic bishops have never been known for their political know-how. Innitzer went over the top on behalf of the Austrian bishops, though, by his personal appeal on a poster signed 'Heil Hitler', for the people to cast their vote for the Greater German Reich, by which Hitler was able to triumph over Schuschnigg's aim of an independent Austria.

Cardinal Innitzer was deservedly reprimanded by the ageing Pope Pius XI for his political naivety. He received an even clearer indication of which way Nazi winds were blowing when, in the autumn of 1938, thuggish Hitler Youths broke into the cardinal's residence and they did a good deal of damage. He had to hide in a wardrobe and one of his clerics was thrown from a first-floor window, but fortunately only broke a leg. After that the cardinal made a lame appeal to young Catholics not to be provoked into discarding their faith.

The Austrian *Anschluss* allowed Hitler to proceed to his next target, Czechoslovakia. As far as I was concerned, I met an unexpected rise in my good fortune, though of limited duration. Aged not yet 18 I got a job on the editorial staff of *Amtliche Wiener Zeitung*. Admittedly, I owed it to a fluke of fate. A vacancy had arisen because the local news editor, known for his anti-Nazi stance, had been arrested and sent to Dachau concentration camp. He and the editor-in-chief knew me from my earlier contributions and the distinguished old newspaper happened to be on my weekly cycling circuit for delivering short items to one of its supplements. I was offered and gladly accepted the job of local news hound. My unfortunate predecessor had left his books behind and one of them was by my revered F. W. Foerster. Although now among the books the Nazis had banned, I remember taking it as my lunch-time reading and proudly sitting on a bench on nearby Ringstrasse that had just been marked *Für Juden verboten* (Forbidden for Jews). However, with my new press pass issued by Vienna's Nazi authorities, I fully enjoyed such licence.

To convey something of these early Vienna *Anschluss* days I recall walking home with a friend from the last weekly meeting of our Boy Scouts group – it was a sad occasion after the inevitable Nazi ban on all youth activities besides the Hitler Youth, to which it was now obligatory to belong. On hearing shouts from a crowd outside a well-known café near the city centre, we came closer and saw a big brown-uniformed storm trooper swinging a whip to the tune of the Blue Danube waltz sung by the assembled throng. Meanwhile, the terrified shirt-sleeved Jewish owner and his tearful wife were made to daub swastikas on their marble-topped tables and wipe them clean again afterwards. It was a ghastly scene, reminiscent of feeding Christians to lions in the ancient Roman arena. Its worst feature was the grinning faces of the onlookers, who were clearly enjoying the spectacle. 'For God's sake, can nobody stop this?' I said under my breath to my friend. 'You must hold your mouth', he whispered back, 'otherwise they'll rope you in too.' I shut up. Not long after I heard, on Good Friday, the story of the Passion read in church, with the Jerusalem crowd clamouring for the release of Barabas instead of Jesus. I remember feeling ashamed both of my silence and of the cruelty of my fellow men.

Leaving Vienna with my mother late that September was bound to be a traumatic experience. My father had already gone to Milan to find a place for us to stay. It fell on me to get the obligatory exit permits for our passports from the new Vienna Gestapo headquarters located in the former Hotel Metropole on the Danube branch canal quay. It was bombed in 1945, so did not survive long enough to acquire the evil reputation of its rival establishments in Albrechtstrasse in Berlin or the Moscow Ljubljanka, which was the Soviet Union's equivalent. Nevertheless, in the few months since March it had acquired a reputation as a notorious place with soundproof cellars for interrogations and many of its victims never seen again.

Compared with my mother, with her gutsy and experienced stage presence, I was a born softy. One can imagine with what trepidation I went there, pretending to be smartly German and worthy of our Führer. After all, born in Hamburg, I was more of a German than the Austrian painter to whom they refused a professorship in the Austrian Academy of Arts. Moreover, I had a German passport and was entitled to feel among the new victors, not to be mixed-up with those *Sauösterreicher* (Austrian pigs), the contemptuous superior invective arrogant Germans traditionally reserved for Austrians. But in my heart, and increasingly my mother's son, I had felt truly at home with them, tacitly hoping that their newly discovered enthusiasm for their fellow countryman, Hitler, would prove a temporary aberration, which it did.

I strode up to the guard at the entrance, presented my papers and was shown to a ground-floor waiting room. Eventually, my turn came. Nonchalantly, I called out 'Heil Hitler', clicking my heels under wobbly knees. A business-like black-uniformed SS-officer beckoned me to an opposite chair. He asked a few questions and checked my form. What was the reason for our journey? Making my voice sound firm, I said that my father was already in Milan representing German firms and that my mother was a professional opera singer. Not for the first time I thanked providence for having provided me with an important name in the Nazi hierarchy. 'I see that you are the son of Rudolf Hess! Any relation of the great man?' Smilingly I said no, making it sound as if I wished I were. The saving grace of a lighter note had been introduced and at that moment I felt an irresistible stream running down my trouser leg, clearly the product of my inner tension and fear, but he had not noticed anything unusual. Two large desks stood between us and he would have been unable to see that I had wet the dark carpet in the room. The mention of Rudolf Hess seemed to have put him in a good mood and, with a kindly bang, he rubber-stamped my own and my mother's passport and gave them back to me. I pronounced a deeply-felt *Ich danke sehr* and possibly more intensely another *Heil Hitler*, in which I might have included everything from Hitler down to the skulls on the nice SS officer's lapels and his rubber stamp. The whole procedure had lasted no longer than a few minutes, but seemed an eternity. I walked out of the room on a happy cloud, wafted through to the exit and quickly disappeared among the pedestrians on that sunny day, hoping that nobody would notice my wet trouser legs.

By way of an incidental postscript, which, after so many years, may be said to have assumed historical proportions, the awkward incident above has come to link me, though upliftingly for me rather than for him, with my famous German contemporary, Günter Grass, the postwar German Nobel prize winner. He was hitherto widely regarded as one of those select 'few good Germans', exempted from the Nazi evil, unlike most others, even members of his own family, had been.

In later years I came to know him a little through our common journalistic interests. As their German past caught up with many who might have hoped to escape it, so also with Grass, through the revelations of the captured former East German Stasi or SS files captured by allied troops in what is now the Czech Republic after May 1945. To forestall these revelations Grass disclosed in his autobiography that, before being taken prisoner of war, he had once been a member of the Waffen SS. His autobiography has the apt and ironic title *Peeling the Onion*, evidently laying open the unknown layers underneath. Not having seen his book, I do not know if Grass mentions the related anecdote from Ibsen's *Peer Gynt* about a woman condemned to hell who had, as one good deed in her life, once given an onion to a starving beggar. This was remembered in her favour on Judgment Day and the said onion was let down to her on a string as a last chance to hold onto and thus escape eternal punishment. She clings to it, but it peels off and helplessly she falls back to hell.

That one onion, her good deed, was evidently not enough to procure salvation.

In the postwar Nuremberg war crime trials, the Waffen SS was exempted from the criminal charges that branded Hitler's elite corps responsible for many of his regime's major crimes. Understandably, with the general mobilization in the Second World War and Third Reich, the distinction sometimes became blurred. While German soldiers were drafted to a number of different fighting units, they were sometimes also used for other purposes. The kindly SS officer who stamped my passport with an exit visa after the Austrian *Anschluss* of 1938, to whom I evidently owe my life, clearly belonged to that criminal part of the regime. However, I hesitate to think how far the analogy of Günter Grass's onion, or the peeling onion of Ibsen's anecdote, applies to what providence has in store for my Gestapo SS officer on Judgement Day.

What concerns me here is not Günter Grass's hypocrital silence, the revered German of clean conscience, which was bound to upset public opinion in today's German Federal Republic, but what strangely unites us. There is a similarity between the wretched Private Grass, hit in the arm by shrapnel and crawling for protection under his tank before the Americans took him captive early in 1945, and me, similarly wetting myself in fright as I faced an SS officer who was clearly a member of the criminal gang. For Private Grass in 1945 the immediate future was brighter, consisting at least of the comforts of American PX-goodies like cigarettes and chewing gum, whereas I was confronting a greater unknown in Vienna's prewar Gestapo headquarters.

A few days later, my mother and I left Vienna after a sad parting from my grandfather and Aunt Mitzi, my mother's third sister who kept house for him. As with our Hamburg departure five years earlier, there was an unspoken fear about what might await those left behind. Like my Hamburg grandmother, my mother's father, a gifted Austrian musician, Sephardic cantor and living embodiment of all that was best in Austrian culture, was taken to the Theresienstadt concentration camp in Bohemia five years later. There, we indirectly heard, like my grandmother, he had died in his bed of old age – an amazing privilege and lucky fate. My poor aunt had to face a worse end, shared by millions; she was taken by cattle truck to the gas chambers of Auschwitz.

My mother and I were silent after the parting, not even feeling like crying. Our train was passing some of the loveliest scenery along the Danube, famous castles and monasteries, but we were incapable of taking in the views. Eventually, we reached the border with customs and passport controls. It was going to be a long stop, we knew. I was fidgeting, finding it difficult to hide my agitation. Sometimes bodily searches were ordered and all the passengers would have to get out for the ordeal. I was aware that my mother had hidden upon her some precious jewels, our only valuables, for no money could be taken out of the country. It was unthinkable what would have happened to us had anything like that been discovered, but my mother was surprisingly cool. She had that morning taken her usual precaution before her stage appearance of sucking a raw egg, which, she was sure, would do her voice good and calm her nerves and spirits. Actors and singers are notoriously superstitious. In German it is customary to express the sardonic and of course not seriously meant wish '*Hals und Beinbruch*' (May you break your neck and legs). We were spared the body search, remained in our seats while our passports were checked and returned to us with a finally polite 'Heil Hitler', and the train moved off.

To help restore our spirits, we went to the dining car for lunch while our train passed the enchanting scenery of the Italian lakes below. Our hearts were still pounding. We could not quite believe that we had made it to freedom, however uncertain our own future was to be. At a neighbouring table sat an elderly couple, evidently English tourists, who were wholly absorbed in the beauty of the landscape. I shall always remember those two, so unconcerned and quite oblivious of the fact that there might be others who had just escaped the jaws of hell.

3

Paradise of Exiles

Arriving from Hitler-occupied Austria in Milan's sunny autumn of 1938 was a liberating experience. My father met us at the magnificent and recently built Stazione Centrale in Milan, reflecting Italian *grandezza* in the late and still tolerable phase of Mussolini's decline and fall. In the small furnished flat reserved for us in the Via Lazaretto near the station, a kind landlady introduced us to Italian cuisine – everything simple and natural, indeed nature at its best. We settled down happily. Despite the uncertainty of the climate of the Italian north, with fog and rain likely, it was easy to adjust to the wonderful feeling conveyed by living under a serene Mediterranean sky. For me it was the beginning of a lifelong affair of the heart, which, decades later, I was happy to seal by marrying an Italian. Falling in love with Italy was, I believe, not a starry-eyed and sentimental affair, like recapturing a holiday image of that country. It was an elected affinity, covering, I like to think, everything, warts and all.

Materially, we somehow managed to get along without any real income, depending partly on the assistance of an organization for helping refugees. It provided a contribution to the costs of our rent and a free meal daily in a good Milan restaurant. One seemed to need little more for contentment in Italy, though having chosen Hitler's *asso di ferro* (iron axis) partner, it was probably another mistaken destination, our third after Prague and Vienna. Although Mussolini was a loyal friend to Hitler and was about to introduce his racist legislation, Italy was still free of the barbarities we had just witnessed in Germanized Austria. Beneath the surface, there was a certain Italian contempt for the *asso di ferro*, much as the Germans had long ridiculed the Italians for being *Katzelmacher,* or treacherous people. The Italians were not slow to give back as good as they got when it came to insulting their northern neighbours. They gleefully compared the Germans with an erect but quickly spent penis, while reserving the partnership's real potency, the *coglioni* (balls), for themselves, again never openly, of course, but with a knowing, eye-twinkling swagger. Nevertheless, behind all this there was also an old Latin admiration for the blond beasts in the north with their efficiency and ruthless power, which the *Duce* was not the first to want to emulate.

Besides, Italy was reputed to be 'the paradise of exiles', which for many seeking to escape to its beautiful landscape and sun, among them the poet Shelley who drowned in the waters between Spezia and Lerici, it was. In the late summer of 1938, Italian fascism was still a lesser evil compared with the German Nazi variety. Above all, through the ups and especially the downs of their history, and sometimes resorting to force, Italians have perfected the art of living. They have had to adapt to changing circumstances, as expressed in *si arrangia*, a remark made with shrugging shoulders and meaning there is no choice but to adapt, to find a way out of apparently insoluble problems, situations and difficulties, the famous *modus vivendi*. Undoubtedly, this ties up with another saying inspired by the great Italian master of political realism, Nicolo Machiavelli (1469–1527) – '*Fidarsi e bene, nonfidarsi e meglio*' or 'to be trusting is good, not to be trusting is better.' In an age when the influence of religion was growing weaker, he was the first to introduce absolute government untrammeled by abstract notions of rights, conscience and religion, finding his Machiavellian disciples everywhere and at all times.

For us there was something European about the atmosphere of Milan, recalling its one-time Austrian and French occupiers. The Milanese local dialect retains certain French sounds, while Austrians left behind a taste of their cuisine, which the Italians skilfully adapted and made their own. Since then, Milan has become a modern industrial city in which one is not even always aware of being in Italy at all apart from the late afternoon bustle in the city centre near the cathedral, the massive and magnificent *Duomo*, which retains the typical Italian touch. Under the old glass dome of the Galleria Vittorio Emanuele there are still shades of the unique liveliness of Venice's Piazza San Marco, of Rome's Via Veneto or of the Via Caracciolo in Naples, but even there, the Milanese sounds seem more subdued, as if swallowed up by the glass roof. However, everything else was as it should be in Italy – appearances mattered more than anything else, promenaders gesticulated animatedly, and elegantly dressed men and women sat leisurely at the café tables lining both sides of the Galleria Corso. Strolling among the crowd, in twos, uniformed *carabinieri* would watch everything through half-closed eyes. Typically, perhaps, Italy has two police forces, the *polizia* and the *carabinieri*, uneasily rivalling and feuding with each other and thereby ensuring that more rather than less liberty is preserved.

I normally spent the mornings studying Italian on a bench in the Giardini Publici, Milan's beautiful central park not far from where we lived and away from the traffic noise, but with ponds, clusters of old trees and cages containing various kinds of animals. After about three hours of work, I would take a break at a nearby *latteria* (milkbar) for a delicious cup of chocolate with a dollop of *panna montata*, fresh thick cream. It was every bit as good as the famous Viennese variety, as was much else in Milan, for example the *Cotoletta alla Milanese*, similar to the famous *Wiener Schnitzel* and allegedly a derivative of it. The secret, according to Sophia Loren, the great beauty and expert Italian chef, is to dip the veal cutlet or fillet in melted butter, then in breadcrumbs, then in beaten egg yolk, and then in the breadcrumbs again; to attain the perfect crust you finish with a final browning in melted butter.

After the break, I would return to my books and to a regular lesson in Italian pronunciation and grammar. Foreigners needed to guard against the temptation to think of the Italian language as easier than it is or to imagine they had mastered it more than they had. To be endowed with a musical ear is a valuable asset and mumbling is not allowed, for one cannot imagine how much those barbaric Northern sounds jar on Italian ears. My aim was to pass an entrance examination for Milan's Catholic University of the Sacred Heart, which I eventually did, though only for a brief period. My afternoons were devoted to journalistic work, writing articles for magazines and newspapers in Switzerland, which I had already supplied from Vienna. Sometimes I acted as an occasional correspondent, reporting for example on car races at the famous track at Monza or other Milanese events. This brought in a little pocket money.

My mother delighted in the Italian environment and its open-ness to music and singing. She was able to improve her bel canto style, having met the famous colloratura soprano Luisa Tetrazzini (1871–1940), with whom she became friendly. Tetrazzini was the Callas of her day and had phenomenal successes in Donizetti's *Lucia di Lammermoor* and as Anima in Bellini's *La Sonnambula*. Through my mother's German colleague, Hanna Lierke, also a soprano, who lived in Milan as the widow of an Italian banker, she managed to give some public recitals and also private concerts. Their friendship proved invaluable for my mother later on, when, during the Second World War, she had to live on her own in Milan. In fact, this brought about one of those bizarre episodes that only seem to happen in times of great upheavals and in Italy. The friend happened to be the mistress of a German SS general who used to come to Milan only on sporadic visits. She invited my mother to share her large villa with her, in a separate flat. My mother's non-Aryan background was a closely guarded secret between them. She knew her friend was opposed to the Nazis, though it was unthinkable what would have happened had it leaked out. The villa came with an armed SS guard, which saluted smartly all who entered or left, including my mother. She told me about this only after the war, mentioning how frightened she had been at first, but gradually accustoming herself to a new role with her innate coolness. In fact, the two women had many a good laugh over how they managed to deceive the authorities. They were both good-looking and in their forties, my mother was purportedly married to Hitler's deputy; nothing seemed more natural than that they should live under heavy protection – in a kind of lion's den, though under the Italian sun. When later in the war the SS lover-general was posted somewhere else, and my mother lost her Milanese 'haven', she thought it advisable to move to Rome, where she had friends.

This was of course wartime Italy and I am anticipating events a little. By then my father had left Milan because of the increasing danger of being arrested by Italian police acting under German pressure. He illegally crossed the border to neighbouring Switzerland, hoping to be safer in Zurich, but was in fact no safer there because of the close cooperation between Switzerland and Nazi Germany, especially in security matters.

A mature friendship

My stay in Milan in late 1938 and early 1939 was entirely agreeable. Aged 18 I was growing up fast physically and mentally. It was then that another friendship became important for me. It was comparable to my Austrian one and also with an older man, the German writer Ernst Erich Baumbach, a German exile, but for political rather than racial reasons. He was 20 years older than I was, tall and good-looking. He had left Germany as a member of the Stefan George circle (*Kreis*) of young writers and literary critics, some of whom (like F. Gundolf and E. Bertram) were to become, after the Hitler years, influential in German and European literature. Stefan George (1868–1933) belonged, with Hofmannsthal and Rilke, to the first rank of early twentieth-century German lyrical poets. Although his best work had largely been achieved by 1920, he continued to be a cult figure and visionary of an authoritarian kind, but was radically opposed to Nazism. His early poetry especially was akin to the French symbolists (Baudelaire and Mallarm) in its aloofness and imagery. In 1892 he founded the influential *Blätter für die Kunst*, a review aiming to reform the German language; in his poetry he largely rejected capital letters and scanning, and insisted on economy in punctuation. His poetry was humanist, mystical and esoteric. 'In his aloofness and rejection George was far more vigorous and deliberate than Rilke, and far more intense than Yeats. Neither of these has anything to rival the insistent quality of the outré present in all George's classical austerity' (*Times Literary Supplement*, 14 August 1953).

Baumbach had followed Stefan George to Switzerland and then gone to live in Milan. When I met him, he was well integrated into Italian life, had been awarded an Italian honour, the title of Commendatore, and, considering his opposition to Nazism, was surprisingly well treated by the Italian authorities. When high-ranking German Nazis visited Milan, the Italian police had naturally to take security precautions. In Baumbach's case this took the form of a courteous telephone call, with due apologies, that he would have to be taken into custody, temporarily, say on the coming Friday, when some high-ranking Nazi like Göring was expected to pass though Milan. 'Would he be ready, please, with his night things at 16.00 hours?' An official in a police car would then collect him, take him to a comfortable cell with all meals provided, plus cigarettes, and

convey him back home again on Monday after the VIP had left.
This was not exactly how, on the other side, the Gestapo would
have behaved! It was typical of the then unofficial Italian attitude
to German Nazis, namely to have a good laugh about them
behind their backs.

Like many of the Stefan George cultists, Baumbach was homosexual, but that did not affect our friendship. He never tried to
proposition me once it had been established that I was not
responsive. We discussed it at length and I came to know some
of his boyfriends. It was a separate chapter of his life. Being so
much younger, I naturally felt honoured to have his confidence.
This was very different from my Viennese friendship with Fritz,
the scout leader to whom I owed my conversion to Catholicism,
where the bond was more like one between teacher and pupil. In
Baumbach's case, it was a more intimate friendship between
equals who trusted each other. It was invaluable for an immature
young man like me to have been so fortunate in these good and
intellectually beneficial relationships. How easily they could have
gone wrong. Baumbach and I used to roam the streets of Milan
late at night, eat in cheap *trattoria*s, and talk endlessly about
philosophical problems, the meaning of life, death, love and
God.

Baumbach was not a Christian believer, but showed great
respect and tolerance for me as a Catholic convert. Literature
and art were his forte and, in Italy, I could not have wanted a
more knowledgeable companion and guide. Together we visited
Milan's wonderful art collections, particularly the Brera Gallery,
and long admired, for example, Mantegna's famous foreshort-
ened figure of Christ, his Pietà, which left one so spellbound both
through its emotional impact and ingenious perspective. Milan is
full of memories of Leonardo da Vinci, who with Bramante came
there to raise it to the pinnacle of its fame – Leonardo with his
'Last Supper' in the church of Santa Maria delle Grazie. Luckily,
during my stay in Milan in 1938–39 a major international
exhibition of paintings, drawings and models of his inventions
was held. Appropriately, it was staged at the Castello Sforzesco,
built by Francesco Sforza, who had then invited Italian and
Byzantine scholars to his court. That castle background provided
an unforgettable initiation into Leonardo's work and art.

Milan's glory is of course *Il Duomo*, its Gothic cathedral.
When the imaginative and frivolous Heinrich Heine visited it in

1829, he compared it with 'a massive cutout of glittering white
paper clippings, which only closer inspection surprisingly reveals
as made of hardest marble, but very pretty all the same, a truly
colossal plaything for the children of giants'. He describes the
countless statues of saints that cover the building and peep out
everywhere from under their panoplies, even topping its heights,
as a sculptured multititude that almost overwhelms the
onlooker's senses. He found it best seen at midnight under a full
moon. This is because that is when all the figures in that stony
crowd 'come down from their dizzy heights to walk with us
across the Piazza, and whisper old yarns into our ears, holy ones
or the secrets of Giangaleazzi Visconti who was its first builder
and of Napoleon Bonaparte who put on the finishing touches.'

I was glad to have a special personal link with the magnificent
Duomo, for I was confirmed in its crypt in early January 1939.
The celebrant was Milan's cardinal archbishop, Ildefons Schuster
OSB (1880–1954), Roman-born but of Bavarian and Tyrolese
ancestry. He combined his monastic profession with a modern
city apostolate and great liturgical scholarship and, as I shall
mention later, standing up for historical truth when it conflicted
with the tradition of the Church. I went to see him for a few
preliminary instructions, accompanied by my *padrino*, Prince
Borromeo, then a friend and Catholic activist in my Milan
parish. He was a little older than I was and belonged to the
famous Milanese family whose ancestor was St Carlo Borromeo,
the great theologian of the Counter-Reformation and the Council
of Trent, canonized in the early seventeenth century. The
Borromeos are among the wealthiest Italian families and their
possessions include the lovely Borromean islands of the upper
Italian Lake Maggiore. I remember visiting its magnificent
terraced gardens with its unfinished palace, and seeing one of the
family's mottos, *Humilitas*, laid out in a glorious display of
flowers, as if ostentatiously contradicting its meaning. We used
to call on the cardinal, usually around midday, and were treated
most hospitably, while the austere cardinal, a tiny and emaciated
figure, was merely served a banana, his usual midday fare.

A different but no less interesting aspect of my outings with
Baumbach was visiting brothels in Milan, which he as an older
Milanese hand seemed to know well, less as 'highlights' of the
Milan scene than, I suspect, as hunting grounds of his own.
These places provided a cheap form of entertainment for young

Italian men who came only for an eyeful of the semi-naked women on show parading behind a barrier. If there were a dearth of customers, the lights would be turned off, the madam would announce they were closing and everyone had to leave. A little later, the establishment would reopen for a new crowd of prospective customers. It brought many young Italian men a lot of fun, an eyeful of female flesh and banter with the women, who did their best to appear alluring and, if the customer were willing, disappeared with him into a bedroom at the back.

There were smarter, higher-class but presumably more expensive establishments where one used to sit down and order a drink, which one of the women of the house would bring. Alternatively, the madam would recommend particular members of her flock. Being in the company of a worldly older man added to my self-confidence, for I would never have seen so much of Milan's night life on my own. One difference between Italian and other prostitutes seemed to be that in Italy an element of old fashioned 'service' survived, which the prostitutes felt obliged to deliver. Undoubtedly, they also played their role, as perhaps expected of them, by being tenderly, motherly, indeed timid, apparently interested in trying to please rather than in the monetary transaction involved. At the initial 'get to know each other' stage in the better establishments it was not unusual for a woman to produce a photograph of her little son or daughter, looked after by her mother, a peasant woman, in the country. That was bound to soften any client's heart.

Leaving for England with £5

In the summer of 1939 I received an unexpected request to present myself for military service at the German consulate in Milan. The call-up evidently arose from false information about my eligibility, perhaps because of my name 'Hess', but I had to come to a quick decision about my future. With my father already in Switzerland, in the hope of being able to earn a living there, I decided to apply for a British student visa. Despite the long queues of applicants, two weeks later I heard that my application had been accepted and so resolved to make use of that chance. In addition, well-meaning friends and my mother were encouraging me to leave; the international situation was uncertain; the Germans and Italians were cooperating more closely and I risked being arrested and returned to Germany at any moment. My mother could not accompany me to England, but seemed safe in Milan. Apart from teaching singing, there were small paid jobs she could do to earn a living and being a woman was an advantage in Italy. I thus arranged a speedy departure to avoid meeting the deadline for presenting myself at the German consulate.

My mother saw me off at Milan's Stazione Centrale. We did not say anything, I clearly remember, but were both obviously preoccupied by the uncertainties of what was to come. Fortunately, neither of us knew how long our parting was to last and that the outbreak of the war, which everybody feared, might turn it into something final. I knew very few people in England. There were some distant relations I barely remembered, a few friends of my own age from Vienna and some friendly priests in Milan had given me some introductions. My knowledge of the English language was certainly inadequate and I knew practically nothing at all of the British Isles and their people among whom I had to make a new home on my own. My mother gave me a precious £5 note, which she had saved, an impressive white piece of paper, on which as though printed by hand it said: 'I promise to Pay the Bearer on Demand the Sum of Five Pounds' and signed by the Chief Cashier of the Bank of England. No other bank chief had ever addressed me in such a friendly way. It seemed encouraging for a new start in my life, amounting to all the capital I had – an iron ration to live on that would, I was assured, last for two or three weeks.

4

Asylum Seeker

On 1 July 1939, a blazing summer's day, I stood on the forward deck of a Channel ferry bound for Dover. I looked especially hard to see the famous cliffs emerging from the distant mist. What did they portend of what that unknown island had in store for me? I was unable to discern what the language or wild cries of the sea gulls signified, but I knew what I had left behind, what was dear to me, and what a continent in fear of a couple of powerful dictators represented. I also knew what drew me on and inspired me with hope, for imprinted on my mind were the lines of an English poem by Arthur Hugh Clough (1819–61) called 'Say not the Struggle Nought Availeth'. He wrote it during similarly desperate times, less than a century before, when, after the failure of the revolutions and popular risings of 1848, authoritarianism and oppression returned to Italy and other parts of the continent. It had always moved me and I then quoted it to myself by way of a prayer:

Say not the struggle naught availeth,
The Labour and the wounds are vain,
The enemy faints not, nor faileth,
And as things have been, things remain.

If hopes were dupes, fears may be liars;
It may be, in smoke conceal'd,
Your comrades chase e'en now the fliers,
And, but for you, possess the field.

For while the tired waves, vainly breaking,
Seem here no painful inch to gain,

Far back through creeks and inlets making,
Came, silent, flooding in, the main.

And not by eastern windows only,
When daylight comes, comes in the light,
In front the sun climbs slow, how slowly,
But westward, look, the land is bright!

And I knew that I, too, after a struggle that at the time was
impossible to gauge, was finally and on my own at last going
towards a strange new and free world, and having to cope with
that as best I could.

On my journey from Milan I had spent a few days in Paris
with my older French cousin Marguerite. As a gangling youth of
nearly 19, my outward appearance seemed to her to need
improvement, so she simply took me to her boyfriend's well-
stocked wardrobe to take my pick. 'You must at least look your
best in England,' she said. England at that time was not only a
worldwide empire but also a hallmark of male elegance. It all
went back to the Prince of Wales, later King Edward VIII, whose
abdication caused such a stir and who afterwards, as the Duke of
Windsor, continued to charm the world with his winning smile,
old-boyish looks and perfectly cut clothes. The story of one of
his shopping trips had made the rounds in Vienna. He had asked
a young sales woman in his halting German: 'Küssen, bitte.'
Saucily, she obliged by bestowing a kiss on the famous face, to
which he replied, apologizing: Nicht küssen hier (pointing to his
face) 'Küssen hier, bitte' (pointing to his behind) and adding
embarrassingly to the linguistic confusion between kissing and
Kissen (cushion). The 'Windsor Knot', which I sported with my
Parisian suit, probably best sums up his paricular contribution to
civilization. I was correspondingly desolate when, not many
months later, already into the Second World War, I lost my
precious suit. This happened in the internment camp on the Isle
of Man where, since it was too nice to wear in rough conditions
behind barbed wire, I entrusted it to a soldier, one of our guards,
to post back to my London address for safekeeping, but it never
arrived. I had to make the ancient bidding more or less my own:
'Naked I came out of my mother's womb, and naked shall I
return there, the Lord gave, and the Lord hath taken away;
blessed be the name of the Lord (Job 34).

At Victoria station, London, I had the unexpected pleasure of being met and welcomed by three Viennese ex-scouting friends. They, like me, were 'Refugees from Nazi Oppression', the official status stamped into our passports, but having already been in England for some time, they were mines of useful information. How good it was to see them! Little Alfons Bellak (Ali) was always so quick and funny, being our Monopoly expert and propagator. We all remembered Hasi (Hans) Frank's home in the centre of Vienna for its good kitchen smells, for their cook was widely famed for her baking skills. Hans Furth, nicknamed 'Tall Jumbo', was a 'boy wonder pianist', who had already given acclaimed public piano recitals in Vienna, then aged only 15. He studied at the Royal Academy of Music before deciding to become a monk of the strict Carthusian order, which he then left to go to the United States where he married and, as though to make up for lost time in the monastery, had seven children. He eventually ended up as a professor of psychology at Washington's Catholic University.

Everything about my arrival at Victoria station remained memorable. It seemed so different from any other journey's end, as so many others had noted through the centuries. Whereas nineteenth-century immigrants like Heine and Karl Marx, landing by steamer, were overwhelmed by the sheer size and noises of the port of London, to me Great Britain's capital seemed surprisingly small, not at all what I had expected. For instance, the famous Victoria station seemed dwarfed compared with Mussolini's grand Stazione Centrale in Milan, from where I had just departed. It seemed unworthy of a big capital, though I was unaware that it was only one of many railway terminals linking London with other parts of the country. The English trains, too, seemed more suited to a smaller world, though with comfortably upholstered seats even for third-class passengers, compared with the hard wooden benches of that class on continental trains. One was almost tempted to ask if this was possibly a country without any particular class distinctions.

Unlike the continental system of state railways, Great Britain's network was then privately organized in regional companies. My Dover train had arrived well on time and the English railway personnel struck me as equally polite and friendly as those on the Continent. What surprised me most about my first impression of that huge city of then nearly eight million inhabitants was that everything seemed to be on such a small scale. Unlike other familiar capitals, such as Paris, Vienna and Berlin, where big is considered beautiful, here they wanted to conceal it. I was then, of course, ignorant of London's real size, of other railway stations, or of London's history. I was unaware that it had not grown from one centre, like Paris, but had haphazardly spread in an unplanned way, swallowing up surrounding habitations, towns and villages, with each keeping its own characteristics, like small towns of their own, and also their old romantic-sounding names like Knightsbridge, Belgravia, Pimlico, Earls Court and St John's Wood. London seemed agreeably small, one was not daunted by it, though that eventually proved, as much else in England, deceptive.

After my arrival, my friends took me for an unexpected treat, an English high tea. Afternoon tea at five o'clock, which was fashionable on the Continent, was naturally a world institution. I even knew that the eighteenth Duchess of Bedford had introduced it to bridge the yawning gap between luncheon and dinner, and that it had soon become established with the whole gammut of table napkins, exquisite silver teapots, small silver forks and spoons, thinly cut cucumber sandwiches and toasted teacakes. High tea, being more plebeian, attracted less enthusiasm from the outside world than was usually expected from all things British. High tea in England evidently replaced the late dinner of the upper classes. Served at about 6 p.m. when the family's breadwinner came home from work, it consisted of something like beans on toast or fish and chips with which the British were unlikely to impress.

They took me to a Lyons Corner House opposite Victoria station, which, along with all the others, has sadly long disappeared. And gone with these vast tearooms and restaurants on different floors was another very English feature that impressed me then – friendly good 'service', not at all standoffish, as the island race was expected to be and this applied equally to the sales personnel in shops. Here nobody seemed keen to sell you anything; indeed, they were even likely to suggest that if you cared to go to another shop round the corner, you could obtain the desired article much more cheaply. Was that how a nation of shopkeepers ought to behave? Napoleon must have made a mistake. Was he perhaps thinking of the much more efficient Dutch?

Anyway, at my first high tea we were cosseted by amply built waitresses who called us 'Duckie' or 'Darling', which no self-respecting continental waitress would ever dare to do. These nice 'dears', as I learnt to call them, carried huge trays with tea cans, jugs of boiling water and milk, and mountains of buttered toast. Then there was another surprise, something gooey called lemon curd; it was so unfamiliar that I bought a whole jar of it to gorge, but with such unpleasant consequences that it served to end my lemon-curd passion as quickly as it had begun.

London traffic, at any rate, as I discovered outside Victoria station, was reassuringly familiar, though English drivers did seem unfamiliarly courteous. They actually stopped at zebra crossings rather than make a beeline for the unfortunate pedestrians, as I remembered them doing in Milan where it had seemed a popular sport for motorists. Not new to me was driving on the left. It was, after all, the old European practice before the Napoleonic occupation. The Austro–Hungarian Empire returned to it, but later changed back when Hitler took over. Having never been occupied by the French, Great Britain kept to the left all along.

A land of such dear souls
In other respects, however, England presented me with a vast tableau of unfamiliar impressions. As an early cigarette smoker, no doubt because I felt it would accelerate the growing-up process, I decided that in Sherlock Holmes territory a pipe enhanced the admired if remote English equanimity. So, having acquired one, I sat down on a Regent's Park bench, surrounded by sheep, then still grazing there, to inaugurate it. Unfortunately, the shag brand the tobacconist recommended was too strong for me, with effects that were reminiscent of my lemon curd initiation. The 'Go Easy' advice from my book of English idioms was commendable.

Later that day my friends took me to the place they had found for me to stay. It was called the 'Westminster Catholic Club', but it was not the august gentleman's club about which one had heard so much. Clubs in England evidently came in different kinds. Mine, which Father Carr, a priest at nearby Westminster Cathedral, ran, was a modest hostel for young civil servants working in the government offices of the area. The housekeeper was a rough-sounding woman called Mrs Whiffin, but said to have a heart of gold; since her most frequently served sweet was rice pudding, a pet aversion of mine, she was not so dear to my heart. The hostel was in quiet St George's Square near the Thames. The rooms had two, three or four beds, something to which I was not accustomed, so on my first night in London I felt very far from home. However, I was learning from my English idioms that 'beggars can't be choosers' and resolved 'to grin and bear it'.

What I nevertheless liked about these first days was how considerate English people seemed to be. For a start, there was not the hostile glare that, however involuntarily, seemed to mark faces on the Continent unless one had been properly introduced. The English, so good on formal occasions, seemed also able to do the other thing, not 'stand on ceremony'. Indeed, a smile in public places was not uncommon, but unknown on the Continent. I had not yet come across the English stiff upper lip. What could possibly have happened to it? On the other hand, a British smile did not connote familiarity, but did facilitate human contact and overcame all those ordinary human barriers. It was nice to think that it was this island that had produced John Donne's famous denial that 'no man is an island, entire of itself' and, on the contrary, that there was a 'Continent, a main', of which man was a part. As a stranger in my hostel, I was welcomed by everybody and without the slightest fuss. The English habit of using Christian names helped, even though it would extend to all and sundry, even those one did not have to like. The French 'tu' or German 'du' might be more intimate, but the British middle way had its advantages. One did not have to go in for those excrutiatingly fraternal relations, which, from Cain and Abel via the French Revolution to British trade unionists, made a mockery of human brotherhood. The leftist Bertolt Brecht hit the nail on the head with his ditty *'Und willst Du nicht mein Bruder sein, dann schlag ich Dir den Schädel ein'* (And if you refuse to be my bother, I will knock your block off). The British, I discovered, had what none of us continentals knew about, respect for other people's private space, and more tact and discretion, so necessary for human relations. In other words, they were part of a civilized culture and not just following mere outward norms of social etiquette.

My Westminster hostel was also cheap, according to the prices of that time, 22s 6d a week, which comprised breakfast and an evening meal on six days of the week, with an added lunch on

Saturdays and Sundays. Even this was above my means. I was glad to learn of Mr Micawber, filling a gap in my literary education, and his very English optimism expressed in 'Annual income twenty pounds, annual expenditure nineteen pounds six, result happiness. Annual income twenty pounds, annual expenditure twenty pounds, ought and six, result misery.'

Soon Bloomsbury House came to my rescue. This was then the centre of the various aid organizations for refugees from Hitler's Europe, situated near the British Museum. From then on I collected a weekly allowance of 25s from the Catholic Committee for Refugees, which covered my board and lodgings. This even left me with 2s 6d, half a crown, to spare and to be able to follow the old injunction: 'Who loves not wine, woman and song/Remains a fool his whole life long' (Martin Luther). It went quite far in those pre-inflationary times when the cost of living was so low, a packet of cigarettes costing 6d or a cinema ticket a shilling. I was also able to earn something on the side from the well-paid contributions I made to Swiss newspapers and magazines.

The five-floor staircase and passages of Bloomsbury House were constantly abuzz with German, Austrian and Czech sounds as people, all on similar errands, queued for assistance or advice on how to find somewhere to live in London. It seemed that they were all speaking or trying to speak something that occasionally sounded like English. They even addressed strangers in their new lingo, so as not to let on that they were 'bloody Germans' and as though the strangers would not have been able to tell. It was funny to listen to their 'English' politeness, to hear them constantly apologizing when they bumped into one another: 'Soooo sorrry, madam' or 'Beggg jour pardong, sir.' It sounded odd coming from the lips of people not normally given to such 'good English manners'. Perhaps, they were in their newly assumed 'English' ways, paying unconscious tribute to the country that had offered them refuge and to which they owed their lives; 'Excuse me, Sir, where is the ladies toilet?' Or 'Pardon me, Sir, where does one go out?' meaning where is the exit?

'Refugee English' became a new variation of English. Even the Cockney bus conductor passing through Swiss Cottage had learnt to call it *Schweizer Häuschen*. The large green hilly area of Hampstead Heath and Golders Green, reminiscent of Vienna's Grinzing, was now a popular bedsitter region. The German and

Austrian cafés and restaurants sprouting up in the Finchley Road were always full of customers. Goulash, *Schnitzel* and *Schweinshaxe mit Knödel* were on the menu and, then rare in London, it was possible to get an excellent cup of coffee *mit Schlag* (whipped cream), which customers had been used to in Vienna, Prague or Berlin. In that part of London homeless people could feel 'at home', could exchange *Tratsch* (gossip), complain about the English food or weather, or tell one another the latest refugee joke like: The gasman rings a Hampstead doorbell, saying 'I have come to see the meter.' Continental lady: 'I am the *Mieter*' (German for tenant). A man in the bus carefully enunciates his destination: 'To Marble Arch, please.' This elicits two tickets. Annoyed, the passenger shakes his head and tries again: 'For Marble Arch, please. This results in four tickets. *Nein, Marble Arch, please,* and nine tickets are produced. Near tears, the passenger groans, holds out a pound note and, giving up the unequal struggle, says: 'Can you change me, please.' 'I wish I could', mutters the conductor.

The Austrian poet Felix Braun (1885–1973), a friend in my early London days, once gave a reading of his poems in a London university hall. A large German speaking audience came to hear him, the most gentle of men, read in his delicate voice. Encouraged by the applause, he finally ventured into English, announcing: 'And this poem I have found in the drawers of my secretary.' It needs explaining that, in his Viennese generation, at the end of the Habsburg Empire, a *Sekretär* also meant a writing desk with drawers that had nothing to do with women's underwear.

In the last 60 or more years all this has changed totally, and London with it. The first wave of Hitler refugees has long passed away via the Golders Green crematoria; and a second and third Anglicized generation has followed them. Newcomers from other parts of the world have changed the formerly continental atmosphere of London's Hampstead. Chinese and Indian takeaways have replaced the Austrian and German restaurants. London has done what it has always done throughout the centuries. Germans, Poles and Czechs have replaced Hungarians and Jews from Russia and eastern Europe. London has housed Catholics persecuted by Protestants and vice versa, revolutionaries and the victims of revolutions, Huguenots in the late seventeenth century, Normans, Danes, Saxons and Romans, all destined for the ultimate melting pot that the island of Britain has always been.

One of the introductions I brought with me from Italy was to the then bishop auxiliary, later bishop to the forces and archbishop, David Mathew. He was a well-known historian of English Catholicism. Eventually, I was to share his interest in the Liberal Catholic historian Lord Acton (1834–1902), about whom he wrote two books. David Mathew and his inseparable younger brother Gervase, an Oxford Dominican priest became good friends. Both were blatantly eccentric. David Mathew, moreover, was then the rare specimen of a Catholic liberal. His cultural and intellectual qualities deemed him out of touch with ordinary British Catholics who were rather short of these traits, though he proved to be a wise and practical priest with a great sense of genuine charity.

Unconcerned about their outward appearance and, sometimes embarrassingly, also about their personal habits, the Mathew brothers were refreshingly direct and original in everything they said and did, and remarkably clever. Unashamedly, David pleaded guilty to his snobbism by saying how much he 'appreciated the rich', but he combined that, as he put it, 'with a deep love for the poor'. He had been a midshipman in the British navy before entering the severe monastic life of the Carthusians, which, however, did not last. He was apparently unable to wear the heavy boots that the monks wore for their long weekly walks.

On my first visit David Mathew, then a bishop auxiliary of the Westminster diocese living in Woburn Square near Bloomsbury House, spontaneously wrote out a cheque for me for five guineas. It was to enable me to participate in a course in English studies at the Regent Street Polytechnic and I remain indebted to him for that act of generosity. Among my fellow polytechnic students was a German Jewish physician who had been a prisoner in Dachau concentration camp. Quite extraordinarily, he was released and made it safely to England. Moreover, he won first prize in an essay competition held in our class. The subject was 'My ideal form of government' and we were all astonished when he made out a fairly convincing case for the old Germanic Utopia of 'a good dictator' who was of course quite unlike the other, real one. Celebrating his prize essay afterwards, we got a little carried away and toasted our sandwiches on the electric fire at the polytechnic library. This, of course, was strictly forbidden and I, as the culprit, was duly caught and severely reprimanded by the librarian.

The four weeks granted to me of prewar and peacetime England passed all too quickly. I used them as best I could to learn some 'basic verities' like, for example, the importance of the British weather, which, because it was so changeable on these isles, was noticed and talked about more than anything else. The reason was undoubtedly that it was always there, or as André Maurois, a foreigner of course, had said, 'It is always bad, though the climate is good'. Or, according to Spanish philosopher George Santayana, 'Because the Englishman is governed by the weather in his soul'. It is not only constantly available as a subject of conversation, but also as a means of establishing human contact while remaining on the impersonal level the English prefer: 'Nice day, isn't it?' or 'What terrible weather we seem to be having.' It provides an agreeable way of taking notice of one's fellow men without a commitment. The weather exists of course in other nations, but they have not even remotely discovered its human possibilities.

Then there was all that queuing up at bus stops, stations and in shops where people waited patiently to be served. Once or twice I tried the untrue gambit of 'Excuse me, I have a train to catch,' but that 'wasn't cricket' either, whatever that strange reference to a game meant. In those days people merely gave you a strange look if you jumped a queue. They would rarely shout 'Hoi' to make you aware of your offence. People were more disciplined then and would converse happily about the weather or the international situation while queuing. Non-queuing foreigners, poor things, just didn't know any better, did they? Their lot was not a happy one either, as illustrated by what happened to a friend with little knowledge of English. As the caretaker of the Austrian Cultural Institute in London, he was sent out to buy stamps at the nearest post office and rehearsed what he was going to say on the way. When his turn came he said, carefully enunciating each syllable: 'A shit of three penny stamps, please.' The man behind the counter, enjoying the scene, replied 'What was it you wanted?' and again 'louder, please' so that everybody would get the full benefit of the poor man's slip.

The English queue was probably the sign of a rich country, I decided, for in England even the last one in a queue is rarely disappointed. Why bother to exert yourself, as others did in less disciplined regions where the devil was sure to get the hindmost and people knew that unless they fought for it they would get nowhere? I was surprised to learn that the British had by no means always behaved thus. According to Alexander Herzen, a Russian revolutionary who lived in London with his family from 1851 to 1865: 'Nowhere is there a crowd so numerous, so dense, so terrifying as in London, yet it never in any circumstances knows how to queue.' John Bull evidently changed his habits. Not even 100 years later George Mikes established that: 'A man in a queue is as much the image of a true Briton as a man in a bullring is the image of a Spaniard.' National characteristics, like all fashions, evidently tend to change. Erasmus, in the sixteenth century, was surprised by the liberality with which English women in his day seemed to bestow kisses on everybody, as I would have been in 1939. Yet not a decade later Londoners astonished outsiders with the so-called 'Kensington kiss', by which English women, old and young, held out their cheeks, mumbling an almost bored but orgiastic sounding 'Hmmmmm' as men bestowed their kisses on them.

Minding my manners

Then there was the remarkable difference in table manners, with strangers sitting at the same table in a restaurant automatically passing the saltcellar, while on the Continent one would have to ask. Continentals expect their food to be properly seasoned, whereas not to add salt is almost regarded as a British freedom. I have often wondered whether the difference in table customs between Britain and the Continent might have something to do with full retinues of domestic servants continuing for much longer in British upper and middle-class households than on the Continent. They had to be given something useful to do like laying the table. In my prewar London days and even in the early days and months of the Second World War, when attending formal dinners I noted that my English hosts had more domestic help than their social equivalents on the Continent. Of course, this changed speedily in the war. Later the British seemed to go to the opposite extreme by shunning domestic service altogether, as if it were a degrading form of slavery. Even regimented factory work was considered preferable to the old 'patriarchal' system in which nannies or domestic servants remained into old age as respected members of the household.

One had to get used to rounded English soupspoons after their pointed Continental cousins. English table manners also required squashing peas against the back of a fork rather than shovelling them onto the front. Salt was poured (therefore the large hole in English saltcellars) in little heaps on the side of the plate, not sprinkled over the dish, and each morsel dunked into it with the fork; this allowed British manufacturers of salt and mustard to get extremely rich from the wastage left on the edge of plates. Placing bread and butter plates to the left of a cover instead of the right was another source of trouble, when Continental guests, unaware of the difference, were present and helped themselves to their neighbour's roll and butter. As for the pudding, a spoon and fork are laid out on the unwritten understanding that if only one is used it has to be the fork rather than the spoon, which is more convenient if liquids are involved. All this evidently had to do with differing ideas of civilized behaviour and culture with the English meaning the latter when they use the former term and vice versa on the Continent. Still, I always liked the story told of King George V who, when an African guest was present who did not know what to do with the bowl of water and lemon after a fish course, raised it in drinking a toast to His Majesty, who courteously responded in the same way.

Above all, a puzzling sphere of cheerfulness and optimism extended over every aspect of British life. 'How are you?' one asked and automatically responded 'Can't grumble', 'not too bad', or 'could be worse'. People wanted to be positive. Even when the sky could not have looked more miserable, 'Nice day, isn't it?' seemed the required reaction. Having read much of pessimistic Germans like Schopenhauer or Nietzsche, I thought that this thinking the best of human nature, imputing good motives even to totalitarian dictators, was flying in the face of reality. For instance, a popular English Catholic newspaper ascribed Hitler's vegetarianism to some praiseworthy relic from his Austrian Catholic past and Friday abstinence, or those well-meaning English lefties who until very late in their day explained Stalin's murders as motivated by his wanting to introduce an element of social justice into backward Russia. My innate pessimism seemed to me the more natural. At least I was rarely disappointed.

In court reports in the British press, terms like the 'alleged' chicken thief were often associated with the 'benefit of the doubt' applied to defendants in common law. When *The Times*, then the representative organ of appeasement, reported what 'Herr' Hitler

had said about 'the Jews' or about 'world peace', it applied that
courtesy title to him as if it were apparently deserved. It would
be understood in the same reassuring way as Neville Chamberlain's gesture when, on his return from Munich, he waved a piece
of paper with Hitler's signature on it as though it were proof of
'Herr Hitler's' honesty. 'Herr Hitler' I ask you, that 'really got
my goat', as I had just usefully learnt as my latest English idiom.
In those last days of peace in 1939, and not through any later
retrospective wisdom, the criminal nature of the man with whom
the world was dealing, seemed to have dawned even on the
British.

There was something both attractive and deeply ingrained in
British optimism and I was fascinated to discover what a
venerable tradition it had. It had an almost sacred quality,
comparable to the common bond between the English and Jews
as God's 'chosen people'. Perhaps, because of their tragic history,
Jews were forced into their peculiar optimism to deal with 2000
years of constant persecution. But what could account for the
optimism of the English? Was it some muddled thinking or the
traditional English preference for moral ideas over all the
metaphysical nonsense that seemed to trouble people elsewhere?

I was glad to discover that the root cause went back nearly
2000 years to a British monk called Pelagius and his powerful
heresy. He may even have been a Welshman named Morgan. The
effects of his heresy were remarkable when one considers that
theological metaphysical ideas are the last thing anyone on this
island could want to be influenced by. Even in our post-Christian
age, an average British person today who is completely ignorant
of the religious, theological and moral notions people cared
about all those centuries ago would still share that optimistic
view about the nature of man with that old tonsured Morgan
and believe, rightly or wrongly, that man, not God, is the master
of his fate.

Pelagius, responsible for that English heresy it has become *par
excellence*, was active in Rome in AD 410, when Alaric's
Visigoths were threatening to overrun the city, then the capital of
Christendom. As a Christian missionary and moralist, he preached
the simple and familiar English doctrine that the ordinary 'man
in the Roman street' could pull himself up by his own boot
straps from his human mess, unaided, as it were, by divine grace.
Pelagius thus denied the traditional Christian teaching of original

sin, the idea that man was not good, but born with a serious crack or taint in his nature, a view that the English have always thoroughly disliked because of their preferred belief in the goodness of man. Holding that view involved Pelagius in a long ideological quarrel with Augustine of Hippo, one of the greatest minds of the early Church. As a one-time adherent of the Manichaean heresy, Augustine, after his own conversion, emphasized the extreme opposite view of man's absolute dependence on God, comparable to a child's dependence on his or her mother. Augustine found the Pelagian notion that man should rely on his own moral efforts for his salvation totally abhorrent.

Augustine and Pelagius did not know each other personally but depended on others to learn of their views, which was unfortunate but not unusual at that time when communications were difficult. In fact, Pelagius did not wholly reject original sin but regarded it as a minor blot on man's nature that goodwill could easily wipe out. He was a pragmatist, as the Romans were, which explained his success under the tough conditions of beleaguered Rome. As a missionary from Britain, he was anyway more interested in good works and deeds than in dogmatics. Augustine was not satisfied with that and also had a deeper insight into all the hidden springs of human nature that were to inspire Aquinas, Luther, Calvin, Pascal and Newman. Had Freud been less dogmatically anti-religious and anti-Christian, St Augustine's frank revelations about his own sinfulness in the *Confessions,* namely keeping a concubine until his conversion and famously praying 'Give me chastity and continence but not yet', should have made the inventor of psychoanalysis more understanding of the Augustinian belief in original guilt and his denial of human freedom.

Pelagius's preaching, however, did not prevent Rome and the empire falling to the Barbarians. The influence of Augustine, the bishop, prevailed upon the pope. Thus, Pelagius, unquestionably a holy man but also a Celtic oddball, was condemned by the Church, which made the British people throughout the ages into his devoted, if unconscious, followers. St Augustine, on the other hand, went on to write *The City of God,* which played its part in helping Christian civilization to rise again from its ruins.

I loved my first days of English impressions, with the men in Whitehall doffing their hats when passing the Cenotaph, a respect shown in public good manners. I was struck by the remarkable absence of the police, not so much as guardians of public order, but as the friendly Bobby on the beat, whom one could ask for the way and who would respond politely, even pulling out his little book and showing you the bus route or pointing to the nearest tube station. Comparably continental policemen were not of course unfriendly, but German police were traditionally more given to expressing the state's authority, and Italian police were always elegant, even in the thick of traffic chaos. Only in England did one not go to the police to register when changing one's address; identity cards were unknown, in fact, they were something English people instinctively objected to as curtailing their freedom. There were long discussions in the newspapers when, all those 60 years ago, ration books were introduced at the outbreak of war and people were requested, indeed ordered, to carry their gas masks. What struck me most about the British way of life then, compared with my own two decades of continental experience, was its unfamiliar and most agreeable absence everywhere of the supreme powers of the state.

Also unfamiliar to me then was the still admirably functioning British Parliament with someone called 'Mister Speaker', so different from presidents as they were called elsewhere. Another very significant difference then was something called 'His Majesty's loyal Opposition'. It made me wonder how one could possibly be 'opposed' and yet 'loyal' at the same time. There was, furthermore, an apparent honesty about public life in that faraway England, which was quite new to me. Cheating the state was tantamount to cheating you or me, English people used to say. That was why they told customs officials truthfully whether or not they had any dutiable goods to declare. They did not delight in cheating the state as we continentals did. I remember, even after the war when conditions had changed somewhat and I used to send food parcels to continental friends, the dirty looks I encountered from English friends when I put the wrong descriptions on the outside list of contents, in other words I lied. I did it, of course, to stop the parcels being pinched, which they would have been if 'chocolate', 'coffee', 'tea', or other desirables virtually unobtainable in post-wartime Europe, had been written there.

The story was told of a Jewish rabbi who had written a letter to a friend, but on finding someone to deliver it by hand, tore up a stamp so as not to cheat the public purse. That was perhaps overdoing it, but he was edvidently a victim of that 'English hypocrisy' one heard so much about. Friends and foes abroad were convinced of its existence, and it was certainly not a myth invented by Puritans.

Then came 3 September 1939 – a beautiful Sunday morning of that fateful Indian summer; London church bells were ringing and people in the streets seemed cheerful. Did any of them realize that the war that everybody had talked about for so long was upon us? Outwardly, people seemed unconcerned, as though they would accept it if they had to, but with reluctance and certainly without enthusiasm. A war with honour was better, however, than Chamberlain's peace with dishonour turning to bitter shame. I was alone in my hostel room that morning, having climbed onto a chair in order better to hear our radio loudspeaker placed on top of a wardrobe. My English was improving, but I wanted to ensure that I caught every word of the broadcast by Prime Minister Neville Chamberlain, scheduled for 11.15 that morning. German troops had invaded Poland on 1 September. In keeping with the Anglo–Polish treaty of mutual assistance, the British government, true to its past policy, had half-heartedly protested at first, holding out to Hitler the chances of another conference if he *agreed* to withdraw his forces; in diplomatic terms that did not necessarily mean actually withdrawing them. For weeks, the daily message on the front page of the *Daily Express* had been 'There will be no war in Europe this year or the next'. Backing Chamberlain's appeasement policy was a reflection of the large body of British public opinion's wishful thinking.

Others in the government, feeling the shame of always cravenly giving in, insisted then on making a stand. 'Speak for England, Arthur,' they had shouted to Arthur Greenwood, the acting Labour leader in the House of Commons, and Berlin received an ultimatum rather than the customary spineless protest on that Sunday morning at 9 a.m. It expired at 11 a.m., though Poland, being too far away to help, was hardly a good case for making it stand. Yet it was better than doing nothing, for on the two previous occasions when Austria and Czechoslovakia fell, the Western powers had failed to intervene.

In my pocket I kept a cartoon by David Low that I had cut out of the *Evening Standard*. It seemed to express brilliantly, if with irony, what many people, I among them, felt. It was based on the first limerick I ever learnt about 'the young lady of Riga who smiled as she rode on a tiger; they returned from the ride with the lady inside, and a smile on the face of the tiger'. The cartoonist had drawn a tiger with swastikas devouring Chamberlain, tossing his moustache and top hat aside and about to eat that symbolic appeasing umbrella. I liked the fun the English language was capable of extracting from the deadly serious business of politics. By then the real Chamberlain was on the air, speaking from 10 Downing Street in an old man's sad, gloomy, tremulous, yet dignified and moving voice. His political dreams had finally been shattered. He spoke briefly, saying that no reply had been received to the British ultimatum and that therefore this country was now at war with Germany. Listening closely up on my chair, I thought of my mother in Italy, my father in even more danger, as we had heard, in Switzerland or France. Then suddenly there was the wailing noise of an air raid warning. How familiar that sound was soon to become. Meanwhile, some silvery, cylindrical barrage balloons had gone up into the blue London sky.

Someone shouted 'Everybody down to the basement at once.' Was London to suffer the fate of Warsaw? I wondered. We assembled downstairs, surprisingly cheerfully I thought given the uncertainty of what lay in store for the world. In *The Gathering Storm*, Winston Churchill described this 'English way' of effacing troubles as he too was making his way to a similar basement on that Sunday. Soon afterwards the 'All Clear' went and we learnt that it had been a false alarm, a mistake. During this 'phoney war' phase of neither peace nor war, which had begun for us in western Europe and was to last six months, Hitler, with his new ally, the Soviet Union, concentrated on carving up eastern and northern Europe – Finland, Latvia, Estonia, Lithuania and Norway – and sinking ships in the Atlantic along Great Britain's vital supply lines. It was as if providence, in the unlikely disguise of the dictators, had granted the British and French a last respite. Since they had been so reluctant to enter the inevitable final settlement, we were given time to adjust to what was yet to come. I thanked God for the phoney war.

A few evenings later I was invited to attend a patriotic music hall show in a Chelsea theatre. The audience joined in when they sang the funny song then becoming popular in the British army and suggesting that war in all its seriousness had not really started: 'We're going to hang out our washing on the Siegfried Line/Have you any dirty washing, mother dear?' After that everybody got up up and sang Elgar's 'Land of Hope and Glory'. I had never heard that hymn before and it moved me deeply; I resolved to send the words and music to my mother in Italy on the first chance that presented itself, but five years had to pass for that to happen. The custom of standing up for 'Land of Hope and Glory', or for the national anthem at the end of all theatrical performances or films, was another unusual experience for me.

'Land of Hope and Glory' has since been criticized for glorifying Britain's chauvinist imperial past, but hearing it for the first time that evening early in the Second World War was for me an unforgettable experience. My fortunes, for better or for worse, were now bound up with those of England and I had no regrets about being on the side of my country's enemy. Was I following the fate of Shakespeare's Roman patriot, Coriolanus who had gone over to the Volscian enemies? Traditional loyalties no longer applied in the age of totalitarianism. I had every reason to thank my lucky stars that I had been cast on the side of the free world. I prayed for it in the same way as I prayed for my father and mother, now on the other side. I felt no hatred for the other side, only sadness that good people there were being dragged along by the tide of events. They had no choice to opt for freedom, as I had. When the war began seriously with the bombing raids on London, a funny incident illustrated my dilemma. A fellow German who was loyal to the anti-Hitler cause exclaimed excitedly: 'Have you heard the latest news? Twenty of our planes were lost last night.' 'You mean *ours*?' asked his British host coolly.

New in wartime London was the blackout of all street lighting. Not a chink of light could shine through the curtained-off windows and, at night, air raid wardens, wearing tin helmets, would knock at doors and windows, shouting 'lights'. The light evenings of that late summer made moving around easy, but when darkness fell traffic became dangerous, with buses and cars creeping along at a snail's pace, with only tiny points of light showing. People in the streets were no more than passing shadows. Many carried little torches, which suddenly and frighteningly shone into your face. Everything was hushed and subdued, especially when the thick London smog descended. Once walking alone, I almost bumped into the Albert Hall.

Piccadilly Circus, London's centre of brilliant lights and illuminated advertisements was plunged into darkness. The underground functioned well, and when the bombing raids began in earnest, the underground platforms became London's dormitories, a nightly refuge for thousands, as so memorably recorded in Henry Moore's's drawings. Gas masks were issued; soon everybody wearily had to carry the obnoxious cardboard boxes on string around their shoulders, though they secretly also served other uses like carrying one's sandwich lunch.

My early journalism came in useful. I became the assistant of Eric Kessler, the London correspondent of the distinguished Swiss *Neue Zürcher Zeitung*. He had moved from the country into a room in the Dorchester Hotel, and my job included sending daily dispatches by telephone to neutral Zurich. The first story I wrote was about the evacuation of schoolchildren from London as a prospective danger zone. I went to Waterloo station and saw large batches of young children, only some accompanied by their teachers or parents, being sent to stay somewhere far away in the country. They all had little suitcases with a bare minimum of clothes, their gas masks, and cards with their names and addresses around their necks. They all looked fearful and lost. Sending them away was a great feat of organization, but it was at their destinations that the problems arose. The helpful future foster-parents who were to receive them into their homes in the country were not necessarily equipped for the challenge. The social conditions of some of those poor children from London's East End were appalling. Some had insufficient warm clothes or shoes with them and, separated from their families, felt homesick. There were also those who were vermin infested, difficult to control, bed-wetters or general troublemakers. Most of them had never been in the country, had never seen a cow or farm animals. Until then outsiders had not realized what real poverty meant in that big city.

I liked my reporter's job. It gave me a first insight into life in England, not least through its contrasts, my hostel, my place of work, the smart Dorchester Hotel with the long gone Gunter's, a fashionable tearoom next door, where Kessler and I often recovered from our day's work. I acted as his secretary, took down dictation, and wrote my own news stories, which I then telephoned to Zurich. In London nothing much seemed to have changed; 'business as usual' was the earliest slogan of the war,

the first expression, as it were, of the famous 'bulldog spirit' that
enabled the British to stand alone against the initially victorious
Germans, but in the early days there was a rather morose,
fatalistic and petulant tone to it. Walls of sandbags went up at
the entrances of shops and offices, even at the National Gallery
in Trafalgar Square from where the paintings had been removed.
Soon the famous lunchtime concerts were held there, sometimes
given by my brilliant pianist namesake, Myra Hess, even during
enemy air raids.

As an 'enemy alien' I had to appear before a Home Office
tribunal, which was to decide on my wartime status. Having
come armed with letters from my bishop friend and others who
testified to my friendly feelings towards this country's cause,
despite my suspicious German name – fortunately Rudolf Hess
was an uninteresting figure until his surprise 'peace' mission
flight to Scotland – I was classified as a 'Friendly Alien' and
given 'class C' status. This meant that, apart from being foreign,
I was neither considered to be an enemy suspect nor subjected to
travel restrictions. However, when I once visited the Royal Naval
College in Dartmouth, where a Russian friend of mine, Count
Nicholas Solohub, taught Russian, someone from MI5 questioned him afterwards about what I had been doing there, but he
managed to satisfy them that I was not a Nazi spy. I also had
another part-time job helping to edit a new magazine, *Free
Austria*, published by Austrian friends linked with the last
Austrian ambassador in London, Sir George Franckenstein who,
having been knighted, remained in England after the *Anschluss*.

Franckenstein chaired the so-called Austrian Office, which
consisted of representatives of all the Austrian political parties in
exile. *Free Austria* was an early attempt to form a kind of semi-
official body to support Great Britain in its war effort and work
for a new and democratic postwar Austria. It was the first of
many similar bodies like the free Poles, free Czechs and free
French. London became their wartime centre and they were
working for the day when those countries had got rid of their
German occupiers. The Austrian Office later presented an ambulance to Prime Minister Churchill, but the organization did not
survive Franckenstein's death. The many feuds among the exiles
of different Austrian political parties, with a preponderance of
communists, made cooperation difficult. Moreover, the early
stages of the Second World War, with Hitler's victories, were not

the time when anyone could or would make plans for the uncertainties of postwar Europe.

Nevertheless, in 1941, when I had already joined the Pioneer Corps of the British army, I published an article in *Free Austria* entitled 'Voice of Youth: Patriotism'. In it I identified with the Austrian cause and, rather pompously asked: 'Can a man lose his home or exchange it with some other place he prefers to the old home?' I answered:

> No external force can prevent us from loving our country in its agony, if we really loved it once. No Nazi brutality can destroy that love. On the contrary, it will only strengthen our determination to prove our love by fighting for it. If, however, we only liked our country as long as it gave us shelter, work and comfort, we are justified in abandoning it as rats leave a sinking ship.

Meanwhile, I continued my English studies and my links with Swiss newspapers, as well as the English Catholic weekly *The Tablet*, whose editor Douglas Woodruff befriended me. He was another of the English eccentrics I seemed to collect. He had the habit of literally 'growing' books around him. Wherever he was or had to wait, he had a little book in his pocket, which he would pull out to read, sharing with Chesterton not only his physical proportions but also wide pockets for books in his jacket and complete absence of mind. Such habits could be disconcerting. After my first meeting with him, we went to some second-hand bookshops in the Charing Cross Road. I saw him deep in a volume held close to his shortsighted eyes, but when I looked up again a moment later, he had disappeared without saying goodbye or exchanging another word. For a man of his size this was no mean feat. English eccentricity, I came to understand, was different from showing off. It was, on the contrary, almost part of an unconscious way of life. 'That so few now dare to be eccentric, marks the chief danger of our time,' wrote John Stuart Mill in *On Liberty* (1859), regarding it as an endangered species of a truly free society, but evidently it had survived.

What to do with early morning tea?

Around Christmas 1939 I was invited to stay with Oxford friends Robin and Mabel Laffan. Robin was an historian and

Fellow of Queens College, Cambridge, but was then working at
the Royal Institute of International Affairs (Chatham House),
which had been evacuated to Oxford for the duration of the war.
Laffan had been an Anglican army chaplain before the First
World War in parts of the Austrian Empire and was full of
admiration for it. He was particularly fond of royalist Serbia and
used to pass on as a useful tip from that time that when camping
one should always sleep outside one's tent. You might otherwise
find it riddled with bullets the following morning.

Laffan, later a Catholic convert, produced a paper proposing
that postwar liberated Austria might take a leaf out of the
English seventeenth century, namely to restore the Habsburgs
following the Stuart precedent. Just as, in 1939–40, a liberated
postwar Austria, in recreated sovereign independence, could
not have been farther away from anybody's thoughts, it seemed
equally impossible to envisage a Habsburg comeback in a world
dominated by the tyrannies of Hitler or of the Soviet communist world empire. Nor did it seem that a return to a Divine
Right of Kings had much to recommend it, even though the
Habsburgs, concentrating on foreign marriages rather than
annexations, remained relatively free of such corruptions of
absolute power.

My Oxford weekend, another first in my life, passed without a
hitch. Laffan was another of those lovable English eccentrics, not
only ex-Eton and Balliol but also an ex-president of the Oxford
Union. He possessed other marks of the British elite, such as
having at least three initials (standing for Robert George
Dalrymple), as well as wearing a signet ring on the little finger of
his left hand. Not least of the finer points of British academe,
into which I was initiated, was to learn the difference between
his Queens' College, Cambridge, of which he was a fellow, and
mere Queen's College, Oxford. Since then I have been proud that
my ignorance of many things in this strange island at least did
not include that distinction. I was mortified, therefore, when,
half a century later, the eminent Asa Briggs, reviewing my
biography of Lord Acton, reprimanded me for my ignorance of
it, as it was 'a test for both Oxford and Cambridge men as well
as outsiders'. I found it even more wounding because I could not
even plead guilty of ignorance; he had been sent an uncorrected
proof copy in which an over-zealous editor had wronged my
right version. No doubt, that was a deserved punishment for

embarking on the impossible, wanting to beat the British at their own game.

One of my weekend surprises was that an early morning cup of tea arrived along with pretty china and biscuits. Since drinking it so early in the morning seemed abhorrent and leaving it untouched seemed inappropriate behaviour for an honoured guest, I was in a quandary about what to do with it. There was no washbasin in my room so I had to resort to the bathroom, which was some distance away and involved all sorts of contortions like hiding the teapot under a towel and dressing gown, not to mention contending with the additional anxiety of encountering my hosts on the way. However, I managed to dispose of the tea and get back to my bedroom without any mishap and, indeed, repeated the operation successfully on the next two mornings. The relief I then felt would undoubtedly have been more than equal to the reviving effect of the beverage I have since learnt gratefully to appreciate.

Sack race at Balliol
The highlight of that Oxford visit was a Christmas party with games organized at Balliol College, which I knew traditionally to stand for brain power as well as world influence. The idea, however, of eminent academics playing frivolous games at Christmas was quite new and strange to me. Would any continental scholar worth his salt want to be known to go in for such lightweight amusements? None the less, the party proved to be enjoyable as well as instructive and I was even persuaded to enter into the spirit of the occasion by taking part in a sack race held in the Balliol dining hall.

Aged 19 and probably the youngest among the guests, I thought I had at least some chance of winning. I was quite wrong. The most senior and aged of the contestants, the eminent Byzantinist Norman Baynes, who was amazingly good on his legs, beat me to the post and won first prize, a bottle of sherry. He was then engaged, he told me afterwards, in making use of his German by translating Hitler's speeches for the British government. That added another surprise to what little I knew of English academic life and what revelations its scholars held up the sleeves of their gowns. I evidently was on my way to becoming familiar with the notion that England's oldest university was more than the city of dreaming spires, though it took me much longer to learn about its reputation for also being the city of spite.

Then, after a very cold London winter and beautiful spring in March and April 1940, the war got seriously into its stride. Finland capitulated to the Russians; Hitler invaded Denmark; and there were naval campaigns in Norwegian waters. The first clash between the German and Allied armies at Trondheim ended with the rout of the Allies. Early in May, newspapers in London were predicting that a German attack on Belgium and Holland would begin soon. An Austrian friend studying at Cambridge and staying with an English don's family had invited me to come up for a few days. On my way to Kings Cross station on Friday 10 May, I saw posters proclaiming 'Holland and Belgium invaded'. When I got to Cambridge in the early evening, I heard of Chamberlain's resignation and that Winston Churchill was prime minister. I also heard that the Germans had dropped parachute troops, some disguised as nuns, in Belgium and the Netherlands. That Sunday Churchill made a short statement in the House of Commons. It was the first of his great speeches to come, which so magnificently summed up the spirit of the time and inspired everybody's confidence:

> I have nothing to offer but blood, toil, tears and sweat. You ask, what is your policy? I will say: It is to wage war, by sea, land and air, with all our might and with all the strength that God can give us. You ask, What is our aim? I can answer in one word: Victory, at all costs, victory in spite of all terror; victory, however long and hard the road may be.

These words charted the history of England for the next five years, my own history included. At that moment in 1940 I felt immensely proud of that little island about to stand alone against the mighty enemy.

A little later on that Sunday morning the doorbell rang. A police officer had come to collect my friend for internment, since Cambridge was now a protected war area. 'Who are you?' he asked me, and then 'You had better get your things and come along too.' He took us to Bury St Edmunds, where we spent the night in a church hall. Count Lingen, an undergraduate whose English was remarkable for its clipped German accent and who turned out to be Prince Friedrich von Preussen, heir to the Hohenzollern throne, was in the bed next to mine.

The next day 100 of us were taken by train to Liverpool and then made to march a short stretch to the port and to a ferry bound for the Isle of Man. On the way there, some people lining the streets shouted at us. 'Why are they shouting?' I asked. 'Because we're bloody Germans,' answered the Kaiser's grandson grimly. It was a nice spring day when we got to Douglas, Isle of Man, where we were accommodated in boarding houses and hotels; part of the promenade was our walking area secured towards the beach by barbed wire fencing. I shared a house with various German Catholic missionary priests, a Benedictine monk, a Jesuit, with whom I soon made friends. University teachers among the internees organized classes. I decided to improve my neglected Greek and to learn shorthand. There were some excellent musicians among us like Norbert Brainin, Siegmund Nissen, Peter Schidloff, who afterwards formed the Amadeus Quartet, the pianist Paul Hamburger and the composer Egon Wellesz. All of them gave concerts.

Another inmate was Hermann Brück (1905–2000), an astronomer who held the post of junior observer in the Cambridge Solar Physics Observatory. He too was a convert. He joined the Catholic Church in Berlin in 1935 under the influence of Romano Guardini, and left Germany the following year engaged to a Jewish woman. They were married and, before coming to England, spent some time in Rome at the Vatican observatory at Castelgandolfo. Among our priests was Father Clement Sandkuhl, a Benedictine monk from Maria Laach who now belonged to Prinknash Abbey in Gloucestershire. We had no shortage of liturgical celebrations in the camp; there were several daily Masses, with Compline and Benediction, which I enjoyed attending. On Sundays there was a sung mass accompanied by cello and flute, which the officers and soldiers guarding the camp attended. Brück was released that summer through the efforts of Sir Arthur Eddington. The Irish Taoiseach, Eamon de Valera, later invited him to move to Dublin where he headed the Dunsink Observatory before becoming professor of astronomy at the University of Edinburgh and Astronomer Royal for Scotland.

Our camp life naturally afforded time for endless debates and I was surprised to discover what a deep hold German political and national tradition had on the older generation of fellow

German Jewish internees. Having grown up opposed to neo-German nationalism, quite apart from the Nazi variety, their patriotic attachment, especially to the cultural values of the German environment, impressed me. One might almost have thought that, but for Hitler's paranoic anti-Semitism and Holocaust, they might otherwise have been his most fervent supporters, at least in matters of German foreign policy.

Given their outlook, these German exiles, though retaining little religious attachment, seemed to be unconsciously repaying a debt for Jewish emancipation. In 1871, after the victorious Franco–Prussian war, Bismarck's united imperial Germany was the first country in Europe to grant Jews emancipation. From Germany, it then spread to other countries on the Continent. In England, there were the earlier and exceptional cases of Disraeli and the Rothschilds, with Lionel Rothschild returned to Parliament for the City of London in 1849 and 1852, but on account of his faith unable to take up his seat until 1858.

Pre-1914 imperial Germany had been particularly tolerant. Jews enjoyed constitutional rights of legal equality, though the civil service remained barred to them at first, but they prospered in commerce, journalism, the arts, the sciences, and the legal and medical professions. Proud of their country, no fewer than 96,000 German Jews served in the German army in the First World War, in which 12,000 were killed and 35,000 decorated for bravery.

German Jews of that generation identified with the country's national and social values so completely that these almost replaced their religious attachment. They thus remained deaf to the distinguished Franz Rosenzweig's (1836–1929) warning not to become politically too involved but rather to remain true to their own religious and spiritual traditions. In the 1880s and 1890s extremist German anti-Semitic and radical nationalism were on the increase and prepared the ground for what was to follow in the 1930s.

However, the German Jewish cultural attachment had older roots still in the the Age of Enlightenment. Their cultural ancestor could almost be said to have been the great Gotthold Ephraim Lessing (1729–81), contemporary and fellow sceptic, with his drama *Nathan der Weise* (1799). It is difficult to convey the impact of that play on German Jews who identified with the process of German–Jewish *Akkulturation*.

The play, which is based on a medieval legend, is about Sultan Saladin who, needing money, asked the rich Jew Nathan which of the three monotheistic religions was the true one. He was trying to catch the Jew out by incriminating him to whomever he awarded first place. Nathan then tells the story of the ring a father always passed on to his eldest son until it came into the possesion of a father who had three sons whom he loved equally. He then has two other rings made, exact copies, and gives one to each of his sons. After the father's death, all three have equal claims.

Nathan applies the moral to the three religions. Saladin gets what he wants and treats the Jew henceforth as his friend. Lessing's contribution was to link his plot to a real person, the stammering philosopher hunchback Moses Mendelssohn (1729–88), revered in the Jewish Enlightenment. Having suffered persecution in the Frankfurt ghetto, Moses personifies the wise Nathan of the play who, after Christians killed his wife and sons, practises the difficult Christian virtue of loving his enemies. He adopts a Christian child, Recha, who turns out to be the Sultan's niece and sister of one of the Knights Templars. Christians and Islamists are thus united in one family and a Jew becomes part of the bond by the power of his noble heart rather than by ordinance of natural religion: 'You are the real Christian, better than any Christian that ever was,' Nathan is told. The powerful drama has even greater significance for the twenty-first century since 9/11, with the growth of Muslim terrorism and the modern embarrassment of some Christians trying to practise what they preach.

Cleaning the loos with the Kaiser's grandson
We kept in touch with the war behind our barbed-wire fence through radio news. June 1940 saw the extraordinary evacuation of Dunkirk, with tens of thousands of British troops saved by small boats. The inevitable German occupation of the whole of northern France and the coastline down to the Pyrenees followed the fall of Belgium and Holland. Italy entered the war in June, and London and other British cities were bombed. In July, while the Germans were preparing to invade Great Britain, the authorities decided to send the younger internees to Canada and Australia. Some ships transporting them like the *Arandora Star* and *Duneira* were shipwrecked to disastrous effect, but we, in a

modern liner, crossed the Atlantic safely under convoy protection.

On board, my Hohenzollern companion and I were put in charge of cleaning latrines. This chore proved less unpleasant than it sounded, for the bathrooms and toilets on our modern liner were easy to hose down and keep spotless. Besides, our ship's captain was keen to meet the Kaiser's grandson and we were thus favoured with drinks from his bar. Our journey lasted over a week. Landing at Quebec, we were taken to a camp at Trois-Rivières, one of the oldest French Canadian settlements. To our surprise, it happened to be a normal prisoner-of-war camp. The Canadian authorities were apparently oblivious of the important difference between German prisoners of war, Hitler's soldiers and sailors, and us, the civilian internees who mostly, as Jewish refugees, had of course escaped from Hitler's Germany.

The German prisoners of war, who were from the merchant navy, knew the difference. By way of 'welcome' they stood at their camp gate chanting the infamous Nazi song: *Und wenn das Judenblut vom Messer spritzt, dann geht' nochmal so gut* (And if only once the blood of Jews gushes from our knives, then we'll be really happy!) It was unlikely that our Canadian hosts had understood what it meant, but separate camp accomodation quickly materialized. Our lot had good reason to fear for their lives and made their misgivings known.

We then went to a modern camp in New Brunswick where, though we had to wear blue POW jeans and jacket with a red spot on the back, our different status was recognized. There were heated debates about whether wearing these clothes meant that we were accepting legal POW status. Most of us had no particular objections to wearing prison clothes, for they saved our own and reaffirmed Richard Lovelace, the English seventeenth-century poet who wrote: 'Stone walls do not a prison make/Nor iron bars a cage/Minds innocent and quiet take/That for an heritage.' And it made no legal difference to what we were.

Conditions in the Canadian camp, especially the food, were far better than on the Isle of Man. We were taken outside the camp to work as lumberjacks, as the approaching Canadian winter made itself felt through its bitter cold.

After a few weeks, we were given an opportunity to be interviewed by British officials who held out the possibility of

freedom and repatriation by joining the British army, or rather
the non-combating Pioneer Corps, as it appeared at first. Many
of us, including me, applied. I had probably given insufficient
thought to all the pros and cons of returning to wartime Britain,
with victorious German armies poised along the coast of fallen
France and an invasion threatening. Some people we heard, like
W. H. Auden and Christopher Isherwood, were abandoning the
sinking ship. Others preferred the safety of remaining on
Canadian soil on the assumption, which we could not foresee,
that sooner or later they would be released. However, another
factor influenced others and me, strengthened no doubt by letters
from friends in England, namely the chance 'to do my bit' and
stand up to Hitler. My hope of doing that two years earlier, of
helping little Austria resist, had come to nothing, so doing 'one's
bit' sounded like a typical English understatement. It might turn
out to be unpleasant, like doing penance, but I was sure it had to
be done, especially since Churchill's England was at that moment
having to do it alone. So, I gladly waved goodbye to our
Canadian barbed-wire encampment and its watch towers,
however much better it might have been than the concentration-
camp equivalents.

For our return passage we were again fortunate to have the
protection of an armed convoy, for this was a time when German
submarines were attempting to starve England into submission.
Nothing worse happened to us, happily, than having to line up
on deck on stormy cold nights wearing swimming vests, but the
dreaded order 'Abandon ship' never came. Instead, we passed
Christmas Eve 1940 in our comfortable ship's lounge listening to
records, among them Dvořák's Ninth Symphony, appropriately
entitled 'From the New World', though we were moving in the
opposite direction. Whenever I hear that wonderful work now
with its recaptured flavours of Negro spirituals, Buffalo Bill's
Wild West Show, even folk melodies such as 'Goin' Home', as it
became later, I am stirred, as I was on that Atlantic crossing back
to wartime England, by its melancholy and religious fervour. We
made the journey safely and disembarked at Liverpool on the last
day of the year 1940.

5

Labor Omnia Vincit

The Pioneer Corps proudly served the general purpose of being the British army's 'heavers of wood and drawers of water' (Deuteronomy 29.11), good for any dirty job and serving as its 'navvies'. They were not yet 'Royal', as were Britain's 'Engineers', but were given that honour after the war. They comprised what in army parlance might be described as 'foreign riff-raff', such as colonials, Asians, no African 'blacks' as yet, but ex-French foreign legionnaires who, on the whole, were treated honourably and decently.

They were given some elevation through their motto *Labor omnia vincit* (work conquers all) from Virgil (Georgica, 1, 145), which was somehow fitting for a bunch of continentals, mainly German and Austrian refugees from Nazi oppression. In British eyes (and officially) they were of course 'enemy aliens' and at first it was noted with surprise that they were keen to fight, imagine, 'on our side'. The British quickly discovered the convenience of such large numbers of willing hands and of emptying costly internment camps. In any case, the Second World War was soon seen as different from ordinary national wars in that, by standing up to Hitler, Britain was leading the nucleus of an alliance of freedom-loving people against the threat of his world domination.

Whoever had chosen Virgil's motto, and whether to sweeten the pill or not, had omitted from *Labor omnia vincit* the word *improbus*, which actually qualified such work as 'unremitting', 'unrelenting' and 'hard'. Virgil's meaning was that 'unremitting work and the stress of hard circumstance conquer all.' This might be said to link the traditional sense of all toil as 'in the sweat of thy face shalt thou eat bread' (Genesis, 3.19) with what Winston intended to convey to the House of Commons on 10

May 1940 'I have nothing to offer but blood, toil, tears and sweat.' Happily, we were not aware of a similarly 'improved' maxim in German: '*Arbeit macht frei*' (work makes you free), which soon after the war I saw in big letters over the railroad entrance to the Nazi concentration camp Buchenwald (beech wood), near Goethe's Weimar. The portals of other German death camps also bore that sadistic sentence. What added to its harrowing Buchenwald meaning was that on an outing Goethe had actually rested there in the shade of one of those beech trees to dream a poetic dream. Most of the forest has been cut down, but the camp survives as a terrible memorial.

After 1940 the social composition of the Pioneers was raised somewhat by a middle-class element, which included the so-called 'conchies', the conscientious objectors who, for religious or other reasons, wanted to join a non-combatant unit, as the Pioneers were intended to be at first. The foreign, German, Austrian element soon dominated; somehow they were paying off a debt to this country for having offered them a new home and they were 'working their passage' for a common and worthy cause. They were a very 'civilian' lot, clearly not born to be soldiers, or, as the English sergeant-majors who trained them might have said of them in polite moments, 'a horrible shower of men', products of foreign schools; not all spoke fluent English.

Different countries – different four-letter words

Swearing, using drastic language in communicating, is no doubt customary among any large group of males making a show of their masculinity. Among us (foreign-born) 'Pioneers' this became, per force, a kind of linguistic initiation, an intriguing theme for long debates while at work, say, carrying cement bags. What was the psychological explanation, for example, of those linguistic German concerns with the anal region, as against the British preoccupation with the frontal sexual parts? The great Goethe, as all Germans certainly knew that of him, had not disdained such drastic terms for giving dramatic effect to his late medieval knight *Gotz von Berlichingen* and thereby hallowing their use in all the best literary circles. Shakespeare, though certainly not lacking quotable material, was more hesitant in the particular respect of four-letter usage. What did that convey, we philosophized, about the respective national psyches?

The Pioneers were commanded by their own NCOs and

officers in junior ranks, who rapidly advanced to captains and majors. Sooner or later all of us were disciplined into what was known as 'proper soldiers', though some never managed to discard their 'civilian' look, say coming on parade in their habitual waddle.

A tricky question against which we learnt to guard from one of our British sergeant majors was 'Who of you men can play the piano?' An unusually high number of cultured hands would have gone up before the inevitable retort, 'All right, you, you and you – off with you to the cookhouse for potato-bashing (peeling).' Unusual among ordinary soldiers might also have been the fastidious use of expensive soaps, shaving lotions or soft toilet paper instead of His Majesty's Government's (harder) issue and, because men in those days still tended to want to appear masculine, this was likely to cause derisive epithets like 'bloody sissies'! None the less, army life undoubtedly helped to overcome social differences. In my training days, I learnt, for instance, to put up with the nightly whiff of sweaty feet mixed with the fumes of strong pipe tobacco that rose from my lower bunk, occupied by an elderly ex-miner, otherwise the best of mates.

Among us there was no shortage of proverbial 'barrack-room lawyers', who might even have been real ones in civilian life, but they certainly ingrained in us the notions of 'just lump it' and 'complain afterwards'. An unusually high number of Pioneers went far in attaining distinction in their later professional lives as publishers, lawyers, academics, or as 'top people' in Whitehall. It was probably part of that life to think up some deserved revenge for those who often so sadistically seemed to order us about, if ever we should run into them after the war, say, as hotel porters or doormen. Not until later did we, the ex-Germans or Austrians, realize how much worse off we would have been, banish the thought, on the other side. My friend Karl, the care-taker of the Austrian Cultural Institute, after the war told us how he had been drafted into the German army and sent to the Russian front where he had the misfortune of being constantly teased by his north German *Feldwebel* (sergeant). When one day the sergeant abused him, calling him *'Du Sau-Osterreicher'* (you Austrian swine), Karli, as he became for me by way of endear-ment, a sturdy little chap, simply reacted by knocking him out. In frontline conditions this was considered a grave offence, but in the ensuing court martial Karli managed to get off by making the plausible point that the man had offended the Führer's nation, an unbeatable defence.

In my early days in Great Britain, I was aware of a widespread sense of right and wrong in British life. If some injustice happened in public, say, on a bus, there always seemed to be someone to react indignantly on behalf of the victim. In German there was even a good word for this sort of behaviour, rare though it was – *Zivilcourage* (civic courage), or the quality required not necessarily in battle but in ordinary day-to-day contacts in a democratic society to stand up to a harsh or unjustified exercise of authority. Nowadays, and in England too, people are more frightened to become 'involved' in an unpleasant public row. Indeed, even the police advise members of the public, 'don't play the hero or you'll get hurt'. People cross over to the other, safer, side of the street to evade trouble. It is a frightening development for any society.

On the whole, middle-class people seemed to accept the discipline of army life more readily than those from lower-class social backgrounds, who tended to grumble and miss 'Mum's ways', particularly 'Mum's cooking'. We moved about the country a good deal, sometimes to very attractive parts. 'Join the army and see the world' was indeed our experience. I thus had the chance to see areas around Chester, Shrewsbury, Breconshire and other parts of Wales, as well as the Oxford region. What added to the enjoyment of army life was the great kindness and hospitality I received everywhere from local residents to whom I was introduced, sometimes by the Catholic parish priest, and who became permanent friends.

They would allow me to read or study in a warm room in their home after my day's work and, later in the evening, I would share a cup of tea with my hosts. How good such English kindness felt. It saved me from hanging around canteens or pubs, and no doubt through these meetings my hosts and I learnt something about our different backgrounds. The British were fervently patriotic in those war years. They really believed in themselves, thought they were the greatest in the world, that others were outsiders, strangers or aliens. This self-confidence certainly helped people through the war years. When long afterwards I wrote a German biography of Margaret Thatcher, she told me about an Austrian Jewish refugee girl of her age whom her family had taken in at that time. She said that what she had learnt from her had helped her for the first time to understand what it meant to live in fear and oppression.

Then, of course, there were the various wartime girlfriends who, with all the problems they sometimes caused, made an impact on my soldier's life. In Chester this turned out to be quite strenuous. I had to cycle 20 miles to accompany one young woman back to her home and then, after a brief kiss, I had to make my lonely and disappointed ride back to barracks. Then there were the elaborate arrangements I went through to book two rooms for a weekend in a beautiful part of the Lake District that turned out to be equally disappointing. Another very attractive girlfriend was an officer in the Wrens, engaged on secret work near Oxford. Meeting her alone to dine out, unless in a private home, was full of problems for a mere private like me. Then there was the young woman from the Land Army in Wales who left such an indelible impression on me when we passionately embraced behind the cinema in Haverfordwest and I suddenly felt her dentures giving way. The memory still makes me shudder. I used to cycle all over these parts in my free time visiting country houses, monasteries and old churches. Occasionally I would get invitations to grand friends of friends of mine, for instance to a tea party given by Lady Theresa Berwick who lived near Shrewsbury, but whom I had not met before. She had merely signed her invitation letter Theresa Berwick, so when I arrived by bicycle at the appointed time at the gatehouse and asked for Mrs Berwick, I was politely shown the big house further down the park. England seemed to have an unlimited store of social surprises for someone like me.

Most enjoyable was my introduction to Scotland's Perthshire and the adopted home of an Italian Pioneer Corps fellow, Nino Webster who, being a liberal and refugee from Mussolini, had been taken in and more or less adopted by a well-known Scottish Liberal family. He also had a good baritone voice and sang the leading part in Mascagni's *Cavalleria Rusticana*, which was staged under army auspices in Chester. Miss Ruth Webster lived at Arbroath until the Royal Air Force requisitioned her house for its aerodrome. I spent my twenty-first birthday there and they made me feel very much at home. Through one family I thus came to know Perth, Pitlochry with its theatre, as well as Aberdeen, and lost my heart to that beautiful part of Scotland near the river Tay. I met many of the Websters' friends and neighbours, and came to share their interests and lives. It increased my attachment to Scotland and its people, which was later strengthened when I was transferred to a Scottish regiment, the Highland Light Infantry. I remember as an unfamiliar delight those old-fashioned breakfasts then still customary in big country houses, with the various fried dishes kept warm on hotplates under large silver covers on the sideboards of huge dining rooms. Those were really meals for the day and I learnt to appreciate delicious Scottish porridge eaten with salt rather than sugar – and there was always delicious heather honey.

Mixing concrete and theology

I have very good army memories of Shrewsbury where my work, connected with building toilets for a women's army camp, was usually finished in the early afternoon. After that I was able to relax in the splendid library of Monsignor Ambrose Moriarty, the Catholic Bishop of Shrewsbury. He had a grand residence in a council house in the old part of the town overlooking Shrewsbury. He became a good friend, allowing me to have my letters franked with his mail and indeed partake of his asparagus, which he grew so expertly in his sloped garden. Before returning to camp at night, we sometimes had interesting theological and philosophical arguments. I had applied for a job in the special operations branch and was called for an interview with an anonymous colonel in London's Northumberland Avenue. Since I had relations in enemy-occupied Europe, the idea of my being dropped somewhere behind enemy lines to blow up bridges was rejected, not without a certain relief on my part. Similarly, a WOSB (War Office Selection Board) weekend, to which I went with the prospect of getting a commission, proved unsuccessful. I was told that I lacked the leadership qualities required of an infantryman, so my hope of taking my Wren officer friend out to dine in style at the Mitre Hotel in Oxford was shattered.

In 1942 I was temporarily transferred to the Border Regiment in Carlisle. Its catchy tune addressed the great historical local hunter:

> Do ye ken John Peel with his coat so gay?
> Do ye ken John Peel at the break of day?
> Twas the sound of his horn brought me from my bed,
> And the cry of his hounds, which he oft-times led,

For Peel's view-hallo would waken the dead,
Or the fox from his lair in the morning.

My duties in Carlisle consisted of weapons training, scrubbing
dining room tables and being attached to the motor transport
section, which involved learning to ride a motorcycle, a particularly inglorious chapter of my army life. I had my practice
rides on the road around the camp perimeter, while the sergeant
instructor stood at the main gate shouting orders to me as I
whizzed past him, but too fast to understand what he said, which
was clearly about slowing down on my fairly heavy machine. I
had to go round the whole campsite twice again until I
understood what he said. After that he treated me with the
contempt I deserved in his eyes: 'a bloody monkey trying to ride
a camel'.

Benefits of the kitchen sink
With the Border Regiment, I then moved to the little village of
Overstrand near Cromer in remote Norfolk. It was on the very
edge of England, with bits of its eastern coast unfortunately
gradually washed away into the sea. I came to know the Norfolk
countryside and its endlessly winding lanes through our night
driving runs. Meeting a local family more than compensated for
the routine and dreary side of army life, and we became great
friends. As a retired civil servant of the Admiralty, Percy Daniels
had been evacuated from London to Bath and had then settled
there with his wife May in a charming bungalow close – in fact
dangerously close – to the sea. It was called 'Buckthorns' after
the hedge that surrounded it. Their children were of my age, the
son an officer in the Royal Marines and the daughter in the
Wrens, and they occasionally came home on leave. Hospitably,
they accepted me out 'from the cold' to their sitting-room circle
around a large red-bricked open fireplace, but I soon advanced
into Buckthorns' true centre, the kitchen–dining room with an
Aga stove and wonderful sea view. Guests unfamiliar with that
part of Norfolk were assured that the healthy breeze blew there
straight from the North Pole, missing only Norway on the way,
which was hardly a consoling thought.

My friends had a special routine devised by their mother, a
devout Catholic and wonderful woman whom everybody loved
because of her common sense. She believed that people revealed

their true character at the kitchen sink, where of course everyone had to take his or her turn at washing-up. Long before the kitchen-sink drama became a theme of angry social protest in London theatres, we had put it to better and more constructive use. John, the son of the house, used to invite his girlfriends home on leave, not necessarily for mother's approval but, unbeknown to them, to test their family acceptability. The pretty things often saw through their guinea pig function and provided a convincing show of domestic competence, while everybody else was part of the secret jury, awarding points in the use of scrubbing brushes and drying-up cloths. Marylou, whom John eventually married, clearly deserved first prize because their happy marriage lasted a diamond span.

Overstrand village boasted a tea and cake shop, fittingly called 'The Singing Kettle', and a mock Tudor stately pile, the former rich German owner of which, it was popularly believed, signalled to passing submarines in the First World War. Modern residents included village originals like some genteel old ladies, an 82 year-old squire, who entered the records by siring an heir with his younger wife, and a mentally backward postman intriguingly said to be the son of his sister. Buckthorns became a real home for me. Nightly prayers or the rosary were customary before the statue of Our Lady of Walsingham, and we all made many walking or cycling trips to that old place of pilgrimage from England's Catholic past, which boasts also a modern Anglican rival.

In those faroff days before TV, the enjoyable home atmosphere for me and other homeless soldiers stationed locally consisted largely of playing silly guessing games. In one, called 'Coffee Pot', we had to say 'coffee pot' instead of an agreed word. After Big Ben had slowly struck nine o'clock, which allowed everyone to think of someone dear to them near or far, we always listened to the wartime news on the radio. Then there were Churchill's magnificent speeches, which had such a comforting and uniting effect. Neither in Germany nor in my maternal Austria had I ever encountered similar feelings of genuine national loyalty, which even an outsider like myself could fully share, though of course I was proud to wear the uniform that went with that feeling.

Listening to German Nazis depicted as comic figures over and above the brutality of their violence somehow reduced their strutting menace and power, and provided an additional uniting factor. Glued weekly to the loudspeaker, we laughed with literally the rest of the country at one of the best anti-Hitler weapons, Tommy Handley's Sunday radio show 'It's That Man Again' (ITMA), meaning Hitler of course but dealing rather with a whole series of very British comic characters. It was perfect for radio and everyone knew and imitated the entertainers' voices. For instance, Mrs Mop, the Cockney cleaner, was always bursting into the middle of everything saying, 'Can I do you now Sir? There were others known as 'Moan-a-lot' or 'Sophie Tuck Shop' or the valiant 'Colonel Chinstrap' with his clipped accents. Another uplifting moment for me was the annual Christmas address by King George VI with his occasional little stammer, which he tried so hard to overcome. My friends would rise when the national anthem was played, even in their own home. I found it very embarrassing, probably because of the awkwardness I felt as a child and teenager when my mother sang at a party or other function. That I felt stupidly self-conscious when 'God Save the King' was played in a private home did not of course mean that, having received the King's shilling, my soldier's allegiance to His Majesty was in any doubt. I solved my problem by remaining standing throughout these occasions so that my awkwardness would remain unnoticed.

Invading Normandy

From Norfolk I was drafted yet again to another regiment, the tenth battalion of the Highland Light Infantry; it was part of the 15th Scottish division under Montgomery's command and was preparing for the Normandy landings. I was assigned to the intelligence section of the battalion headquarters, where it was thought my knowledge of German might soon prove useful. I loved my 'elevation' to an honorary Scottish status, as I took it, shown by my khaki tam-o'-shant'er with a tuft on top, or the black Glengarry cap. In wartime, only real natives among our officers and pipe majors wore kilts on parade.

Most of my HLI mates were little dark-haired Lowland Celts from Glasgow, known by the enemy as 'ladies from hell'. In the postwar British army of occupation in Germany they were also nicknamed 'poison dwarfs', presumably because it took a very small quantity of wine to bring out the worst in their explosive temperaments, including their knives, with the use of which they were particularly handy. Many years later, when I was president of the Foreign Press Association in London, I had to chair a meeting with a chief of the Metropolitan Police. He was a Glaswegian through and through and I enjoyed reliving my HLI memories by introducing him as 'a poison dwarf', which, being a six-footer, he was able to take in good spirit.

Our Channel crossing to the beach of Arromanches took place in small landing craft on 18 June 1944, 12 days after the start of the D-Day invasions. We were thus fortunate in having to put up with nothing worse than getting wet when wading to the shore with our rifles held up high to keep them dry. The ruined houses of the coastline were testament to the terrible battle the initial onslaught had been. Dead German army horses with swollen bellies and smashed vehicles still littered our route into France.

A fine white dust from the road surface, ground down by the relentless traffic of armoured vehicles over the previous few days, covered everything. It gave it an uncanny wintry landscape for the second half of June. The Germans had already been beaten back hundreds of miles and we followed behind in army lorries. I remember the ghostly stillness of that snow-like landscape while on guard duty on a moonless Normandy summer night when suddenly I saw tiny glimmering lights coming suddenly out of the white darkness. My vivid imagination immediately conjured up enemy soldiers smoking cigarettes while creeping closer in attack, but I was happy to conclude that they were merely a host of glow-worms.

Over the next few days we stopped briefly at devastated Caen, then at Falaise with its castle a ruin, though I was unsure if this was real or caused by the terrible aerial bombardments of recent days. As a local souvenir, I was able to find a little ceramic statue of Our Lady, the work of a local artist whose kiln we had passed on the way, which I sent home to friends in a little parcel along with a round box of Normandy Camembert, then a precious rarity in wartime England. When the package arrived, I heard later, the cheese had melted but, miraculously, it had saved the small statue from shattering, even in the army post.

Our next stops were in southern Holland, where everywhere we were welcomed as liberators with flowers and drinks. The reception in the small town of Tillborg, which had suffered much under its Dutch Nazi regime, was particularly joyful – an

11. Private R. J. Hill, 10th battalion, Highland Light Infantry, 15th
Scottish Division, in a Normandy orchard, June 1943.

especially happy welcome by a Catholic family overwhelmed me.
Their joy was indescribable.

They made me join them in their house, where we drank
champagne and toasted their liberation, while their daughter, a

gifted pianist, played a moving Schubert and Mozart piano welcome for the soi-disant Scottish liberator with some tacit family links of his own bridging the national divide to those two great Austrian musicians. It nearly made me miss my convoy, which had already moved on, but which crowds in the streets had held up. We took up positions along the River Meuse, with German troops occupying the opposite bank. My intelligence section managed to 'liberate' – the term became fashionable – the larder of an old castle at Maasbree, well stocked with homemade jams, while the castle served as our company headquarters.

We could only reach our forward positions along the Meuse under cover of darkness and, moving there one night, I stumbled into a barbed-wire fence and injured my face so badly, through profuse bleeding of my lips, that I had to be stitched up at the nearest army hospital, which put me out of action for a few days. It was fortunately my only war wound and the scar disappeared eventually. One of our section, a good friend, was fatally shot at that same spot while carrying a bottle containing a special brandy ration for our people. We naturally mourned his death, but with typical army callousness everybody praised his last good deed, which was not to have spilled a drop of the precious liquid he was carrying as he fell.

Raised to three stripes and crown

My relatively comfortable fighting war ended as my battalion prepared to cross the Rhine in February 1945 and I had to stay behind for transfer to another unit. Again, my guardian angel may have been active, for my HLI battalion suffered heavy casualties that night, but managed to cross the Rhine successfully. Meanwhile, I was on my way to recently liberated Brussels. I had to report to the 21 Army Group headquarters for an interview with Colonel de Beer, in charge of the new information control units that were just being set up and for which my knowledge of German and journalistic experience would be useful. I got on well with the colonel who in his academic life had been a distinguished zoologist. When I left, he told me to put on the crown and three stripes of a newly fledged staff sergeant. It was an unusually quick changeover from one camp of the 'other ranks' to what we were used to looking upon as the 'enemy', namely the higher NCOs.

Our new units comprised a lieutenant colonel, a captain, a

staff sergeant and five other ranks. One section went to Hamburg, but mine was destined for Rhineland-Westphalia. The officers were Lieutenant-Colonel Christopher Dilke, formerly of the BBC European service, Captain Nigel Caley, a former journalist from South Africa and me. We were to hold quite powerful positions, being responsible for handing over the licenses to the future German newspaper publishers or editors. These were practical monopolies at first, and of great financial benefit to the future German holders, the equivalent of an official British blessing.

Controlling the German press

The new German press that was first set up in the Western occupation zones was different in some ways from its predecessors. The British handed licences to individuals as representatives of a particular political party. The Americans appointed people from different political parties to run one newspaper, but once they had handed over the licences, the new German editors were fully independent. The free market system of the future Federal Republic later introduced many changes in the press, though in the Soviet occupation zone one totalitarian system merely succeeded another. In the media, the changeover presented many unforeseen problems. The method of simply dismissing Nazi Party members did not work there, for those previously licensed by Dr Goebbels were not necessarily members of the party at all, but selected for their ideological reliability. They were made to join the *Reichsschrifttumskammer,* the writers' official Nazi trade union, and were naturally often more extreme Nazis than the ordinary party members who, like postmen, might have been affiliated as a body and, individually, were often politically harmless.

Many complex problems confronted the victors, for which they were quite inadequately prepared. Most of us spoke no German and knew little of the defeated enemy's history, so, inevitably, we made many mistakes. To the vanquished, the victors often seemed little better than the Nazis. The proverbial one devil, it seemed to them, had merely been replaced by seven others.

Thus, the Allied military government's policy was often a mixed bag of good as well as bad measures, which was understandable given the terrible conditions of the immediate aftermath of war. Apart from verbal misunderstandings, the victims felt the foreign occupiers' prejudices acutely. The British generally tended to dislike Roman Catholics and, unless they were Catholics themselves, instinctively regarded them as fascists. Ignorance made things worse. They saw German Protestantism and the Church of England as equivalents, but had no knowledge of the fundamental difference between the Lutheran Reformation and the changes Henry VIII introduced to England. The Third Reich had produced two kinds of Lutheran Churches – the minority 'Confessional Church', which opposed the Nazis and backed the courageous Pastor Niemöller, and the thorougly Nazified others with a bishop of their own.

Some well-meaning if ill-informed British occupiers of Germany were unusually sympathetic to the newly emerging German socialists, or even the new communists. They probably thought that Brigadier Barraclough deserved the palm for having sacked Dr Konrad Adenauer, the very popular Catholic mayor-in-chief of Cologne. Since Hitler had originallly removed him from that position, to which the British restored him at first, his dismissal at least served Adenauer well by allowing him time to build up the interdenominational German Christian Democrats for their later electoral triumphs. Adenauer apparently magnanimously forgave the British, but it probably rankled with him and coloured and impaired the uneasy relations between the two countries for decades to come.

Because of their initial reserve and correct behaviour, the British were popular occupiers, at first ahead even of the Americans in their zone of occupation. Being richer, however, and more remote from European political entanglements, Americans soon became more popular, not least because they proved easier going in the slow and difficult process of German democratic re-education. Some Americans, after all, were of pre-First World War German origins and readier than later generations to let bygones be bygones. Some among all the Allies were keen to have their revenge on the Germans, but as often happens, took it out subconsciously on the wrong people.

The postwar British Labour government's fellow feelings for the new German Social Democrats and even communists concealed the important fact that 12 years of the Third Reich had been enough to ensure that all former German democrats, regardless of their political adhesion, were either dead, imprisoned or eventually persuaded to support Hitler. This certainly had something to do with the real meaning behind Hitler's National Socialist Workers' Party, for its literal significance was taken insufficiently seriously, especially abroad. Inside Germany, having once reached power democratically, the party succeeded through totalitarian methods to remove all obstacles to absolute rule. It was then able to emerge, historically correctly, as the maintainer of Bismarckian German nationalism, and indeed of the Prussian state with its exemplary workers' welfare schemes. Long before Britain's first postwar Labour prime minister, Clement Attlee was elected and the British welfare state was born, Bismarck had already implemented exemplary, albeit authoritarian, state legislation for the benefit of workers and of their health and pension schemes. The changeover from the Prussian state to Hitler was eased not least through a genuine emphasis on what 'national socialism' meant once its German historical premises had been accepted.

The British military governors of Germany, whom civilian administrators later replaced, went about their tasks in pragmatic fashion. Some were not particularly interested or versed in politics, or aware of Germany's historical development; and the linguistic barrier proved a major obstacle. German Christian socialism was quite unlike the form that William Morris had produced in England; it derived from the French revolutionary model with its state-centred, anti-Christian or at least anticlerical origins, and later Marxist or Leninist additions. German liberals, who had little in common with freedom-loving Gladstonians, had been the major state-controlling, extreme nationalist force behind the Bismarckian achievements of the nineteenth-century German empire.

That we did not stay long enough for any of the political blunders committed by the military governments at the time to have done lasting harm probably minimized any harm done by us as press controllers, but the desperate paper shortage was the best force for good. There was no toilet paper anywhere, or indeed even wrapping paper in shops, so newspapers were needed for more than the information they furnished. For the first time since 1933 the Germans had their local and national news untainted by Hitlerite censorship, now replaced by ours. Under our democratic rules we made some ludicrous decisions, such as issuing 100,000 copies each of three new political newspapers to the almost wholly Catholic rural region of West-phalia. The Catholic population alone could have read 300,000 copies, but Social Democrat and Communist newspapers had also to be supplied. Communist Party membership in the entire British zone would then not have amounted to 100,000, but its newspaper sold like hot cakes. Toilet paper requirements happily knew no political barriers.

Later generations can barely imagine the extent of the material devastation from aerial bombardment we faced when we first arrived at zero hour (*Stunde Null*) in defeated Germany. How was it possible, we asked ourselves, that life had functioned at all under such appalling conditions? German women in the cities were renamed '*Trümmerfrauen*' (rubble women) because of the chains they formed to remove debris and broken bricks from the destroyed areas. Then, the next moment, having changed into pretty dresses, they were unrecognizable. Despite the scarcity of soap, standards of hygiene were still high. In the towns, people got used to keeping starvation at bay by growing a few potatoes, fresh fruit or vegetables themselves or paying high prices and taking regular buying sprees to the country. A few real coffee beans were worth their weight in gold – or cigarettes and pipe tobacco, which served almost as a new currency. The reformed currency, a few years after the war, saved the country from the devastating inflation after the First World War.

One of my own treasured 'war trophies' is a bronze sculpture of my head made by Zoltan Szekessy, a well-known Hungarian artist who with his wife lived in a garden cottage on the outskirts of Düsseldorf. He had studied in Budapest, then in Paris as an apprentice of Aristide Maillol, whose style he adopted. The Szekessys had then settled in Germany, but had retained all the charm, humour and *joie de vivre* of their native Hungary. We became good friends and I paid Zoltan for my head with smokes, covering his needs for probably more than a year. There was a tremendous thirst for all forms of culture, the arts and literature. Theatres and concert halls, even though bomb damaged, were always full and not just because they were among the few public places allowed to be heated. The collapse of the Hitler regime produced an extraordinary demand for untainted civilized values of the mind.

If not exactly welcomed as liberators, as the Allies were else-where in Europe, the Germans nevertheless accepted them, grudgingly at first and much criticized as 'no better than what was there before'. Some of the victors might have enjoyed their role as a new master race, lording it over the 'natives' and reminding them and themselves of their past colonial glories. Stretching their legs over polished mahogany office desks, they enjoyed their new powers as they indulged in a briefly extended empire of their own on the European continent, which the subservient Germans rarely challenged. It was feared that hardened Nazi werewolves would attack the victors, but that happened nowhere. Subconsciously, a few Germans were beginning to see that by having supported Hitler they were responsible for what had happened, but no one would openly admit it yet, partly because they feared punishment from the Allies. Millions of Hitler pictures and other incriminating evidence suddenly disappeared; and people claimed ignorance of the concentration camps and of what went on in them, which may even have been genuine. The hatred of Jews was less widespread among Germans than Nazi propaganda had made out, but that propaganda was as effective within Germany as outside. Behind all this the real questions were what a whole nation knew or 'really wanted to know'.

A few of the Allied troops would, given their plentyful supply of cigarettes, smoke only half of each cigarette while watching a small German crowd gathering to pick up the stumps, then, as they prepared to pounce, slowly and sadistically pulverize the cigarettes into the ground with their boots. This had a telling equivalent in a typical Jewish joke of the time about an SS officer in a concentration camp. 'I'm in a good mood today, Cohn', he said to a prisoner. 'I'll let you go free if you can guess which of my two eyes is glass.' The man looks at him briefly and says without hesitation: 'The right one, Herr Sturmbannfuhrer.' 'Amazing, how did you guess that?' 'It looks so kindly, Sir!'

6

Being a Liberator

Early in April 1945 our five-man team, transported in a big army truck and smaller van, arrived at Ölde, not far from Münster, the capital of rural Westphalia in the north German plain. Historically, it had belonged to the elector-archbishop of Cologne, but in the Napoleonic sequestration of church lands this region, bordered by the Netherlands, Hanover, Hessen and the Rhine, had gone to Prussia. In the Second World War Münster, like most other German cities, suffered massive destruction from air raids, but almost next door Ölde, a pleasant little country town, was miraculously undamaged. It suited our purposes ideally, for it also contained a large modern newspaper printing plant, the only one in the vicinity in perfect working order. Having requisitioned a large garden villa, we started to get ready to produce one of the first postwar German newspapers. Only our CO, Christopher Dilke, knew German well, so the basic organization, like finding a new German editorial team, arranging local news supplies and other editorial sections, and getting the advertising department and distribution to function was left to me. Telex and telephone had not wholly broken down, but luckily, we had our own army outlets.

About a week later, the first edition of *Neue Westfälische Zeitung* produced under British auspices was rolling off the linotype press. Moreover, I then went round in the early morning hours with a driver in a three-ton lorry to various delivery points, from which local agents, mainly on bicycles, took over. I had engaged a secretary who was both attractive and intelligent, spoke excellent English and was able to coordinate with the staff in the printing and editorial departments. She became my girlfriend and contributed to my basking in relative new importance as a combined publisher–editor, surely the first ever

23 year-old staff sergeant of any Scottish regiment playing that role in two languages. On 8 May 1945, I gave my own cheers for V-E (Victory in Europe) day by firing three shots into our lawn with a Lueger pistol I had confiscated from a German officer who had surrendered with his men and been taken as a POW. I felt that my survival and the official end of the war were surely worth such an exuberant private celebration.

Tea with the 'Lion of Münster'

At Münster, the cathedral city of this staunchly Catholic region, I was soon to meet the bishop, Clemens August Count von Galen, who was famous for having opposed some of Hitler's anti-Church measures. Earlier, in London I had already met members of the family who then asked me to look up some of their relations, refugees from the communist parts, who were then living in comparatively straitened conditions. I was able to look them up and provide them with some of the things that were then so scarce like coffee, tea and cigarettes, of which we had plenty. They introduced me to the bishop and I thus came to be on closer terms with him because of those family links. He was a man of tall, imposing stature and presence, was immensely popular in his diocese and, because of his anti-Nazi 'roar', was named the 'Lion of Münster'. He had been a high-ranking officer in the First World War and made no secret either of his right-wing views or of his criticism of the British as the occupying army. At that time, he was particularly incensed about foreign civilian workers who, released from their camps, were roaming the countryside breaking into houses, robbing farm stores and generally taking their revenge on the Germans. The British authorities were in a dilemma. These people had been victims of the Nazis and atrociously treated as forced labourers and, while their lawless behaviour was of course condemned, there was no means of controlling them. This added grist to the bishop's mill who regarded it as typical British hypocrisy to favour democracy and, simultaneously, condone anarchy and disorder.

Ruled by self-discipline and a sense of order, he was an authoritarian of the old generation. However, he would neither admit openly that the Nazis had undermined these traditional values nor accept my views about the preparatory role that extreme German nationalism had played in laying the ground for the historical nonsense of a 'First Reich', leading to the German imperial

'Second Reich', followed by Hitler's 'Third Reich'. According to the bishop, my views were wrong-headed, but at least over many cups of tea, which I gladly provided, we agreed to differ.

I had to admire his courage, compared with that of other German bishops, in having openly denounced particular Nazi policies, but I was also aware that in 1933, in his first pastoral letter, he had, naively welcomed Hitler's fight for an apparent new political moral order based on anti-Judaism and anti-communism. Soon afterwards he rejected the pagan Nazi philosophy of Hitler's ideologue, Rosenberg. To me he would privately concede that had Hitler achieved final victory, he would not have hesitated to turn fully against the Church.

Count Galen's great hour came in 1941 when, in reaction to his sermons condemning the Nazis' euthanasia and other medical experiments, the Gestapo called to arrest him. When he came down to meet them in his full episcopal regalia, however, they refrained from taking him away, for this might have caused a riot in Catholic Münster. Bishops were given more consideration than ordinary priests and nuns, for it helped strengthen the Nazi propaganda message to leave the Church unmolested. However, I did not feel bold enough to rub this home. As far as his criticism from the pulpit was concerned von Galen's courage was unde-niable. Since Clemens Count von Galen's beatification has recently taken place, 60 years later, I may thus pride myself on having had many 'cuppas' with one of God's future saints, and perhaps have a claim to his special intercession on my behalf.

Still, he is not quite there. Making saints sometimes takes a long time, no fewer than 400 years in the case of Sir Thomas More, Lord Chancellor of Henry VIII, but that was probably because Rome did not want to offend the mighty though Protestant British Empire. Some lucky candidates make it more quickly than others do; Mother Theresa had to wait only seven years after her death, whereas Cardinal Newman is still waiting.

According to the theological encyclopaedia, one need not be a perfect man or woman, or even good-tempered, as those many rather curmudgeonly saints during their lives on earth proved. What the Church requires is that one is very ordinary indeed, 'almost' like you and me but in a special way. That is the ecclesiastical hitch. The Bishop of Berlin, Konrad Count of Preysing, a distant relative of Bishop von Galen, said of him at the time that 'brave as he was, he had only average intellectual gifts'. Sanctity does not even require a special spiritual or priestly superiority. He or she just has to show his mettle where he is placed, 'to make the understanding of Christianity relevant', as a modern theologian, Karl Rahner, has said, or, perhaps more basically, as the Old Testament suggests: 'I am God Almighty, live as in my sight, and be whole' (Genesis 17.1).

We also started up newspapers in other German cities like Düsseldorf and Essen. I found it interesting and constructive to travel around the country and meet many of the new generation of German opinion makers. Overall, they were keen to work with us and play their part in their country's democratic renewal. We were supposed to base the system we introduced on Fleet Street usage, the centre of most of the big newspapers. However, since that bore no resemblance to German ways it was natural that eventually the Germans would want to do things their own way. After the German totalitarian experience, the British contribution was to insist on some standards of fairness, even-handedness, and a stricter separation of news and comment in an attempt to diffuse the old ways that were to continue among the east German communists for another four decades until the 'peaceful revolution' of 1989.

Keeping in touch, as I have been, with the new press in the Federal Republic, I am impressed by how much that seemingly insignificant democratic lesson of keeping comment to strictly relevant parts of a newspaper have become accepted practice. This applied also to consulting the staff, or voting on disputes over how best to run these papers. A functioning democracy has of course to be concerned with more than the rights and respon-sibilities of majorities. Matters become more complicated when it comes to the rights of minorities, especially unpopular ones. One cannot deny that German authoritarian thinking suffered a severe setback at 'zero hour'. It was at any rate the beginning of what, many years later, became known as *Vergangenheits-bewältigung*, meaning managing to cope or come to terms with ones country's past. The Germans had to achieve this by themselves and, looking at the German press today, they have.

Permission to fraternize
As a member of the occupation forces, I was officially 'permitted', as it were, to 'fraternize' with the former enemy. I even carried an official permit to this effect, though I actually

never had to produce it. What an extraordinary symbol of the times that was! However, it did not apply to the opposite sex. I was not yet 25, certainly not distinguished by any special maturity in this regard, or indeed alone in making the most of the *embarrass de richesses* always on offer in a conquered land. Apart from girlfriends of my own age, there was something very special in my encounter with three women, devout Catholics and much older than I was. Their friendship made a great impact on me, as I seemed to have made on them as their 'liberator'.

They lived together as an inseparable trio, first in Ölde, where we met, then later they returned to their flat in Münster, which they had had to leave when it was bombed. What struck me at our first meeting was how nice and natural they were, highly educated and cultured, but with no hang-ups – intellectual, religious, social or otherwise. Their spiritual emancipation was something one did not encounter frequently then. They were certainly not the familiar type of pious activists, aptly known in German as *Sakristeiwanzen* (literally bugs that infest the sacristy). They in fact belonged to a generation of women who were emancipated earlier, at about the time of the First World War. Also, then rare among educated Germans who tended to be closer to French influences, they were agreeably Anglophile. They spoke English well and were familiar with English ways and English literature.

The eldest was Dr Idamarie Solltmann, then headmistress at the School of Social Welfare for Girls at Münster. She was born in 1897 in Berlin, brought up as an agnostic, then studied philosophy at Göttingen university. One of her fellow students, the great love of her life, was tragically killed in 1915 before they could marry. She then became a close friend and follower of Rosa Luxemburg, the revolutionary socialist, who was murdered in Berlin in 1919. These two experiences jolted her from her original materialism into Christianity, chiefly under the influence of writers like Dostoevsky, Berdyaev and Paul Claudel. Then the Bach chorale No 78 became something of a personal call for her:

Lord, I trust thee, help my failing.
Let me never know despair.
Thou can'st give me strength, availing
Strife with sin and death to bear.
In thy grace my soul believeth,

12. Fraternizing with higher permission, interviewing a German refugee
from the communist zone.

Till with joy mine eye perceiveth
Thee Lord Jesus, then in war and in peace for evermore.

(The German original seemed to have an even more simple
sound:

Herr, ich glaube, hilf mir Schwachen
Lass mich je verzagen nicht;
Du, du kannst mich stärker machen,
Wenn mich Sünd und Tod anficht
Deiner Güte will ich trauen,
Bis ich fröhlich werde schauen
Dich, Herr Jesus nach dem
Streit in der süssen Ewigheit.

Claudel's '*O monde entier, je t'accepte avec mon coeur catholique*' (O entire world, I accept you with my Catholic heart), was finally, in 1922, what made her enter the Catholic Church. By the time I met her she was not only the popular head of a leading school for girls, but also a scholar of repute and much in demand as a lecturer and writer in the newly formed postwar Catholic women's movement of that part of Germany.

Her two younger companions, also unmarried and Catholics by birth shared her religious outlook. Luise Heinemann, who acted as the housekeeper, was an excellent cook and pastry maker, and was well capable of making what little food they had in times of real shortages last as long as possible. She was very knowledgeable about English literature, especially nonsense books and had a great sense of fun. Anni Borgas, the third and youngest, was a well-known photographer of the art treasurers in the old Westphalian churches. She also had a sharp tongue and used it refreshingly when encountering the sometimes condescending ways of the German clergy in their dealings with women.

They were greatly pleased that I was able to supply them with English weekly reviews and magazines. They became enthusiasts about G. K. Chesterton, Graham Greene and Evelyn Waugh, and loved and laughed about Ronald Knox's spurious proof that Queen Victoria rather than Tennyson was the real author of that great Victorian poem, 'In Memoriam'. Their laughter showed the relief they felt after years of being fed totalitarian propaganda, but these three highly cultured women were exceptional in that they had not lost their ability to think for themselves.

A letter that Idamarie Solltmann wrote to me in July 1945 illustrates the German situation:

How difficult living seems to be these days. Under the

Nazis it was of course dangerous to be 'anti'. But it also was very simple. You risked your life, but somehow you had no choice; besides, the Nazis were really rather stupid, so deceiving and working against them was also fun. It was no problem, but nowadays everything becomes a problem, and we are so tired of these problems. Not that we are disappointed with the British, and you know that. How could we be? We are immeasurably glad to be rid of the Nazis. We can see very well how furious the ordinary British or Americans must feel having to sacrifice their sons, their money and all sorts of other things, because we Germans could not liberate ourselves on our own. Of course, an occupation army will do all sorts of wrong things, but now they get criticized out of all proportion.

My friends were very attached to the Westphalian Benedictine abbey of Gerleve, which the Nazis had disbanded but which was restored again in 1945. The three regularly attended the Easter and Christmas services, liturgically done to perfection by the monks belonging to the renowned Benedictine Beuron tradition. Of the Easter night service, 1945, Idamarie wrote:

> It was an overwhelming experience when the whole congregation burst into the threefold alleluia. It was as though we had all waited for that moment when the monastery was closed down. I wept tears of joy, and more than joy, tears of sorrow. *Resurrexit sicut dixit*, and at the beginning of threefold Lumen Christi and then the Exulted and the Prophecies, just those twelve, with Nebuchadnezzar and all those Nazi *Gauleiters* and *Kreisleiters* and *Celleiters* who had similarly prostrated themselves before the Golden Calf.

Then a shadow fell over the abbey's rebirth. With the three women cramped into small guest rooms with numerous other visitors, that Christmas she wrote:

> I can't stand it anymore, these people's silly talk and constant grumbling about the awful English. Not one word of relief about yesterday's much worse lot. But the Nazis have been swept from their memory. People don't want to

think about them anymore, and how it all happened. They are back happily in some remote past and wondering what the 'damned English' are doing 'on German soil'. It is sickening, and I hate having to be sick at Christmas! And in our beloved Gerleve, they have relapsed to pre-Nazi days as though nothing has happened since. Of course, they were expelled, and feel jolly proud over that, talking of their persecution as 'a blessing'. But they also fail to see that they would still be persecuted if Germany hadn't been defeated. They can't bear to face this defeat. So they simply ignore it. Of course, they don't want the Nazis back, but Nazism was just some pardonable 'mistake' in the past, not a ghastly crime, all due to the Treaty of Versailles and so they go on and on.

And there was another blow to come, as she wrote again:

I was so used to joining in the choir. The liturgy is of course intended not as a performance for the benefit of an audience. Naturally, we did not join in singing the studied parts like Introit, Graduate, Offertory, but in the others, the psalms, at Laudes, Vespers and Compline. But, lo and behold, the Prior came the other day to tell us that that was also against the monastic rule, for the abbey guests to sing, too. And now I am considered an alien in the house of God and don't like to attend a performance rather than a service. And now in the night of all nights, at Midnight service, we are supposed to sit there as though we were dumb, having ears, but no mouths. Not me!

St Hildegard, women's lib or *omnia vincit amor*
My friends were close to some Benedictine nuns who came under the jurisdiction of the Gerleve monastery. They had been expelled from east Germany but had nowhere to go. Then the senior of the Galen family offered them the moated *Wasserburg* castle, where Bishop Clemens von Galen was born. Serious obstacles existed, however, due to the authority exercised by the Gerleve monks over the nuns. Idamarie Solltmann supported them in their fight to regain their independence and wrote:

Incredible as it is, precisely the same things are happening

as when St Hildegard of Bingen tried to free herself and
her nuns from the jurisdiction exercised over them by the
monks of Disibodenberg. But this was in the eleventh century, yet basically nothing seems to have changed since.
Why can't these men tolerate the spiritual independence of
women? Hildegard was also in the right then. When her
nuns left the monastery at first, things were hard, they
were poor, the monks would not return their dowries to
them, daughters of noble families. There was a brief time
when all seemed lost, but Hildegard was sure that God
was on their side. Gradually things improved. There were
too many women in Hildegard's foundation at
Rupertsberg. So she founded a second convent at Eibingen
near Rüdesheim, which famously exists still. I am also sure
that in the end the Dinklage nuns will prevail, for they are
simple, straight and sane.

And so it happened.

The German winter of 1946/7 was unbearably cold. It is 'five
degrees below zero and we have no heating at all', wrote Luise to
me who had already returned to London. In February Anni
described how they were sitting 'with chattering teeth' round
their little stove and that the postman had told her that on his
round that morning there were only seven people with heated
homes, and that all the others had stayed in bed at minus two
degrees.

Luise and Anni both died ten years later from cancer. Idamarie
spent her last years at Kloster Dinklage where the nuns, with her
help, finally achieved their independence from the bigoted monks
of Gerleve. They had behaved exactly like their monastic
ancestors in the twelfth century who were reluctant to allow St
Hildegard and her nuns their independence from traditional male
domination – and nor would St Hildegard's modern successors
have wanted her to be 'silent in church'.

So I was glad to have begun and completed my own British
wartime experience, as it were, within the Western and Virgilian
tradition, first through *Labor omnia vicit* and then, more
directly, by way of *Omnia vincit Amor: et nos cedamus Amori*
(Love conquers all: we too must yield to love) (Eclogue, X.69).
Later, when I was already a graduate of London University and
the British military establishment, I invited Idamarie to England,

I was able to show her around, the highlight of her visit being a lovely summer boat trip on the Thames.

Later I discovered what Sir John Denham (1615–69) had written in praise of London's river, 'the most loved of all the ocean's sons':

> Oh, could I flow like thee, and make thy stream
> My great example, as it is my theme!
> Though deep, yet clear, though gentle yet not dull;
> Strong without rage, without o'erflowing full.

I sent it to my dear friend, believing that the words applied also to her. She died on 23 February 1980 among the nuns assembled around her bed and praying with her the dolorous rosary; the repetitive responses 'and in the hour of our death' and her own finally inaudible 'Amen' were re-echoing around the room, as one of them wrote to me afterwards:

> And though people were wondering if heaven had perhaps forgotten Idamarie, she had not forgotten it. The words 'And in the hour of our death' perhaps characterized her and her life with its ups and downs and the expectation of that hour of our death. What she used to say was not always to be taken seriously, as she well knew herself, but but what linked her with eternity was. Her mind knew no formula, she had never learnt these. She had only learnt what she could make her own, and that was also her way to life eternal. Not the usual way of nostalgia or longing, but in the honest happiness of one who had found her faith as a convert.

How my parents survived the war

The end of the war enabled me naturally to re-establish contact with my parents after a six-year interruption, in which only the briefest messages through the Red Cross were possible, so at least I knew they were alive. A long letter I wrote to my mother, which she kept, may have been the first such renewed exchange. Written in the summer of 1945, I gave her all my news – what had happened after my internment on the Isle of Man and return from Canada to join the British Army of Liberation, as it was then called, after the defeat of Hitler. All she had known was that I was doing 'a useful job in England'. With German–Italian censorship, one had to be careful what one said so as not to endanger the recipient's life. I wrote:

> I still can't believe that you and I have been spared. Having heard of the air-raids on Milan I was of course worried about you. But now merely to be alive is wonderful. In spite of all the miseries this war has caused, it was right and just to wage it, for its ends were not to be attained in any other way. Such a conflagration can of course produce no real victors. Injustices have been committed on all sides, and many I have had to witness even on our Allied side. So I feel disillusioned, though not in despair for having been on the side of right and freedom, though what the future has in store for me seems uncertain. ...
>
> Years of army life have meant living just from day to day without thinking what the next day will bring. I shall probably get out of the army some time next year and return to civilian life in England. I wouldn't mind at all returning to Germany or Austria, where there is now a great need for people to help rebuild all that has been destroyed, and who also know the language and something of the background and way of life of what used to be 'our enemies'. And I have already made many friends among people who had never been Nazis, but living there had no other choice. But whether it will be possible for civilians to return, I can't say now. I have really had enough of soldiering, although I managed quite well to adapt myself to that life. But I would like to be my own master again, able to make the best or worst of things. ... As a soldier in the Normandy invasion I was certainly no hero, and often surprised at what I was capable of doing. But once in uniform you just have to do what needs to be done. Fortunately, British people are always individuals first and soldiers second. And what helped me no doubt was the conviction that it was all a worthwhile cause.

Then I told her how I had come to meet my father again in liberated Belgium and of his illness and sad last days in March 1945. Ever since he had left Milan and entered Switzerland without a permit, he had led a dangerous life. The greatest risk was that the Swiss police would arrest him and return him to Nazi Germany as an illegal immigrant. Incredible though it may seem today, seemingly neutral Switzerland, that model of liberal democrats and land of the free, was very much on Hitler's side early on in the war, at least its German-speaking parts. Hitler's initial successes impressed the Swiss, who sympathized with Nazi views, particularly anti-Semitism.

Inevitably, the Zurich police caught my father without a residential permit and took him to the German border for handing over to the German SS or Gestapo detachments that regularly met these unfortunates. The Swiss authorities were of course aware of what fate awaited the people whom the Nazis sent to the death camps. By some incredibly lucky circumstance or, indeed, divine ordinance, on that night the German reception party was late and the Swiss police just left them, 20 men, on the German side of the frontier. So, in the darkness they speedily scrambled back to Swiss territory and safety.

The danger of course was not over for them, for they had to avoid being caught again. My father then thought it safer to make his way to France, but this time, in 1940, the victorious German army occupying Vichy France caught him. Luckily, he was released, apparently because of his German bearing and stature and because he had the same name as Hitler's deputy, which not for the first time proved a godsend. He decided to make for Belgium, doing odd jobs and, because his French was quite fluent, he thought it advisable to assume the more inocuous French name of Georges Mercier. Not surprisngly, these ordeals affected his health. He went down with angina pectoris, was nearly turned over to the Germans again by the doctor of a Catholic hospital, but manged to evade them. After further anxious days, he found another hospital where the nuns protected him; they even facilitated his escape during an unexpected Gestapo raid and took him in again when the danger had passed.

That experience, added probably to what he knew of my religious change, decided him eventually to be received into the Catholic Church. I still have his little pocket book, in which he had copied all the Catholic prayers in his neat handwriting. By then the Normandy landings were taking place, but he would not have known that I was an Allied participant. We were able to correspond by occasional Red Cross messages, limited to just 25 words, he always wrote in English, of which his command was limited and he ended them feelingly, wanting to send me his love by expressing it: 'Your lovely [loving] father', which was of course no less movingly acceptable.

In Belgium he lived in sparsely furnished accommodation, first in Antwerp and then in Brussels, where I managed to trace him after its liberation. That is how we met again. Physically, his condition could not have been more depressing. Having had his personal documents taken away from him, he had no valid papers, but I was able to help him with the Belgian authorities. He was of course immensely proud of his son for being among the victorious Allies and also his liberator, but soon I had to move on into Germany with my own British unit.

With some shame, I have to confess, I felt guilty about not having done more for him. Looking back, I seem to have behaved rather heartlessly; perhaps I unconsciously resented his stricken condition, for he seemed to have done nothing about rejoining my mother in Italy. The reason was perhaps a younger Belgian woman he had met and grown fond of, and who cared for him in his illness. I felt stupidly annoyed at his physical condition and sense of helplessness, probably because he was a father about whom there was so little to feel proud. Maybe it was part of an old and typical father–son conflict, from which I certainly would not seem to emerge well. Young people can be very cold and cruel. The next I heard was a message from his Belgian friend saying 'Your father died on 25 March 1945'. Apparently, she was with him. Left to my contrition and shame, I put a simple tombstone with his name and dates up on his Brussels grave.

Meanwhile, my mother had survived under brighter circumstances. In December 1945, my unit in Germany granted me compassionate leave to see her. She had moved from Milan to Rome after the war ended in Italy. Getting to Rome took three weeks by troop military train, first from Germany, then slowly down wartime-battered Italy. I had to cross from Montgomery's army sector to Field-Marshal Alexander's Fifth Army, the advantage being that the changeover to another army bureaucracy would make it easier for me to extend my leave.

I arrived in Rome in the early evening of Christmas Eve 1945. My mother knew that I was coming, but not when I would arrive. She would anyhow have been unable to meet me at the station because of an important concert engagement, a Lieder recital in one of the Vatican church halls, organized for her by the Austrian ambassador to the Holy See. It started at 9 p.m. and I went there straight from the station, but was able to see her only during the interval. What a strange reunion that was for both of us after six years of war. The hall was crowded and somehow the ambassador, Baron Fröhlichsthal, must have made the news of our meeting public. I was thus included in the thunderous applause she had earned for her singing and that greeted both of us as she embraced the khaki-clad British staff sergeant.

Her musical programme consisted of her favorite arias from Mozart, Verdi, Schubert, and Johann and Richard Strauss, and at the end she led the whole audience in singing 'Silent Night'. Tears welled up in me, and no doubt many others. Among the guests that evening were Dr Kurt von Schuschnigg, Austria's prewar chancellor who had just been released from Dachau concentration camp, and Jacques Maritain with is wife Raïssa. He was soon to take up the post of French ambassador to the Holy See, and a mutual bond was our common friendship with Friedrich Wilhelm Foerster, my German mentor. He was anxious, Maritain told me, to try to get the Latin Missal cleansed of its references to the 'perfidious Jews'. Alas, this was not to happen apart from minor changes until after 1958.

After that memorable Roman evening I heard about my mother's extraordinarily adventurous survival of the war, which, being a woman on her own, was even more hazardous than it had been for my father. She managed to earn a living in wartime Italy giving bel canto lessons to young Italian singers sent to her by her Milan prima donna friend, Luisa Tetrazzini. She also taught German and found occasional jobs as a housekeeper in well-to-do Italian families where her Austrian cooking and baking talents proved popular, not least her *Mehlspeisen*, Viennese puddings and desserts.

She finally plucked up courage to leave her 'gilded cage', the grand villa she shared with her friend the singer and mistress of a German SS-general. She felt she had to make a break with such a dangerous lifestyle in case it became known that lover-boy had also hosted a non-Aryan. She then moved from Milan to Rome, where, with more inner peace, she could live with friends in greater safety.

Before that happened she lived through the Italian drama of Mussolini's fall from grace and power, the first stage being on 25 July 1943 when the king, Victor Emanuel III, summoned him to the royal palace to dismiss him. He was subsequently arrested and kept in various places of detention, including the Abruzzi mountains from where, in a daring raid, a German parachute force carried him off. He was taken to Vienna's Hotel Imperial, a rallying point of resistance for the so-called Fascist Republic of Northern Italy under Hitler's protection and from its head-quarters near Lake Garda, he would have been able to escape across the Brenner Pass to Germany. Now a sick and broken man, he tried once more to appeal for support to the Milanese who had only recently fêted him. He kissed the hand of Cardinal Schuster, who wanted to hide him in his palace, but he preferred to flee, not wanting to face the bankruptcy of his policies. An Italian partisan caught him hiding in a German truck, dressed in the heavy coat of a German NCO and wearing a German helmet. His long-time mistress, Clara Petacci, was with him. They were both shot and their bodies taken in triumph to Milan. This was on 28 April 1945, two days before Adolf Hitler's suicide in his Berlin bunker.

While loyal supporters burnt the bodies of Hitler and Eva Braun to ashes, a grim episode from remote history was being acted out in Italy. Like the reformer, revolutionary and tribune Cola di Rienzi in 1354, the Duce and Petacci were hung upside down for public display from the roof of a petrol station in Milan's Piazza Loreto. We had lived near there when we came first to Milan from Vienna in 1938. Describing that gruesome day with some sense of shame, my mother said that, caught up in a vast crowd of thousands, she, along with everybody else, had filed past the horrible scene.

For me that Roman visit was unforgettable. It was wonderful to find my mother looking so good in her fifties and I was glad that she felt so proud of her Scottish Highlander son, even though that did not extend to a real kilt.

At the papal university, the Gregoriana, I made some friends among the German Jesuits who surrounded Pope Pius XII. Among these was Father Gustav Gundlach SJ (1892–1963), the papal adviser on social and moral issues. One could always 'nose out' his room, off a vast Gregoriana corridor, from afar by the fumes of the thin Virginia cigars with a straw mouthpiece to which he was addicted. It became known only much later that he had also been the co-author of a planned papal encyclical to deal with the (Hitlerite) 'heresies' of national-socialism and racialism, including anti-Semitism. This was the famous so-called 'suppressed encyclical', which I shall mention elsewhere. Commissioned by Pius XI, an English text was supplied by the American Jesuit, La Farge, a French one by Gustave Desbuquois and Gundlach's German version. It was supposed to be called *Societas Uno: Unity of the Human Race*, but owing to Pius XI's death and the succession of Pius XII nothing more was heard of it.

The submitted texts, it was said afterwards, were not what was wanted. Perhaps it was just as well because those three Jesuits were natural stalwarts of the old 'orthodox' Catholic theology. Gundlach, in particular, was responsible in various papal writings for the traditional distinction in pre-Vatican-II Catholic thinking between the Church's anti-Judaic attitude going back to the Crucifixion, and the new racist anti-Semitism that had emerged in France and Germany only at the turn of the nineteenth to twentieth century. The Catholic Church did not of course subscribe to the latter, but was clearly involved in the logical and theological confusion of what basically amounted to some kind of anti-Semitic outlook, one so to speak with a human face and allowing for conversion to Christianity, and the other leading to the death camps of the Holocaust. Only Vatican II was finally to settle that theological Catholic dilemma.

At the Gregoriana I befriended Pius XII's private secretary and confessor, Father Robert Leiber SJ. He was a man of tiny stature but great personal charm and humour, and every day in the early evening a huge papal limousine would arrive to take him to the Vatican, literally swallowing him up as he waved to his friends from the windows. At the time, these German Jesuits must surely have seen me – an ex-German–Austrian Catholic convert and the HLI staff sergeant – as quite a freak. The Pope's 'German' surroundings in Rome reflected the years 1917 to 1930, which Eugenio Pacelli spent in post-First World War defeated Germany and which decisively marked his character and his authoritarian outlook.

As a papal diplomat, he had never had a priestly pastoral office. His preoccupation with diplomacy and the numerous concordats for which he was responsible (Latvia, Poland,

Lithuania, Italy, Hitler's Germany and Austria) meant that his knowledge of these countries remained largely theoretical, legalistic, and remote from their historical and social realities. From years of residing among them, he knew and loved the German Catholics and their religious customs probably better than any pope before him had done and, although a Roman of the lower nobility, he never felt the same way about the Romans.

There was also the German nun, Sister Paqualina who took care of the eating restrictions to which his stomach ailments condemned him throughout his life. He was deeply attached to his two Persian cats, which had German names – Peter and Mieze; when driving to Castelgandolfo he nursed the cage containing his beloved German canary on his knees.

With no fewer than 17 huge volumes of speeches and writings to his credit, his life (1876–1958) could not have been more active, but with his self-imposed 'diplomatic silence' as pope at a critical phase for the Church in modern history, it remained curiously empty. Even after 1945, despite his undisputed efforts to help Rome's persecuted Jews, who were after all part of his flock as Bishop of Rome, he kept on saying that he had not wanted to confuse the consciences of 30 million German Catholics by publicly protesting against Hitler. He did so only in the most general and meaningless terms, condemning for example 'the satanic spectre of national socialism', which was merely a way of driving it underground, just as he had never once in any acceptable scholarly fashion defined 'materialism', 'socialism', 'communism' or 'Marxism' as seriously wrong. His religious faith remained linked to the primitive and basic Catholic teachings of the Church and Church Fathers, the destruction of the Jerusalem Temple in AD 70 and the dispersal of the Jews as part of the divine punishment inflicted on Jews for the Crucifixion.

My Rome visit, which extended into January 1946, also marked the end of my wartime service. I was 'demobbed', as it was called, in July 1946, released into 'civvy street' with the army's farewell gift of a double-breasted pin-striped grey suit and a brown felt hat that made me look like a follower of Al Capone.

What was I to do next? No home or job waited for me, as for some of my mates. There were various possibilities, which I tried one after another. First, to become an interpreter for the Nuremberg war crime trials, but I failed for being seconds too slow in the automatic talent of simultaneous translation. To listen with earphones in soundproof boxes in the courtroom and then automatically reproduce what one had heard in the requisite language required a special knack. There was no time to search for the right phrase, for the words had to come out of your mouth as soon as they had gone into your ears.

Then there was the European Service of the BBC, but again I failed compared with my competitors. Perhaps I should consider teaching in a private school, but for that, too, I was evidently not particularly well suited. Finally, I decided to complete my interrupted studies by working for a history degree at King's College at the University of London. For this, I was entitled to a British government grant provided I first passed the intermediate examination.

With that aim in mind, I settled down at Swiss Cottage in bedsitter land in northwest London's attractive continental atmosphere. I had a tiny bedsitting room with a communal bathroom next door. A small gas ring on the floor near the fireplace served my cooking and heating needs. One fed the gas heater and gas ring by dropping shilling coins into a meter, which had the enfuriating habit of expiring in the middle of trying out an eleborate Italian dish from the great cookery book by Elizabeth David, who taught postwar Britons how to eat properly. In my case, this meant having to work on my hands and knees. I still have her book with some of its pages sticky from the apprentice's long usage of the pasta section. Still, I did produce one-pot meals approved of by the connoisseurs among my friends.

However, in those postwar years eating out was still comparatively cheap and affordable on my limited budget. There was a good choice of restaurants in Hampstead for those with continental tastes, among whom I was forever included. Wartime rationing continued into the postwar years and this meant a weekly spectacle of a nearby store's huge van arriving to deliver my ration. The driver would open his rear flap door and take out a tiny package, my allocation – two eggs, some bacon rashers, two ounces of butter, five ounces of margarine, some tea and some sugar. Yet, I seemed to manage quite well on that.

My landlady, an artist with high standards of order and cleanliness, admirably put up with me for nearly two years. Then something dramatic and unforeseen happened, but I do not remember whether my exuberance as a self-made host and cook got the better of me. I had prepared an excellent meal on my gas ring; it consisted of spaghetti as a first course, followed by lamb chops with two vegs, a delicious local Viennese Apfelstrudel and ending with a perfect Italian espresso. My guests and I behaved in exemplary fashion, making no excessive noise, as was the rule of the house after 10 p.m, despite our high spirits. I saw them off in the early hours, having suppressed any exaggerated gaiety.

Then the host faced the washing up and clearing away of debris and, perhaps overcome by tiredness after the exertions of the occasion, did something unpardonable. Rather than dispose of the chop bones in the dustbin outside on a cold winter's night, I dumped them down the loo, which was an old-fashioned, possibly Edwardian or Victorian type. It worked well when one pulled the water lever near the seat. Then I dropped off into a sleep of the just, only to get my come-uppance the following morning when my chop bones had upset the system as never before, but worse still, my artistic landlady. It was the last straw for her as far as I was concerned. She gave me notice and I had to find another place with cooking facilities, but having learnt another of those lessons of which life is so full.

7

An Elderly Student

Like others who had spent the war years in the forces, I did not find it easy to return to a civilian occupation of books and studies. I was nearly 27 and found it tedious to live on my own in the bedsitter-land of northwest London and in other suburbs. While it was pleasant to receive invitations to the homes of friends for glimpses of close-knit family life, it always made me sad to have to leave them late at night to go back to my digs. I spent my days working in university or public libraries such as the British Museum reading room. This was where people met their friends during breaks for a stroll under the museum's colonnade entrance and where Continentals were generally recognizable from the clouds of cigarette smoke in which they were enveloped and from the way in which they waved their hands and arms about during their eager discussions.

In those days, the British Museum's rotunda attracted far more weird characters than it does now since it has moved into the streamlined British Library premises in the Euston Road. What, I wonder, has become of all those people who seemed to spend most of their time there? I remember an elderly little woman bent over piles of Chinese books who wore in all weathers the briefest of shorts, naked legs and a pelerine and probably came by bicycle from somewhere far away. She was always the first to get to her corner seat in Row C, close to where Karl Marx used to sit. In my time, there was also a bearded man with shoulder-length blond hair – the Jesus-look long before it became fashionable – who wore a mackintosh with, so one was told, nothing underneath.

I also learnt to appreciate the excellent British local lending libraries and the facilities they offered in their public reading rooms for consulting reference books, encyclopaedias and daily and weekly newspapers, as well as for obtaining books from other libraries. My happiest discovery was the London Library in St James's Square, which I joined later when I was able to afford its annual fees. Sir Isaiah Berlin described it as 'easily the best in the world', and he kindly supported my application to join after only a brief meeting through common friends. Situated in the midst of London's clubland, it had existed for over a century along those lines, owned by and answerable to its members only, like a club. However, with Westminster Council's rising rates in the 1960s, it eventually had to become a registered charity. Now with over a million books, an additional annexe, and needing half a mile of new shelves every three or so years, its continued existence in that desirable part of London remains surrounded by uncertainty.

Surely, no private library has remained as cherished by its readers. It was founded in 1849 by Thomas Carlyle with 2500 books in two rooms on the first floor of 49 Pall Mall, lack of space soon forced the move to its present site. The irascible Scot, then aged 46 and at the beginning of his fame, found the disorderly working conditions in the crowded reading room of the British Museum frustrating, for it took ages for the pile of books he needed to consult for his *French Revolution* to be brought to his seat. What finally precipitated his departure was a loud sneeze from one of his fellow readers, which disturbed his nerves. Even worse, he infuriated Anthony Panizzi, the Italian architect then at work on the new rotunda reading room, by describing him as a 'respectable official'. Panizzi had denied Carlyle access to one of the shelves, but he had his revenge by saying that he could not allow his library to be 'pulled about' by an 'unknown man of letters'.

Soon Carlyle found about 500 subscribers for his new library, among them Charles Dickens, then 29 years old and known only for his *Sketches by Boz*, though working on *Oliver Twist*, and equally disgruntled about having to work in the old British Museum reading room. Carlyle, moreover, had a daily long ride on horsebasck from his Chelsea house in Cheyne Row. He had to cross what is now Belgrave Square and what was then known as 'Five Fields', a wilderness notorious for the robbing of travellers who had to cross it on foot.

Carlyle deserves our gratitude for having led this exodus,

especially in view of the *French Revolution*, which was perhaps his greatest work. The Carlyles' maid had inadvertently used the first volume of the manuscript to light the sitting-room fire and Carlyle had to rewrite the whole text from memory. He certainly knew what it meant when he said that 'a book is a kind of thing that requires a man to be alone with it.' In the London Library he introduced the then innovative system of allowing members to take several books home with them and, unless required by another member, to keep them for as long as they were needed. Thus, the comfortable reading room at St James's Square was used less for study and more for consulting weeklies or foreign journals and for an armchair snooze after an exhaustive search in the stacks extending over five floors.

Generations of well-known British writers have belonged to it, considering it an honour, if elected, to accept the chore of serving on its governing body. Members were encouraged to write requests for new acquisitions of particular book. John Stuart Mill, for example, asked for *Political Economy*. Early elected library presidents were Carlyle, Tennyson, Macaulay, Gladstone and Leslie Stephen. Stephen's daughter, Virginia Woolf, also served, as did Lytton Strachey, H. G. Wells, Rudyard Kipling, Hilaire Belloc, E. M. Forster and T. S. Eliot. No other library had so many books donated to it by its own author members, or whole libraries bequeathed to it after their deaths. Indeed, the profusion of such offers sometimes made tactful refusal a necessity. And, perhaps unique among such ancient British institution, its staff has remained particularly courteous and helpful.

When, later in the century, Gladstone planned his own library, St Deiniol's at Hawarden in North Wales, he consulted Lord Acton about whether or not to follow the model of their mutual friend, Sir Anthony Panizzi's British Museum reading room. It had an iron gallery all round, as did the London Library, with iron lattices filtering the skylights' gleam ever more dimly down several levels. Acton, who had impoverished himself by buying books for what was then the largest private library in the country, annexed to his Shropshire residence, replied: 'Panizzi was an immense spender of money. The only positive dogma of my own library experience is that books should not be against a wall but in double rows, with nothing between, and the backs looking both ways.'

The relevance of St Benedict

In my belated student days I came to appreciate the atmosphere
of Benedictine monasteries like Prinknash Abbey near Gloucester
or its sister foundation, Farnborough Abbey, in Hampshire. I
had become their 'oblate', a 'worldly' one, as distinct from
cloistered oblates who are linked to monasteries by 'vows'. Such
oblates are a kind of Benedictine 'third order' meant for lay
people or women whose attachment to a particular community is
with a less binding promise. I enjoyed their traditional Benedictine hospitality and was able to study and take part in the
various 'hours' of their beautifully celebrated liturgy, especially
Vespers and Compline at the end of the day.

Prinknash (pronounced prinadge) Abbey was not part of the
English Benedictine congregation, but owed its origins to an
Anglican community founded by Dom Aelred Carlyle on
Caldey Island in 1893. His monks soon realized the illogicality
of their position within the Church of England and the
demands of their liturgy, so, in 1913, they decided corporately
to be received into the Catholic Church. Their priory status was
raised to the rank of an abbey in 1937, with Dom Wilfrid
Upson, of the original Anglican community, as their abbot.
They developed rapidly and soon spread to Farnborough in
Hampshire, founded by the exiled French Empress Josephine,
who is buried there in the tombs of the Emperor Napoleon III
and their son, the prince imperial. Another Prinknash foundation was made in Scotland.

These ex-Anglican monks had originally been attached to the
Monte Vergine Benedictines at Avellino in southern Italy and,
unlike other 'Black Monks', they wore a white habit. They
adopted the *ora et labora* principle of prayer and manual work.
They also strictly applied the Benedictine rule of *stabilitas*, which
meant no educational or other outside activities. At Prinknash, I
shared the monks' meals, which they took in silence in the
refectory as extracts were read from weekly Catholic papers or
newly published books. Listening attentively, they would sometimes emit an appreciative chuckle or shake their heads in dissent
or disbelief. My participation in the community was probably at
that stage of my life caused by uncertainty about my future and
about whether I might adopt it on a regular basis. However,
after long talks with trusted friends among the monks I
eventually decided against it. Sentimental reasons, like how good

the security of the monastic life made one feel, should not of course determine such an important decision.

A fellow internee on the Isle of Man, Father Clement Sandkuhl, came to influence my own later attachment to his Prinknash monastery in Gloucestershire. He was a German Benedictine monk and had, before coming to England, originally belonged to the famous Rhineland Abbey of Maria Laach. It was he who had introduced me to the *Rule of St Benedict*, one of the great practical handbooks of European history written at Monte Cassino in about AD 535. I first read it in the internment camp and it made a deep impression on me. I found its ideals immediately attractive, perhaps because I had always regarded their opposite extremes – excessive vanity and pride, talkativeness and diso-bedience – as particularly off-putting sins. One could easily under-stand how these clearly written and understandable instructions to his monks had given birth to Western monasticism and kept the Catholic Church's ideals no less than the torch of civilization blazing through the Dark Ages that followed the disintegration of the Roman Empire and its world.

One knows little about the life of St Benedict (*c.* 480–547) beyond the edifying account written by Pope St Gregory the Great (540–604). Apparently, he was born of noble parents at Nursia, today Norcia near Perugia, about 30 miles outside Rome where he went to study. He became a dropout, apparently as a protest against the disorderly life of his fellow students, joined an ascetic community and then lived as a hermit in the wild mountains above the Anio valley. In about 529, after he had founded some small monastic communities near Subiaco, he and a few monks settled at Monte Cassino, where he died and was buried. The invading Lombards destroyed the Monte Cassino monastery, but the monks were able to escape to Rome where Pope St Gregory the Great gave them a monastery near the Lateran.

St Benedict's *Rule* is an an extraordinarily powerful practical vision. While the practical *ora et labora* principle as such does not appear, it does so in its sense and in that all the necessities of life came from within the cloistered walls, creating a self-sufficient unit of production and consumption, which was naturally superior to anything outside during the chaotic and lawless five centuries that followed St Benedicts' generation.

The book upheld the old Roman world's image of a majestic and universal Christ, and has particular Benedictine virtues like *gravitas* and *discretio,* called the 'mother of virtues', an ability to distinguish between what is essential and less essential, and the practice of moderation. Every detail of the monastic life, even its seemingly less important offices and aspects are covered, such as that of the cellarer or monastic reader. The latter is advised to adopt a deliberately monotonous tone, so as not to distract listeners from the peculiarities of his person or voice. It was accepted that he, too, had to eat, letting him 'take a little bread and wine before he began to read ... and lest it be hard for him to fast so long. Afterwards, let him take his meal with the weekly cooks and other servers. The brethren are not to read or sing according to their order, but such only as may edify their hearers' (Chapter 38).

At my stays in Prinknash, the Sunday rest period after the midday meal always provided a pleasant opportunity for the abbey's guests to meet and talk with Abbot Dom Wilfrid Upson. He embodied all the congenial Anglican cultured gentlemanly characteristics, including its snobberies, and a taste for good coffee and Turkish cigarettes, which, however, did not detract from his spiritual personality. The *Rule* allows the abbot to add 'something (tasty) to the (monastic frugal) fare', 'even to break his fast for a guest'; Benedictine hospitality is part of charity, based on 'Let all guests who come be received like Christ himself, for He will say: 'I was a stranger and ye took me in' (Matthew XXV, 35).

Dom Wilfrid had a strong interest in filming and one could appreciate how he must have charmed the Hollywood stars, some of whom were his special friends. His reason for cultivating them was linked to his ambition to erect a modern Prinknash monastery and abbey church in the the Cotswolds hills. The old monastery grounds had fallen victim to Henry VIII's monastic dissolution, but in later centuries, it had come back into Catholic lay ownership and was eventually left to the ex-Anglican Benedictines who moved there after 1937. However, it soon became too small for the growing Prinknash community.

The abbot has the pivotal role in St Benedict's monastery. Chapter 2 of the Holy Rule devoted to him is clearly the best written and most interesting of its 73 chapters. He 'holds the place of Christ', he should 'teach by deeds rather than words', 'make no distinction of persons', 'consult the brethren, but then take his own decision'. He is the 'Father', this being the very meaning of the word abbot, and on the basis of the old Roman

and authoritarian principle paterfamilias of Roman law, which is
certainly not unquestioned today. He is the 'Shepherd of God's
flock and will be held responsible for whatever defects the master
shall find in His sheep'. He must be 'a wise Physician, ready to
apply any remedy, correction, exhortation, chastisement for their
spiritual diseases, lest one diseased sheep should infect the whole
flock', and in the last resort apply 'the amputating knife', meaning corporal punishment, even expulsion. This was of course
intended to apply to an uneducated peasant society, with most of
the monks not originally being ordained priests or deacons. It is
doubtful whether St Benedict himself was a priest.

The abbot's special qualities, St Benedict insists on, are to be
'learned in the divine law', he must be 'chaste, sober merciful',
but not 'turbulent or anxious-minded', nor 'overdoing things',
'he must always be prudent and circumspect'. St Benedict seems
not to care too much that he should be a disciplinarian or even a
saint, which is easily understandable when one considers the
enormous powers, untrammeled by any legal limitations, he puts
into the abbot's hands. The only ultimate safeguard against an
abbot's abuse of his powers 'is the account he has to render for
all the souls dependent on him, as well as for his own soul on the
day of judgement'.

Evidently, the Holy Rule of St Benedict was not a school of
democracy, and the countless abbots who used their powers
tyrannically, foolishly, selfishly, is legend, just as there were bad
popes, bad kings or republican presidents, especially in the feudal
ages when abbots had increasingly to take on temporal powers
and became truly 'lords'. Yet, in the sense of the just use of his
powers, the abbot's can be said to be a basis for the true exercise
of authority. Significantly, Chapter 2 devoted to his responsi-
bilities is exceeded in length only by the chapters that deal with
humility (4–7) and its 12 degrees by which man's humbled heart
is lifted up by the Lord to ascend to heaven and by which we
descend by self-exaltation. (The above quotations from the Rule of
St Benedict are taken from the edition by D. Oswald Hunter Blair
MA, Abbot of Dunfermline, 4th edition, 1934, Fort Augustus.)

The funds that Abbot Upson had collected in the USA proved
insufficient for the great building project that he envisaged
together with the eminent Catholic architect Harry Stuart
Goodhart Rendel, based on a design of French Romanesque and
Byzantine inspiration. The monks were to do much of the

building work themselves, but the plan was unfortunately never fully realized. Goodhart Rendel died in 1959, with only the crypt of the new abbey church partly completed. Wanting to finish the project, the new Abbot of Prinknash who had succeeded Upson went back to a modified and cheaper design by Goodhart Rendel's former partner F. G. Broadbent. What was then completed by 1972 now looks more like a complex of undistinguished college or hotel buildings with rectangular windows, with the monks' living quarters consisting of a clumsy cell block, six storeys high, sitting starkly on the steep hillside, detracting rather than adding to the beauties of the surrounding Cotswolds.

Architecture is an art as well as a craft, more than just 'good building' in the sense of sound construction and good materials. According to Sir Henry Wotton's *Elements of Architecture* (1624), three conditions are required, 'Commoditie, Firmness and Delight', the first element being good planning (commoditie), the second using good materials (firmness) and the third (delight) that it must be pleasing to the eye. Taste is evidently a quality that varies with the changing times, and is not one St Benedict in his Rule might have especially wanted an abbot of his monastery to have. There was a joke making the rounds in those early British postwar years concerning a rich American who had paid for the rebuilding of an English church destroyed in the war. The benefactor attended the reopening ceremony at which the local English bishop expressed heartfelt gratitude to him, saying 'thank God for this succour', which did not go down too well with the American who misunderstood him to have said 'sucker'. However, for once, *the force majeure* of declining vocations is to be welcomed in that it compels the Prinknash monastic community to forego its futuristic aspirations, but return to its original abode, meanwhile restored, as more befitting its present-day numbers.

Prinknash was also the original spiritual home of another friend, Dom Bede Griffiths (1906–93). His book *The Golden String* (1954) admirably described his conversion from an Edwardian Anglican background. This was, however, only the beginning of a long spiritual odyssey that was to end with him heading an Indian ashram of a very different kind of religious wholeness from the one he had set out from (see his excellent biography *Beyond the Darkness* by Shirley du Boulay, 1998). I knew him only in his earlier Western Benedictine phase. The seed of his later development lay in his friendship with Dr Toni Sussmann, whom I also knew well for many years. She was a Jungian analyst who, together with the Catholic psychologist Dr Franz Elkisch, both former German refugees, had many patients among members of the Catholic religious orders.

Dr Sussmann was a remarkable woman, tiny in stature, with an indomitable spirit and known to advise her patients to 'go home and meditate on the difference between the important and the essential', which would have been familiar to a student of the Rule of St Benedict. Though not a Catholic, she demonstrated her interest in the unity of religion by the Buddha she placed at one end of her mantelpiece in her Bayswater flat and a statue of the Mother of God on the other. She had a great influence on Bede, interesting him in Jungian ideas and in Eastern meditation.

He set out at first to be a Western Benedictine monk in India, but soon realized that this would amount to a life of unimaginable luxury in that part of the world. According to Shirley du Boulay he came to hold that the monastic ideal needed 'to be freed from its Western Christian captivity, its overweight of words and rules, lack of silence, and become also more accessible to lay people'.

He came to admit openly how repressed sexually he had always felt, and that he had to discard the stifling overdeveloped, rational, masculine, patriarchal, animus in his left brain. At the same time, he felt that the feminine and intuitive mind, the right brain, the chthonic and earth power had to be awakened. India helped him to realize how dualistic thought had always conditioned the Church and how God and the world, God and humanity, are all conceived in dualistic terms. Bede Griffiths died as a Camaldolese monk. He made a unique impact throughout his life as a holy man of great vision, a Christian sage and guru.

A lesson from Sir Michael Howard

I was then in the middle of my history studies at London University's King's College. Among my teachers were Sir Michael Howard, as he has since become, then a junior lecturer, and (unrelated) Christopher Howard, a specialist in nineteenth-century studies. I also took a course in the history of philosophy, a subject that had always interested me, at University College, or UC as it was known. This was the Benthamite, heathen rival of King's representing the Anglican establishment, with the undergraduates of both colleges engaged in mock internecine warfare. Jeremy Bentham, apostle of utilitarianism, had left himself, appropriately embalmed, to University College, sitting as a clothed skeleton in a box, from which he occasionally emerges for an airing and dusting down, a special challenge to all passers-by but apparently hardly noticed by them anymore.

One of Bentham's intellectual heirs was Professor Alfred Ayer, the logical analyst and positivist who lectured there, in challenging disregard to colleagues who were more metaphysically inclined. One of these happened to be the thoughtful Geoffrey Keating, whose fondness for garlic exuded an aromatic spicy touch, not objectionable to me, to his early afternoon lectures on the perennial philosophy. Ayer was the destructive new prophet of analytical thinking, much beloved by those usually ignorant of basic notions of fundamental verisimilitude. Keating upheld, at least as far as I was concerned, the banner of rational thought. The times were against him, however, and many preferred Ayer, the more amusing and destructive lecturer. As an atheist, but unlike Bentham, Ayer startled the world by returning to the living after having apparently died after an illness. He was able, however, to report from the beyond no more than having glimpsed something like a shining blinding light, which was bound to disappoint some.

I much enjoyed the lectures on modern history at King's by Michael Howard who has since become a distinguished Oxford Regius professor and professor of war studies at Yale University. He was two years younger than I was, with a German mother and a splendid war record in the Coldstream Guards. By comparison, I felt rather self-conscious, having no more to show than my desultory exertions in the Pioneer Corps and the Highland Light Infantry. There was about him also a brilliant intellectual superiority combined with fitting elegance, and accents that in those days were anything but subdued. He was, in other words, the distinctive product of an elite school, regiment and Oxford college, the personified gentleman-scholar, with wit and irony that could make me feel miserably inferior. His type would nowadays perhaps prefer to appear more anodyne, so as not unnecessarily to annoy the inferior classes. He used to invite favoured students to reading weekends at his country cottage, which London University undergraduates not used to such refinements were eager to attend.

My own daily commuter's journey took me back to digs in

Kensal Rise, where I tried hard to be comforted by G. K. Chesterton's lines: 'For there is good news yet to hear and fine things to be seen/Before we go to Paradise by way of Kensal Green.' It seemed appropriate there that, walking home late one night, I should totally lose my way. There was nobody around anymore to ask for directions and as I roamed through the still streets, with all the houses and their little front gardens looking alike, I felt increasingly like extricating myself from some Kafkaesque nightmare. Wondering what I should do, I finally saw a phone box and rang the 'Automobile Association', and they kindly helped me out of my dilemma. I only had to turn around two corners to get to my number 137.

My landladies were two nice sisters with office jobs whose retired old dad shuffled about the house in his shirtsleeves, braces and slippers. He always seemed to be in the kitchen reading the *Evening Standard* or doing the football pools. I had rented their ground-floor bed-sitting room, which opened towards the back garden. It was not a very cheerful place and did not encourage one to spend more time there than necessary. I had the use of the kitchen when not needed by the family.

While feeling too old for the boisterous activities of the students' union, I was nevertheless persuaded to act as cheerleader in support of female colleagues in a momentous university debate 'that this House believes in the New Look'. We managed to get a large majority in favour of the latest ankle length women's fashion, which female colleagues had to display courageously by climbing on the table under howls of protesting shouts of 'higher', 'higher'. Though glad to have helped to make history, my elderly heart seemed not quite into such harmless frivolities.

I did enjoy, however, our long summer vacations when I revisited many old haunts in Austria, Germany and Italy. These countries were also recovering from their war experiences, but they seemed to have the additional spur of trusting in a new and common European future, which the victorious British evidently lacked. For one of these holidays, three of us from King's College, London, invested in an old jeep. We were hoping to recover our expenses by profiteering from the continental sugar shortage, of which we had heard reports. With that aim in view, we took a kit bag filled with saccharine tablets, which we wanted to sell on the black market and get rich! However, we were unlucky in this respect and in another, too. Our jeep let us down, being apt to blow its gaskets, which required expensive garage repair jobs at regular intervals in all three countries. In addition, our hope of selling our saccharine tablets in Italy came to nothing. There was a veritable glut of sugar in that blessed country, as we, still used to ration cards, soon discovered.

To lighten our load we decided to dump our bag of artificial sweeteners and Umbria's Lake Trasimene seemed to be the right place in which to do this. Being students, however, we had remembered that in 217 BC the Romans under Gaius Flaminius suffered a tragic setback when Hannibal beat them in an ambush, with the Roman senator slain and Hannibal losing the sight of an eye. The celebrated Carthaginian warrior had been on a march to the south having, according to Polybius, crossed the Alps with his foot soldiers, horses and elephants. It did not occur to us then that a similar environmental catastrophe would result from feeding artificial sweeteners to the lake's fish. In other respects, our trip was great fun, even though we had to sell our jeep afterwards at a considerable loss. We evidently lacked the knack of black marketeers.

On another vacation my friend and teacher Christopher Howard, who wanted to improve his German, accompanied me. His linguistic howlers were legion, but since he wanted to practise on others, he contributed much to the general gaiety. He could never quite get the right formal phrase, for example, for expressing his pleasure for having met someone when parting after a brief first meeting. Instead of the correct *Es war mir ein Vergnügen* (it was a pleasure to meet you), all he managed to come out with was *Viel Vergmügen*, which is the equivalent of 'have a good time'. Fortunately, people with good manners merely responded by politely smiling. However, on one occasion in Italy, Christopher got the better of his opposite number, a medical doctor who decided to speak in Latin, thinking that among academics that should be no problem. During a delightful Neapolitan summer's evening outside the house of this doctor's family, our Italian host wanted to impress his friends and family with the ease with which he tackled international understanding. However, it backfired because the differences between Italian and English pronunciation of Latin proved a real obstacle. Ultimately, temperaments threatened to be involved and there English moderation prevailed over southern irascibility.

As for the progress of my studies at King's College, I had to admit that through the interruptions to my life due to emigration followed by war, I had probably lost much of the drive and inner discipline I needed. A 'letter of condolence' Michael Howard wrote to me after I failed my intermediate examination in 1948 reflected this. He told me of my weakness in various history papers. I had not answered the questions asked, but produced a collection of relevant and irrelevant data not related to any coherent argument. It was not that my factual knowledge was inadequate, he pointed out, or that I had not been good in other subjects. His conclusion, however, was that academic history was perhaps not my forte. 'Examiners may err; if they have done so in your case you will prove it sooner or later,' he added kindly. When, many decades later, I produced my biography of Lord Acton, a book based on original research, I had to recall Howard's final advice: 'Cut your losses and start again.' I repeated my intermediate examination, scraped through it, and went on to my finals. At least I had not thrown in the sponge, but it was time for me to give up being an elderly student and get down to something more productive and worthwhile.

According to my birth horoscope (Sagittarius) produced at that time by a reputable astrologer, some very contradictory features were attributed to me, some of which I was not even aware. I had 'a peace-loving nature', was 'optimistic, enterprising and self-confident'. I had 'a good intellectual grasp', was 'inventive-minded, far-sighted, physically agile and mobile'; and I was 'prudent' with 'good intuition'. I was also blessed with 'a strongly physical love, artistic power of creation, and an extremely magnetic personality with regard to sexual attraction'. 'Endeavour to meet others half-way', it advised. It also claimed that I was 'gallant', 'polite', had 'a passionate disposition' and 'a strong procreative urge'.

I was apparently 'a sentimental talker', 'lively', 'inquisitive', 'curious' and displayed an 'interest in novelties'. I was quick 'at repartee or in the uptake', and showed an 'ability to give a good answer when challenged'. I also showed a 'desire to revel in something or become enraptured', and was 'a person with a sense and appreciation of beauty', and an 'interest in art'. I was, however, prone to 'emotional depressions' and 'pessimism' and suffered from an 'inability to develop emotionally in a proper manner'. I was subject to 'irritability, excitability, an inward unrest, illness caused through excitement or upsets, inhibited sexual expression' and 'a state of being fed-up, faint and feeble'.

I was 'successful at tackling the environment' and 'organizing', and demonstrated an 'ability to work together happily with others'. I had 'a joy of living, love of enterprise, creative urge, procreative powers or faculties'. I possessed 'the power to get sudden ideas' and of 'independent thinking'. I was, however, inclined 'to act rashly and hastily', was disposed to 'nervousness, quick changes of thoughts and moods, an instinctive and quick grasp of a subject and logical thinking'. I had a 'practical disposition, was circumspect, could grasp connective links and relationships correctly and draw logical conclusions from such knowledge'.

I suffered from a 'phlegmatic temperament, a propensity to corpulence, happiness in solitude, inhibitions in mental or physical development, arterial sclerosis, instability, feelings of inferiority, misdirected energy, a tendency to associate with weak or sick persons, and emotional inhibitions when in contact with others'. I was inclined 'to deceive others and to seduce people'. I showed a tendency to live in hopes and expectations, was inclined to speculate, was easily influenced or impressed by others, was impressionable and open to mystical or spiritual influences'. I tended to act 'unpredictably and impulsively, had an excessive self will, was stubborn, strove for absolute independence, was restless and craved sensations'. These, I suppose, are innate dispositions, so what one makes of them might, it is hoped, turn out to be very different.

8

Writing 'Pro Ecclesia Dei', 'Regina et Patria'

After my belated and none too memorable university years I was looking for a job in the one area in which I could claim some experience in this country and abroad. I had kept my links with the new German and Austrian press, particularly the Catholic papers, and contributed to them on a freelance basis from London. Being able to do that at a time when Britain's international standing was still high, and in German, increased the demand for my contributions.

As I have already noted, between Britain and its continental neighbours one could sense a growing divergence of opinion about how to assess the postwar world. Apart from having 'to feed the Germans', the new British Labour government was inclined to turn its back on Europe for the sake of its own social revolution. For the time being, it wanted to carry on its traditional empire and Commonwealth links, or at least to regard these as historical obstacles to any British engagement in postwar Europe. Moreover, France's de Gaulle was increasingly thwarting Britain's role in Europe. Before the war, Hitler and Chamberlain were often accused of missing the proverbial bus. After 1945, with the growing cold war confrontation between NATO and the communist world, it seemed as though Britain was about to miss another bus, the European one. Did Britain's future lie with the United States, with wider free trade world links, or with the new developing European coal and steel community? The answer overshadowed the tug of war between Britain's political parties, to which Winston Churchill's Zurich speech in September 1946 and its 'United States of Europe' theme had first, albeit vaguely, pointed the British Conservatives.

For Douglas Woodruff, editor of the Catholic weekly, the *Tablet*, it was natural as a Catholic and Conservative to feel close to the new Europe's three Catholic founding fathers. Interestingly, they each came from disputed frontier areas with national and ethnic divisions that seemed to be at the heart of the Continent's problems. Alcide de Gasperi was from the Trento region between Italy and Germany, Robert Schuman came from Alsace, and Dr Konrad Adenauer was from the Rhineland; and their origins dictated their personal histories and future hopes. Woodruff, a rare European Englishman in that he was European-minded, had befriended me when I first came to England, and when I finished my studies in 1952 he again offered me a job as editorial assistant on his paper. I gladly accepted and stayed for five years.

Journalist apprentice

The *Tablet's* weekly circulation was then only about 13,000, low enough, but Woodruff envisaged producing 'a weekly review for educated Catholic opinion' along the lines of the *Spectator* or *New Statesman,* as distinct from the more popular Catholic weekly newspapers. Nevertheless, the loss-making *Tablet* could hardly have survived without a subsidy from its financially prosperous stable mate, the *Universe* (with a circulation of several hundred thousands) under the then common ownership of the Catholic publishing firm Burns Gates & Washbourne. Altogether, with the *Catholic Herald* and *Catholic Times,* these papers, which were mainly sold at church doors, were then serving a Catholic minority estimated at five million in England and Wales. Though reading a Catholic paper was still considered a pious duty, it was evidently not observed all that eagerly by the faithful. Woodruff's 'educated Catholic opinion' long remained no more than a pipe dream. The private Catholic schools in those years before the second Vatican Council did not seem to produce that desideratum as diligently as they did recruits for the more profitable legal profession, for the City of London's financial establishment or for the armed forces.

Catholic publishing, apart from prayer books and devotional articles, suffered from the minority status of the Church in Britain. Even Catholic bestseller authors of the mid-century such as Graham Greene, Evelyn Waugh and G. K. Chesterton preferred to have their books published by economically more viable non-Catholic publishers, and could hardly be faulted for that. In 1967, long after I had left the *Tablet,* I was involved in the takeover negotiations for the bankrupt Catholic publishers Burns by the German firm Herder of Freiburg, with which I have had a longstanding link. This Herder connection explained my presence at a disagreeable personal clash between the German representatives and T. F. Burns. I had long known the latter as a gentleman-publisher, namely agreeable but without Woodruff's intellectual stature, but I never thought I would come to feel sorry for the man put under pressure by the German negotiators to substantiate his claim that his firm was a viable business. This clash illustrated how much confidence the new Germany had derived from its postwar *Wirtschaftswunder,* which came from integrating all its energies into the one basket of its European cause, while Britain, the exhausted world power, lacked a similar spur for national as distinct from social regeneration.

My weekly wage on the *Tablet* was low, £2. 10s 0d a week. Every Friday the manager, Mr Bradley, handed it to me in a sealed white envelope, thus seemingly confirming that Catholic employers expected one to work for the greater glory of the Lord. At present valuation, my pay was worth about £50 and, although I was not a member of the permanent staff, which was better if not much better paid, I was quite happy with my first job at the bottom of the ladder. It was an apprenticeship opportunity for me, the more so because, being the equivalent of a three-day working week, allowed me office time for my freelance work for the foreign press. Merely to have access to the major newspapers and magazines was of course worth a lot. My *Tablet* tasks covered only the high-pressure days on Mondays and Tuesdays when the paper was 'put together'. It then customarily opened with two pages of comments on home and foreign affairs, of which I provided the coverage on foreign affairs and on the Church abroad. The weekly leading article written by the editor or assistant editor followed, after which came the major articles and sections on letters to the editor, book reviews, international Church news and obituaries.

Altogether, the *Tablet* aimed to produce a more serious though not necessarily stodgy fare. Writing readable English was one of the unwritten house rules and I had much to learn. Wednesday was press day, which the editor or the assistant editor spent putting the paper 'to bed' at the printers in Reading.

The day was largely free for me in London. Thursdays and Fridays served to prepare for the coming week's issue, including outside reporting jobs, which fell to me as then the youngest on the staff. It meant hobnobbing with the cardinal-archbishop and other bishops, and acting as a reporter. I also did a good deal of book reviewing on international affairs and other matters in which I had a special interest.

It was our experience in weekly journalism that the week passed with amazing speed, as quickly as the day did for those engaged in producing a daily newspaper. One of my occasional chores was to take down the editor's dictation of his weekly leader. Woodruff was a portly, slow-moving man, a modern equivalent of Dr Samuel Johnson or a combined 'Chester–Belloc', as some described him. His dictation emerged, amazingly, almost in the form of ready paragraphs, into which he would afterwards merely insert full stops and commas. I learnt from him not to undervalue the semicolon! He rarely had to do more than add a word here and there, clearly had an 'alpha mind', and was skilled in the word-knitting process, even though that might consist of a good many clichés like 'moderate people of every political complexion' or 'it is devoutly to be wished'. These would evidently go down well when read out aloud in the refectories of the religious orders. Amazingly, Woodruff's paragraphs could be switched around on the printed page, yet still make sense to the reader. He was a master juggler at this game, which he had learnt as a young journalist on *The Times* at a time when top people both read and produced that paper.

A difficult job I disliked was having to decipher and rewrite the manuscripts of Edward Ingram Watkin (1888–1981), the notable Catholic writer on theology, mysticism and philosophy who was a frequent and highly respected contributor to the *Tablet*. He was immensely clever, with excellent German and French, which made his book translations of Halévy's *History of the English People* and Foerster's *Europe and the German Question* most readable. I became quite friendly with him, since we had a common interest in German and French Catholic ideas. We were both converts, and I shared his identification of 'ecclesiastical materialism' as the bane of Catholicism; at the time I knew him, his sympathies were more modernist than mine and he, being more mature, was probably more sceptical than I was about the reforms of Vatican Two.

Occasionally I visited him at Torquay, where he lived, separated since 1937 from his wife and children who had remained in Norfolk. His family called him Edda, though his Torquay mistress Zoe called him Edward. I remember her as a tall, strikingly good-looking woman with dark curly locks, some thirty years younger than he was. He married her after his wife's death, when Zoe was 69. 'The question at the Last Judgement will not be did you commit adultery with that woman? The question will be how much did you love the woman?' He shared his life with his two families on a six-month per year basis; they lived in somewhat shabby gentility largely on independent means as a private scholar.

E. I. was decidedly eccentric, as was Zoe, whose cutting voice always embarrassed me, the foreigner, whenever we rode together in a Torquay bus, for everybody would stare at her while she remained admirably cool and unconcerned. I came to admire his son Aelred Watkin as an eminent Downside Benedictine, and his daughter Magdalen Goffin for her excellent and evidently truthful books about her father.

One of Watkin's peculiarities that affected me was that his typewriter had no space bar, so one had to separate all the words by hand. It fell to me to fit them for *Tablet* editorial usage. In time this became quite an expertise of mine, helped no doubt by the fact that his logic and wording were impeccable. A longer Watkin manuscript thus served as a welcome excuse to take the long journey to Torquay, which the enriching company of his whirling brain assisted.

Newspaper readers tend to favour the politics of which they approve. The erroneous notion persists, however, that the press leads rather than follows public opinion. It has, after all, to please and retain its readership. Before coloured pictures ruled and confused everybody, there was still a great deal of trust in the printed and spoken word. What more unbeatable argument existed than I have seen it with my own eyes? How wrong these eyes could be *vis-à-vis* the dethroned supreme power of the word as man's alpha and omega. Society in the 1950s still seemed to have a unique normalcy about it, especially after the long and exhausting Second World War. Everybody still 'knew their place', whether this was up or down, and they did not have a 'thing' about it. People enjoyed damning the apparent contortions of 'modern' music or art and felt no shame about it. There was respect for age and status before the angry young men and

women arrived, and one wondered then about what it was that
they were actually angry. Moreover, suddenly everybody was
able to play a role formerly confined to the privileged and to a
few 'politically correct' intellectuals. I remembered from my
German postwar experience that neither I nor any other members of my generation were the first to be 'liberated' and that
there had been previous emancipations throughout history.

At that time, working on a journal like the *Tablet,* as well as
reading it, was seen as a kind of superior apostolate, like being
on a court circular. This was psychologically still peculiar to the
English Catholic context, which had a ghetto-like quality from
having half emerged from centuries of oppression, yet feeling a
part of the universal Church. From the pulpit, priests would
remind the faithful that it would be pleasing to God if they were
to leave their copy of the more strident *Catholic Herald* behind
on the bus (in case someone casually picked it up and was
converted by it), though not the *Tablet,* which had too much of
an intellectual whiff about it. However, the equally possible
opposite effect seemed not to have occurred to those apostolic
missionaries.

The *Tablet* office was then situated near the Chelsea end of
London's Sloane Street, when 'Sloanes' were to awaken into a
new juvenile power movement in the 1960s and the 'Kensington
kiss', as I liked to describe it, came into fashion. But with my
juvenility, so much extended by circumstances outside my control,
I was forced reluctantly to agree with Philip Larkin that 'sexual
intercourse began/in 1963/which was rather late for me/Between
the end of the *Chatterley* ban/and the Beatles' first LP.'

The *Tablet* was the oldest Catholic weekly in the world, with
an uninterrupted existence since its foundation in 1840 by the
robust Frederic Lucas, a Catholic convert from the Quakers,
though lacking their pacific qualities. It was intended politically
as a liberal organ, sympathetic to Daniel O'Connell and the
cause of Irish independence, and temporarily even moved to
Dublin. However, it soon fell into conservative hands, lost its
political edge and was, for 68 years, clerically owned by the
archdiocese of Westminster. In 1936 Cardinal Hinsley, one of
the more enlightened Catholic primates of the new century, sold
the paper to a group of Catholic laymen, among them Tom
Burns as publisher and Douglas Woodruff as editor.

The remarkable DW

Woodruff ran the *Tablet* for 31 years, establishing its prestige at home and in the English-speaking world. During the Second World War he subscribed to the BBC's radio monitoring service. This was a clever move, for it enabled the *Tablet* to cover, and knowledgeably present, Catholic Church news worldwide at a time when the dominance of the totalitarian powers made reliable Church information a rarity. Lay control of the Church press and publishing hardly existed outside Britain, and here it had come about through ordinary Catholic development. However, in itself, clerical control of the Catholic press was by no means always detrimental to a free Catholic press. This was demonstrated at the time, for example, by the Zurich Jesuits' excellent journal *Orientierung,* then operating under extreme anti-Catholic hostility, which supposedly liberal Switzerland practised well into the second half of the twentieth century.

The growth of Britain's modern Catholic minority was due mainly to the mid-nineteenth century influx of tens of thousands of poor immigrants occasioned by the Irish famine and the pull of British industrialization. Because the Irish brought their priests with them, they were able to preserve their faith in foreign exile. In Britain too, where they lived in great material poverty in the new urban slums, their faith, which derived from St Patrick whose own history so much reflected the Irish fate, remained their strength. Stern devotion, a popular religiosity and an almost puritanical essence, as though the harder and the more unpleasant it was in terms of human comfort and ease the more pleasing it must be to God, characterized the spirit of St Patrick. Like the toughest of weeds, it helped the Irish retain their religious/national faith in alien and hostile surroundings. While their Catholicism was not remarkable for its intellectual or aesthetic qualities, they sometimes added these elements from English sources, mainly from the constant stream of educated converts in the wake of John Henry Newman and from other influences, such as marriage to a Catholic partner.

English Catholics had to wait for more than a century and a half for their emancipation to have the full effect of practical equality. Today, a Roman Catholic monarch remains the only constitutional taboo. Far into the twentieth century, however, the alienation of English Catholics produced an odd psychological difficulty. As members of the universal Church, they felt they were superior to Henry VIII's 'upstart' Church of England, but they had also become a despised minority in English snobbery terms – theirs was the religion of Irish servants. Catholics in England were different from Catholics in Catholic countries, for an extraordinary loyalty to priests and fellow Catholics, no doubt a St Patrick inheritance comparable to a ghetto clan, united the English ones. Early British, American and Australian Catholics had Mafia-like traits; they favoured their Catholic shoemaker or dentist and subscribed to 'Catholic' causes irrespective of whether or not they were justified. This probably expressed the fact that Catholics, with 1000 years of Catholic Christianity, had become strangers in their own country, as in England where the 'usurpers' ran their old cathedrals beautifully and liturgically as though nothing had changed. On the European continent, however, the changes the Reformation wrought had been much more radical and violent.

Woodruff had an original mind, as well as a sense of history and humour. He had a first-class degree in modern history, was president of the Oxford Union and was a renowned 'debater'. On *The Times*, he had been a leader writer, specializing in dominion and empire affairs, and was the first to start the light-hearted fourth leaders, which have remained a regular feature. They became his speciality on the *Tablet* in the form of his anecdotal 'Talking at Random' and a characteristic expression of his humour. It also started him off as a collector of books, which literally grew around him in their thousands. He was of course totally unlike his editorial and more sectarian predecessors, having not only ample experience but also useful and international social contacts. His wife was the granddaughter of the First Lord Acton, the Catholic Liberal and historian; throughout his life, he was in great demand as a lecturer, debater and brilliant after-dinner speaker. Being childless added to the impact the two Woodruffs, forming almost a composite unit, made on the English Catholic scene for nearly half a century. He was good at the journalistic art of differentiating between 'the wood and the trees', and, to illustrate it, liked telling the story of a young reporter sent out to cover a wedding for his local newspaper, but no story came. On Monday morning, the editor sent for him and asked what had happened. The reporter explained that the bride had eloped with the best man, whereupon the bridegroom had shot himself – 'no wedding, therefore no story'! This was an instructive model for any budding reporter not to follow.

Among Woodruff's books was a funny imitation of the dialogues of Socrates, *Plato's Britannia*, in which he describes Socrates's disappointment, on a visit to modern London, to find that neither the Athenaeum in Pall Mall nor the exhibition hall in Olympia lived up to his expectations as God-fearing places of wisdom. He approves, however, of the seemingly modern democratic touch of equality whereby the poor ride in shiny big red buses while the rich have to make do with humble black cabs. Woodruff had a romantic vision of a Belloc-like Catholic Europe that looked back to Charlemagne and Alfred the Great (about whom he published his earlier books) but with a deep sense of freedom based on English political and common law traditions. Combining an independent mind with great loyalty to Rome, he was a pragmatic conservative to the right of centre for his generation, differing from the British Catholic majority who if they had Irish origins were Labour supporters, partly in gratitude to the Whigs as their heirs in achieving Catholic emancipation.

Under its masthead, the *Tablet* used to carry the motto '*Pro Ecclesia Dei Pro Regina et Patria*' (For the Church of God, Queen and Country). Undoubtedly, this characterized the past Woodruffian era of English Catholicism, for it was later dropped because it no longer fitted the temper of a different age. Shortly before his death, the novelist, essayist and leading liberal E. M. Forster (1879–1970), paid what was, coming from him, a backhanded compliment to the English Catholics for their cultural achievement in having produced in one generation so many outstanding writers. Forster ascribed this to the advantage of putting a persecuting religion under some kind of legal restraint. It brings out the best in them, instead of indulging in their former triumphalism, he said in a radio broadcast in 1968.

Woodruff's sense of English Catholic independence allowed him, long before Vatican Two, to criticize the Vatican when he regarded this to be justified. He did this, for example, when, in a particularly high-handed decision, English Catholics were banned from membership of the Council of Christians and Jews, then one of the first ecumenical organizations under royal patronage. Emphasizing that British people were accustomed to having Roman decisions adequately explained to them with the reasons for and against, he argued that proceeding in such an authoritarian manner was only likely to diminish respect for, indeed obedience to, the Church. In another leading article he similarly objected to the Roman criticism of the Catholic membership of 'Rotary Clubs', as this was evidently and one-sidedly based on their anti-clerical composition in southern Europe and South American countries. He pointed out that these critics in the Vatican were evidently ignorant of the different character of Rotary Clubs in more democratic parts of the world.

In campaigning for freedom of opinion within the Church and against its court-like authoritarianism, Woodruff was really standing up for principles that John Henry Newman had asserted more than a century before. Newman's essay 'On Consulting the Faithful in Matters of Doctrine' was published in 1859 in the small liberal-minded journal the *Rambler*. In it, Newman recalled the Arian controversy in the early Church when, having been let down by the bishops as official guardians of the faith, the ordinary faithful were called upon to come to her aid, which they did. Newman's essay was denounced in Rome by English Catholic bishops of the time, but was later, after the Vatican Council, to play an important part in restoring the balance of Vatican One's one-sided emphasis on papal infallibility. Indeed, Vatican Two became known as 'Newman's Council' in that it developed a new role for the laity in the Church.

It was thus strange that Woodruff, whose outlook was formed by the ideas of the young historian Sir John (later Lord) Acton (1834–1902), whose granddaughter he had married, came to be so opposed to the outcome of Vatican Two. This may have had something to do with Woodruff's Catholic and European conser-vatism, which owed more to Hilaire Belloc's dictum that 'Europe is the [Catholic] Faith' than was justified both historically and theologically.

Michael Derrick, Woodruff's assistant editor and almost twenty years his junior, was very different from the two Woodruffs, especially in terms of the British class distinctions that survived the Second World War. Fittingly, Derrick prided himself on being 'the best beta mind there is', which meant both being satisfied with being a second in command and holding his own against the formidable Woodruff. English snobbery continued to exert its extraordinary hold, with Woodruff and Derrick presenting almost an instructive Tweedledum and Tweedledee model. With his huge head of greying hair, and being immensely talented and attractive, Derrick held his own against his formidable chief, indeed complemented him in his political views, being a Liberal, and in his encyclopaedic knowledge of ecclesiastical affairs. He had a cool head, was good in a crisis and could generate printable copy on the spur of the moment. He probably inherited his talent from his artistic father, the illustrator Thomas Derrick and his Danish-born grandfather, the painter Sir George Clausen, who made his mark as a foremost English impressionist. Michael's death from cancer in 1961, aged only 46, was a great loss, not least to the *Tablet*.

Death, however, was perhaps preferable to the fate imposed on Woodruff who, having reached the requisite age, was forced into retirement in 1967. His successor was the publisher Tom Burns, who for years had waited for his moment, like Eden following Churchill, but similarly proved not to be up to his predecessor's intellectual stature. Burns, however, happened to be socially as well as religiously acceptable, having sided with the coming changes in the Vatican Two Church, whereas Woodruff's opposition to these was well known. Woodruff got his own back, however, when asked to speak at Burns's seventieth birthday. He gave a brilliant and witty penegyric of Burns as a great publisher, then, to loud applause, sat down. The sting in the tail, however, somewhat along the lines of Shakespeare's 'Brutus is an honourable man', was that he failed to mention, even with one word, that the man honoured that evening had also occupied the *Tablet's* editorial chair for the past ten years. I remember well the open-mouthed faces behind that applause.

My spell in Catholic journalism preceded the second Vatican Council by some years, but in a way it served also to prepare me for the changes to come, which, on the whole, I gladly embraced. When that good and simple Cardinal Angelo Giuseppe Roncalli became pope in 1958, he surprised the world by summoning the second Vatican Council in January 1958, having as a papal diplomat found the church wanting, in both organization and habits of thought, for the needs of the twentieth century. His death in 1963 interrupted the Vatican Council, but he had already left a profound mark on it. Its defining principle was '*aggiornamento*' (adaptation to modern conditions, renewal), but this aim was soon extended and deepened under his successor, Paul VI, into a new endeavour, for instance, how the Church was to differentiate between the various truths it proclaimed. When

the fortieth anniversary of Vatican Two was recently commemorated, one of its voluminous innovations was singled out as
perhaps the most important and far reaching. This concerned its
schemata dealing with the 'Church in the world of our time',
which covered ecumenical relations, particularly those to the
three non-Christian religions, Judaism, Islam and Buddhism.
'*Nostra aetate*' (In our time) the Council's declaration on this
theme was, after a lengthy and most controversial debate, finally
passed in October 1965 by 2221 votes for and 88 against. It was
significant in one overriding aspect, the Church's final recognition of the pluralist and secular character of 'our time' and no
longer the rock or bastion and untouched by these elements, as
for instance was the *Syllabus errorum* in which in 1864 Pius IX
condemned the 80 leading ideas of his time.

The diplomatic silence of Pius XII

In the modern world, the Church could no longer occcupy an
outsider's position and this affected not least its ecumenical
relations with other religions, particular Judaism and the Old
Testament, which due to my personal history remained my
special preoccupation. This also covered the alleged wartime
'silence' of Pius XII. Significantly, it arose only long after his
death through Hochhuth's drama *The Deputy* (1963). It was an
untrue accusation, due above all to the way in which he differed
from his predecessor. The latter had been prone to public protests, while he was the diplomat pope *par excellence*, so was
identified with the disastrous concordats policy by which the
Church sought to cling to a legalistic appeasement of the dictators
that differed hardly from that practised by politicians like Neville
Chamberlain. The German concordat of Pius XI in 1933 was
largely the work of Cardinal Pacelli who was nuncio in Germany
for 13 years, as was the Vatican's 1937 protest against Hitler's
violations of it. I have already referred to the meeting with him
in Switzerland in 1921 by my friend, Friedrich Wilhelm Foerster.
When Cardinal Pacelli was elected as Pius XII, Dr Goebbels,
Hitler's minister of propaganda, then noted in his diary of 4
March 1939 that 'Hitler is considering whether we should give
notice for terminating the concordat altogether in view of Pacelli's
election. This will certainly happen if he does anything hostile.'

Hitler's genocide of the Jews, however, did not become clear,
even to the Vatican, until the end of 1942 when news of the

Polish death camps made the Holy See's previous moves supporting Jewish emigration seem illusory. Konrad von Preysing, the
courageous Bishop of Berlin (1880–1950), appealed to Pius XII
on 6 March 1943 yet again to:

> raise his voice in view of the new wave of deportations,
> which began just before 1 March. Thousands are involved,
> many Catholics among them. You have hinted at their fate
> in your last Christmas broadcast. Would it not be possible
> again to try to intervene on behalf of these unfortunate
> innocents? It is the last hope of many and the heartfelt
> request of all men of goodwill.
> (W. Knauft, *Konrad von Preysing: Anwalt des Rechts*,
> Berlin: Morus Verlag, 1998, p.145)

Pius XII replied on 30 April 1943:

> It must be for the chief pastors on the ground to decide how
> far they can go and whether episcopal interventions are
> advisable *ad maiora mala vitanda* [to prevent greater evils
> from happening] or whether restraint should be exercised.
> This is one of the reasons why We have had to limit Our
> own interventions. ... Everything that is economically and
> morally in the Holy See's power has been done on behalf of
> Catholic Non-Arians as well as believing Jews. ... Our
> rescue work has actually encountered warmest recognition
> from Jewish central organizations. ... In Our last Christmas
> broadcast. We have referred to what is now happening to
> Non-Arians in German political domains. ... As far as the
> present situation is concerned, we are unfortunately unable
> to provide more effective help than our prayers.

A few months later, in October 1943, the Gestapo rounded up
thousands of Roman Jews and sent them to their deaths in
Auschwitz. Their train left from Rome's Tiburtina terminal. Many
people have since wondered why Pius XII did not, in his capacity
as Bishop of Rome, go there in person and stop the train from
leaving. It would have made a unique impact, the more so since he
had privately allowed thousands of Jews to hide in Rome's
ecclesiastical institutions, which, according to Pinchas Lapide, in
his book *Three Popes and the Jews* (1967), 'saved at least

700,000, but possibly 860,000 Jews'. Threatened by Hitler and
Mussolini, he preferred to act, in the interest of the Church,
behind the scenes. When a Roman protest to German Ambassador
von Weizssäcker proved ineffective, the matter was raised again
with the German military commander in Rome, Brigadier General
Rainer Stahel, an Austrian Catholic who was known to be
humane. He sent a telegram to Himmler, claiming that Gestapo
arrests of Jews were interfering with his military actions to
reinforce the German divisions then still fighting to the south of
Rome, thereby endangering the situation in Rome. Himmler
responded by stopping any further arrests and deportations of
Jews. At least in this instance the pope's diplomacy had worked.

On the other hand, however, it was also widely known that
the notorious German Nazi bishop, Alois Hudal, was active in
Rome, helping leading Nazis, Eichmann among them, to escape
to South America. This could not have happened without the
knowledge of the *Curia*, the apparent neutrality of which the
pope was so anxious to preserve.

The question ultimately is can the murder of millions of Jews be
separated completely from the ancient relationship between Christians and Jews? Strictly speaking, of course modern Jewish–
Christian relations were outside the Church's direct responsibility.
In the Old Testament God asked Cain 'Where is thy brother Abel?'
and received the sullen answer 'Am I my brother's keeper?'
(Genesis 4.9) Similarly, the distinction has come into use between
the age-old traditional anti-Judaism and anti-Semitism.

Edith Stein appeals to the pope
Anti-Semitism in its modern racist sense developed only towards
the end of the nineteenth century and today the Church, indeed
Christians everywhere, generally disapprove of it. Anti-Judaism,
however, relating to the 'perfidious' Jews, goes back to the time
of Jesus and Pilate. 'And the whole people, answering said: his
blood be upon us, and upon our children' (Matthew 27.25). The
'disobedience' of the 'stubborn' Jews bearing the curse of having
shed the blood of Christ, culminated in the Isaiah quotation of St
Paul's Letter to the Romans – 'All the day long have I spread my
hands to a people that believeth not and contradicteth me'
(Romans 10.21). Actually, this was hardly less racist than
traditional anti-Judaism, which at least allowed for conversion,
which would be excluded by anti-Semitism in its racist sense.

Nevertheless, it is possible to see a direct link between the persecution of Jews from the beginning of the Christian era, via the destruction of the Temple in Jerusalem, to Marcion, the Gnostic heresiarch (c. AD 180) who wanted to abolish the Old Testament altogether. His racist view long survived his condemnation. The Crusades, with their pogroms on the way to and from the Holy Land, added a new missionary tone to the persecution of the Jews. Later still, the 'Jewish danger' was increasingly seen in terms of national sovereignty, and arising from their domination in trade, industry and finance, though it continued to be overlooked that most other professions had remained closed to them since the Middle Ages. Finally, we get the twentieth century's world conspiracy of Jews, Freemasons and Bolsheviks, which forged a common bond between anti-Judaists and anti-Semites, a major aid for Hitler.

In this connection, a letter from Edith Stein addressed to Pius XI has recently come to light. It was among the unpublished papers in the Vatican's secret archives covering the reign of Pius XI (1922–39) that Pope John Paul released in February 2002. While the Vatican documents of the years 1939–45 are not yet open to research, her letter touches movingly, if only indirectly, on the theme of 'papal silence'. It is undated, but was enclosed sealed with another letter dated 12 April 1933 from the Abbot of Beuron, Raphael Walzer OSB, a friend introducing her to Pius XI as 'known to me and everywhere in Catholic Germany as a woman of high renown through her faith, moral integrity and scholarship'. The cardinal secretary of state, Pacelli, acknowledged receipt on 20 April 1933, saying that he had submitted her letter to the Pope. Dr Edith Stein was then still a lecturer in philosophy at the Collegium Marianum at Münster, but was about to be dismissed with all other Jewish public employees following the new racist legislation introduced when Hitler came to power in January 1933. That October she entered the Cologne Carmelites under the religious name of Theresa Blessed of the Cross. Earlier, she had tried to get a personal audience to submit a special plea to Pius XI, which proved impossible owing to the full agenda of what was then being celebrated as a Holy Year. So, instead of travelling to Rome, she put her urgent plea in writing 'as a child of the Jewish people who through God's grace has been a child of the Catholic Church for eleven years'.

She continues:

> For weeks we have witnessed deeds here in Germany that
> pour scorn on any sort of justice or humanity. For years
> the Nazi leaders have preached hatred of the Jews. And
> now that they are in government the seeds of hatred have
> borne fruit. I am convinced that this is a general
> phenomenon that will have many more victims. For
> weeks not only Jews but thousands of faithful Catholics
> have been hoping that the Church of Christ will raise its
> voice.

She went on to say that under pressure from abroad more lenient
measures had been proposed, but that many had been driven to
despair and that she had personally been told of no fewer than
five suicides due to these pressures. 'One may deplore what little
inner reserves these unfortunates have in coming to terms with
their fate. But in the last resort this is the responsibility of those
who have driven them to these lengths, and, indeed, of those
who have looked on in silence.'

Edith Stein's deep personal concern was for the Church to
make her voice heard and call a halt above all to the sacrilegious
use of the name of Christ in that these deeds are committed by a
government claiming to be Christian. Not only Jews but also
loyal Catholics in Germany and throughout the world want this.
She went on to ask:

> Is not this idolatrous worship of Race and State Violence
> the most blatant heresy, especially as put across by
> incessant radio propaganda? Is not this annihilation of
> Jewish blood a profanation of the holiest humanity of Our
> Redeemer, the Blessed Virgin and the Apostles? Is it not
> totally contrary to the way that Our Lord behaved, Who
> even on the Cross prayed for those who persecuted him?

She ended her letter with 'all of us fear the worst for the good
name of the Church, if she persists in her silence. We are sure
that such silence cannot buy peace with the present German
Government.' While the war against the Church is as yet waged
quietly and less brutally than against Judaism, it would not be
long until Catholics too would come to feel it.

In her recollections written five years later, Edith Stein expressed her disappointment at the Roman reaction to her letter, though she and her family received the Pope's blessing. We now know from the Vatican archives that Cardinal Pacelli, as he then was, had sent a telegram to Nuncio Orsenigo immediately after the boycott of Jewish businesses in Germany and at least a week before Edith Stein's letter reached the Vatican. In it he requested that the possibility of intervening against the 'anti-semitic excesses' in Germany be looked into (Pacelli to Orsenigo, Vatican City, 4 April 1933, Archivio della Congregazione per gli Affari Ecclesiastici Straordinari (AA.EE.SS.), Germania, Pos. 643, fasc. 158, folio 4r).

Thomas Brechenmacher, an historian of the armed forces in Munich, revealed this in a lecture given at the German Historical Institute, London, on 7 December 2004 entitled 'Pope Pius XI, Eugenio Pacelli and the Persecution of the Jews in Nazi Germany: 1933–1939'. He said that:

> The Church found that a nationalistic–materialistic move-ment was putting it in the same boat as Judaism, ... found itself mentioned in the same context as Judaism, whose process of emancipation in the previous century the Church, with its defensive battles against modernity, had often seen as the root of all evil. Pius XI and Pacelli were of sufficient intellectual stature to understand that this unwanted coalition was uncomfortable and to be resisted – a resistance undoubtedly responsible, at least in part, for some of the hesitation after 1933. ... The threat to the Jews was inseparably linked with the threat to the Church. The chance of extricating itself from the unwanted coalition for the sake of its own existence must have been tempting indeed.
>
> (Thomas Brechenmacher, *GHIL Bulletin*, vol. 27, no. 2, November 2005, pp. 24–5)

Pacelli then told Nuncio Orsenigo, widely known for his fascist and anti-Semitic sympathies, that: 'It is traditional for the Holy See to carry its universal mission of peace and love to all people, regardless of class or religion and, where necessary, for its charitable establishment to intervene'. Nevertheless, on 8 April the nuncio had to answer that things had changed. 'Since yesterday the fight against the Jews has taken on a governmental character. Intervention by the Holy See would now amount to a protest against German Law.' This was a reference to the new law legitimating the dismissal of Jewish and Catholic civil servants, which affected Edith Stein and which meant that any official protest by the Church could now be regarded as 'interference in internal affairs'.

A move by German Catholic bishops, led by the Bishop of Berlin von Preysing, to make the German government responsive to the Catholic Church's wishes, inspired by Pacelli's 'universal mission of peace and charity' then followed. Cardinal Faulhaber of Munich, referring to the Jewish/Catholic package, wrote to Pacelli:

> At the moment we bishops are asked the question why the Catholic Church, as so often in its history, does not step in on behalf of the Jews. This is not possibble at the moment because the fight against the Jews would also become a fight against the Catholics and because the Jews can help themselves, as the quick breaking of the boycott shows.
> (Faulhaber to Pacelli, 10 April 1933, AA.EE.SS., Germania, Pos. 643, fasc. 58, fol. 11 rv.)

Here Faulhaber was wrong in that the boycott had neither shown that the Jews could rely on international protest nor that the Church would be unaffected if it stood by merely watching as though untouched by what happened to the Jews. Indirectly, it was clearly involved. Orsenigo told an international Jewish representative, who suggested that Jewish children should be allowed to attend private Catholic schools, that this could not be done because it contravened the principle of 'confessional' (Catholic) schools; and Pacelli congratulated him for his polite rejection.

All the Holy See's hopes clearly rested on its concordat with Hitler, which was to be ratified on 10 September 1933. On 1 September the London *Jewish Chronicle* announced that the 'Pope condemns anti-Semitism. The Pope has expressed his concern about reports of continuing persecution of Jews in Germany. He said that such persecution exposed a lack of civilization in such famous people. ... The Aryan race, he declared, had no right to feel superior to the Semites.' The

Vatican neither confirmed nor denied the report, based apparently on a private remark by Pius XI, but agreed to its private dissemination, as it came conveniently to put more pressure on the Nazis to abide by legal agreements.

However, four years later, in the encyclical *Mit Brennender Sorge*, and in view of the Nazi government's consistent breaches of the concordat, the pope had to concede defeat in dealing legalistically with the new race of dictators. As Edith Stein had predicted, this was not how the Church should deal with evil. She would have been unaware of another approach by Pius XI, who in June 1938, after the Austrian *Anschluss,* commisioned the American Jesuit, John LaFarge, to submit a text for an encyclical, which was to tackle the three modern heresies of totalitarian racism, nationalism and anti-Semitism. With the collaboration of the German Jesuit Gustav Gundlach at the Roman Gregoriana and the French Gustave Desbuquois, LaFarge produced a text based on the traditional differentiation between anti-Semitism, as objectionable, and anti-Judaism, as it had always existed in Catholic practice, and allowing Jews the escape clause of Christian conversion. Such a half-hearted condemnation of anti-Semitism would clearly not have helped the Church's cause.

Whether or not Pius XI was shown the English, German or French versions of *Societatis Unio* (Unity of the Human Race), as the proposed encyclical was to be called, he in any case died in February 1939 and was succeeded in March by Pius XII. Nothing more was heard of the drafts except, understandably, that they were not what was wanted. For nearly four decades, these versions appeared first in France and then in German under the suggestive title of 'The Suppressed Encyclical' before being published in 1997 in a book by Georges Passelecq and Bernard Suchecky called *The Hidden Encyclical of Pius XI*. The time of the Munich Agreement of autumn 1938 and of the triumphs of Hitler and Mussolini was clearly not the moment for further Church protests, not least in view of the Vatican's economic dependence on fascist Italy, which was about to introduce its own racist legislation. There was the additional problem that, before the outbreak of the Second World War, the Vatican was divided between the theologians of the Holy Office, in favour of an early condemnation of Nazi racism and anti-Semitism, and the more powerful Pacelli-led state secretariat.

Since Hitler had then also supported the Spanish civil war against the 'Reds' who were murdering priests, raping nuns and destroying churches, nobody wanted to say anything critical about him. Such was the moral confusion of his Vatican opponents that for a time they regarded Nazi support for nudist bathing as a greater moral evil than Hitler's major aims. In *Der Vatican und Hitler*, Peter Godman, a New Zealander at the Sapienza University in Rome, described Pacelli's diplomacy as 'excessive'. Godman concluded that the ostrich burying its head in the sand would have seemed a more appropriate heraldic emblem than the bold eagle and the dove of peace that Pius XI and Pius XII respectively chose as theirs.

Is the Church institutionally anti-Semitic?

Nothing seemed to illustrate better the need for a basic change in the Church's attitude to the Jews than the one eventually made after the second Vatican Council in connection with the Good Friday prayers. It occurred surprisingly unobtrusively, escaping the general notice of the faithful, as though it were something about which the Christian world had to be deeply ashamed, which of course it was. Since time immemorial, the Good Friday prayers have customarily been held on that day and at the most solemn hour in the Church's calendar when Jesus died on His Cross. The intercessory prayers were said for the Church, pope, clergy, head of government, candidates for baptism, those in need and danger, heretics, Jews and pagans. The brief text of the original prayer was followed by an oration, followed by a call to 'bow your knees' and 'rise again', ending with a silent prayer of the whole congregation.

At some stage in the Middle Ages, the customary kneeling down at the prayer for the Jews stopped, probably in the ninth century by way of popular protest and local demonstrations, which subsequently grew to such an extent that, by the year 1570, it was taken up officially, and incorporated into the first post-Tridentine Missal. The prayer for the Jews became then, as translated from the Latin: 'Let us pray also for the perfidious (unbelieving) Jews, that God Our lord may take away the veil from their hearts and eyes, and that they, too, may recognize our lord Jesus Christ.' An instruction followed for the deacon to omit the customary call to kneel down 'so as not to renew the memory of the infamy, with which the Jews at this hour had mocked the

Redeemer by their bended knees'. Then came the petition, phrased in the sense that God may listen to the perfidious Jews that they may 'not be excluded from his mercy despite their delusion and recognize Christ, as the light of truth, and be raised from their darkness.'

However, a particular attempt at reform occurred in 1926, when anti-Semitic agitation was on the increase, particularly in Germany. A priestly association was formed in Rome, called the 'Amici Israel', a name of course unconnected with the State of Israel, which did not yet exist. Its promoter was Sophie Francisca van Leer, a convert from Judaism then living in Munich, where she was friendly with Cardinal Faulhaber, himself an Old Testament scholar. With his support, the association soon became influential, comprising eventually 19 cardinals, 300 bishops and 3000 priests, all agreeing to oppose anti-Semitism in word and deed.

The Amici's special aim was to seek to reform the Good Friday prayer and its objectionable Latin phrases (at that time the Catholic Mass was still held in Latin) like *pro perfidis Judaeis* (for the faithless Jews) and *judaicam perfidiam* (Jewish faithlessness). Having investigated these, biblical scholars among the Amici, led by Abbot Ildefons Schuster OSB, concluded that *perfidiosus* had to be distinguished from *perfidus*, like *ebriosus* (addicted to drink) from *ebrio* (dunken), that is, one who occasionally offended against the faith, whereas *perfidiosus* was someone lacking faith completely. The meaning of these terms had evidently changed through the ages. These scholars thought it unlikely that when first introduced into the liturgy, the Church had intended them in the sense of total depravity, in which contemporary anti-Semites used them. Moreover, the usual justification for the difference between the normal kneeling down and its refusal, allegedly that this had been done by the Jews, was clearly contradicted in the Gospel, which explicitly referred to Roman soldiers having mocked the imprisoned Christ in this way. It was clearly a matter of abolishing some 'superstitious' practice that had been added later.

The findings were submitted to the liturgical commission of the Congregation of Rites, which approved them in January 1928, but first the consent of the Holy Office had to be obtained, which changed matters altogether. Appointed as the pope's special representative to respond, Marco Sales, a Dominican, admitted first that as far as doctrine and faith were concerned, there were no objections to such a reform. However, as to suitability this was quite a different issue, and for the following reasons:

1. The Amici Israel was a purely private body trying to tamper with the venerable liturgy, which was intolerable.
2. The etymological considerations, according to Sales, had to be rejected, particularly the distinction between *perfidus* and *perfidiosus*. The ordinary meaning was of somebody breaking his or her word or agreement, which was precisely what God in the Bible had accused the Jews of having done. 'No wonder *perfidi* and *perfidia Iudaica* is applied to them rather than to the pagans.'
3. As for the refusal to kneel and pray for *perfidis* Jews, this was part of venerable antiquity and therefore beyond what could be reformed.
4. The Jews had assumed responsibility for the Crucifixion of Christ, not least in the words 'His blood be upon us and our children' (Matthew 27.25).

Sales concluded his very deplorable and 'politically correct' reasoning, *Nihil esse innovandum* (Nothing shall be changed).

Worse was to come for the Amici, for among its highly placed members, indeed the secretary of the Holy Office, was Cardinal Raffaele Merry del Val (1865–1930), an Anglo-Spaniard and notorious integralist who had played a leading part in the modernist persecutions under St Pius X. When Merry de Val received an invitation to attend the second anniversary of the Amici Israel, which he seemed to have regarded as a harmless fraternity for the conversion of Jews, his anger was boundless. He had the Amici anniversary banned and started proceedings against them in the Holy Office.

When the cardinals met on 7 March 1928, Merry del Val proposed they reject the Good Friday prayer reform. The Good Friday prayer, he argued, was not about the conversion of Jews but about the curse for their stubbornness. They were responsible for having shed the blood of Christ and he condemned, in increasingly violent racist language, the latest attempt by 'Hebrewism, with the support of Talmudic sects, perfidiously to rebuild the reign of Israel against Christ and his Church'. He then described the 'Amici Israel' as 'infamous' and asked for its censure because of its association, by implication, with all that was evil, namely freemasonry and Jewish ritual murders. His words hardly differed from the worst Nazi vituperations. Finally, he called for the reprimand of Abbot Schuster for having played the Jews' game through his attempt to remove from the Church's sacred rite an 'alleged superstition'. The majority of Holy Office cardinals, who supported their secretary's votum, also decided on the 'dissolution' or 'downgrading of the Amici Israel to a simple prayer group', and called for the severe reprimand of Abbot Schuster.

To become effective, the decree of dissolution needed the pope's signature and Pius XI took an even more serious view of Jewish interference in matters of the Catholic faith, as he regarded it. There was no hint of the expression 'spiritually we are Semites', for which that Pope later came to be specially remembered. To avoid possible repercussions and renewed accusations of anti-Semitism against the Church, careful steps were taken to conceal certain matters from the decree. These were that it was the wretched Amici Israel that had wanted to reform the Good Friday prayer for the Jews, that the proposal had the full approval of the Congregation of Rites and, shamefully, that the Holy Office and pope had been the sole objectors. The affair naturally caused great offence to Jews at the time who found the Catholic Church thus linked with traditional anti-Semitism. Since the Vatican could hardly go on pretending to be both for and against anti-Semitism, Father Enrico Rosa, the Jesuit editor of *Civiltà Cattolica*, the papal organ, was bidden to bridge the painful dilemma. He did so in the Church's manner of those days, with an article already ominously entitled *Il pericolo Giudaico e gli Amici d'Israele* (The Jewish danger and the Amici Israel). Distinguishing between 'the un-Christian form of anti-Semitism' and what he described as a 'healthy estimate of the danger threatening from the Jews', Rosa argued that the 'rascist attitude based on party-political reasons or passions or materialist interests' was clearly damned by the decree dissolving the Amici itself. But 'with similar zeal the Church must guard against the other, no less dangerous extreme, misled through apparent goodness, into which that organization had fallen'.

Humanity, including the Catholic Church, needed another great war, indeed the death of six million Jews, to bring about, in the era of Vatican Two, the changes in the Good Friday prayer that the Amici Israel had sought in vain. With blatant disregard for what the Church had authorized in previous centuries, the controversial terms 'perfidious' and 'faithless' Jews as well as the traditional prayer for the 'conversion' of 'unbelieving Jews' were discarded and dropped as though they had never been used before. Instead, now the people of the Old Testament are directed to find their own salvation. Moreover, the prayer was advanced to sixth place, between the two prayers for the unity of Christians and the prayer for all those who do not believe in Christ. (I am indebted to Dr Hubert Wolf, professor of church history at the University of Münster, for these latest findings concerning the Amici Israel in a lecture to the Bavarian Catholic Academy, Munich, in May 2004. The text of *Pro perfidis Judaeis* also appears in *Historische Zeitschrift,* no. 279, 2004, pp. 611–58.)

The shameful incident seems to confirm the view of Olaf Blaschke, a Catholic historian at Trier University, that anti-Semitism is an 'institutional characteristic' of the Catholic Church, but also perhaps that the Church is willing to learn from the lessons of the past. To highlight the contradictions characteristic of the changing theological notions of the times, even Cardinal Faulhaber, who courageously criticized Hitler's early persecutions of the Jews in his Advent sermons of 1934, spoke of them in the traditional Christian sense as 'divorced from God'. The mentality of that Catholic generation following the First Vatican Council could clearly be regarded as not only traditionally anti-Judaistic but also if not openly as anti-Semitic.

Little over half a century later, Pope John Paul II emphasized in 1980 that God stood by his never abrogated bond with Israel and spoke of Jews and Christians as 'Abraham's children, called upon to bless the world in their common fight for peace and justice'. In the Holy Year of 2000, he pleaded for forgiveness for 'the sufferings which not a few Catholics committed against the people of the Old Testament'. On behalf of his own generation, in which he included the reigns of Pius XI and Pius XII, he sent, in 2005, the year of his own death, Cardinal Jean-Marie Lustiger, himself a converted Jew, to renew the pledge on the sixtieth anniversary of the liberation of Auschwitz. This was that 'Monstrously capable of evil as man is, and as the Bible shows him to be, evil will not have the last word.'

The convulsions surrounding the problem of anti-Semitism include a mysterious element, namely that one cannot ascribe

Hitler's murder of the Jews to German anti-Semitism. According to Daniel Goldhagen's thesis in *Hitler's Willing Executioners*, pre-1914 Germany was one of the most philo-Semitic countries in Europe. Anti-Semitism was then far more rampant in parts of Eastern Europe like Poland and Romania, and in Austria, where Hitler was born, and more public in France than in Germany. How is it that the culture of anti-Semitism did not lead to worse murderous excesses in those countries? The reason must lie, I believe, in the pressures and special conditions of totalitarian rule, with its constant search for new victims, scapegoats, and the need to find a public enemy number one. In Germany, this happened to be the Jews, but other unpopular minorities like gypsies and homosexuals, would have served equally well, as many of them did, as outlets for the whipped-up popular frenzy and fury.

The Swiss philosopher Max Picard came close to realizing this in his book *Hitler in Ourselves* (1945). Fittingly, Picard compared the evil of Hitlerism with a festering boil growing on an infected body. Post-1918 Germany, suffering defeat, social unrest, revolution, unemployment and inflation, provided just such a fertile ground. Picard had already written about the human face and he now used that of the anonymous First World War soldier, Hitler, to demonstrate how such an unremarkable face could achieve universal acclaim. At a time of discontinuity, Hitler's nondescript face, showing neither crime nor insanity, had an enormous and magnetic effect on the masses, especially women. According to Picard, this was not a phenomenon of the political, sociological or psychological orders, but rather the offspring of demons. The atrocities such men committed were merely 'incidental', like by-products of a machine that could be adjusted at one moment to crime, at another to public welfare or even to building autobahns.

It was not surprising that in such a disjointed world Himmler, the head of the Gestapo, would be adept at playing Bach, or Heydrich, the hangman of Czechoslovakia, weep tears when listening to Mozart. Murder, music, the gas chamber and the concert hall were all part of one meaningless whole. No wonder Goethe was a particularly popular author in the lending libraries of concentration camp SS guards. For Picard, the decline of humanity was similarly evident in the shabby rationalizations of anti-Semitism over the centuries – from Bossuet's denunciations of Jews as calumniators of Christ, from Viennese mayor Lueger's

hate objects wielding international economic power, right down
to the ultimate Nazi degradation of reducing people to the
numbers tattooed on their arms. Picard's Hitler lacked even the
makings of a dramatic evil hero such as Richard III. For years, he
stood on the verge of victory; however, being an evil nothing,
ultimate success evaded him. He did not even achieve the
maliciously desired final triumph of a Wagnerian *Götter-
dämmerung* (fall of the gods).

The world was spared that fate, which showed that, as Picard
believed, there is some intervening love of the earth and of
mankind that only religious faith can explain. Having long hesitated to receive baptism, being ashamed to desert the persecuted
Jews, in 1939 Picard and his son were eventually received into
the Catholic Church. As he wrote to his friend, Monsignor John
M. Oesterreicher, also a convert from Judaism, 'my feelings
finally mattered not anymore, I simply had to be where truth
was, and so we both were baptized.'

9

Lord Jones – Alive or Dead?

Journalists rank among the very last in the social esteem scales of British opinion polls, a fate they share in these isles with politicians. Abroad journalists fare a little better, enjoying more respect as belonging to the educated middle classes, though this would naturally also depend on the quality of their particular journals. The British, moreover, are said to be greater newspaper readers than others, which hardly corresponds with the earlier finding, unless purely as a matter of circulation figures where biggest is worst. These findings evidently do not spread much enlightenment. The public's low regard for journalists tends to stop short of foreign correspondents, such as I have been throughout my professional life.

Ignorance, rather than any other factor, seems to explain that state of affairs, as the example of a well-known French correspondent may show. He had not been back to his country, except for brief holidays, but his Maurice Chevalier-like accent sounded very convincing. He was immensely popular on TV discussion panels, where impressions and generalizations matter more than what is actually said. So much for the deceptive nature of the box, though over the radio waves this man's voice conveyed the French touch the audience expected. G. K. Chesterton, who was also a good journalist among other things, was right to observe that journalism consists of saying that 'Lord Jones is dead' to people who never knew that Lord Jones was alive.

Foreign journalists have a slightly different status, given that they come under the protective umbrella of the Foreign Office or elsewhere the ministry of foreign affairs. Being concerned about their country's image abroad, it is customary for these to take an interest in what foreign journalists write about them. Long gone are the days when London professed a superior disdain for that.

However, leading newspapers everywhere naturally carried a particular weight of their own. In the early, more leisurely, days foreign journalists anxious to have policy matters explained to them would submit their written questions to a clerk on duty, who would then ask them to collect the answer a week later. Since then, well-staffed press and information departments have grown up everywhere, whose task it is to look after the needs of journalists and ward off unwelcome outside intrusions.

If foreign correspondents in Britain expected as much deferential treatment as they got in their own countries, they were disappointed. This of course also reflects the different social status of these people – overall foreign correspondents tend to be better educated than other journalists are. I remember well from my own time as president of the Foreign Press Association in London, in the 1980s, having annually to fight for the protection of our members' interests at the British party conference season, usually held at seaside resorts like Brighton or Blackpool. While equivalent events abroad would cater naturally for the foreign interest, in Britain this happened only very slowly in the postwar decades. The Wilson- or Callaghan-led Labour Party, oddly, seemed particularly insular about recognizing the interest abroad in their annual political jamborees, though the Conservatives were not much better. The British party organizations tended to regard these conference rounds as for home consumption mainly. This would naturally be a priority interest in every country. But be it because of the more limited accommodation for that annual influx of hundreds of the party faithful as well as outside observers, or due to seating limitation, government parties abroad would have considered that foreign interest much more readily. For the foreign media, these events of course provided major insights into the particular party political grassroots.

Insularity breeds contempt
Insularity, however, is not a British prerogative. Similar attitudes to foreigners exist everywhere, though here they may be more politely disguised and therefore less noticeable. Every country looks after its own first, and cheers its own teams, which Lord Tebbit once declared was the loyalty test for those who had come to this country from abroad. Still, he drew a line between hard-hitting, yet seemingly more mannerly cricket finals and the mass hysteria engendered by a very different game, football. As

for the famous *Evening Standard* headline 'Fog in Channel – Continent isolated', by which British insularity was forever branded, this may in fact be easily translated into any national attitude, with inhabitants of mountain villages tending traditionally to be the most insular. The inhabitants of islands are at least encouraged to leave them to explore wider horizons, as the British have shown in their history.

But national differences are liable to change. Queuing, for example, is an evidently newish characteristic of the British. Similarly, nowadays we would find it strange to share the view of the Venetian ambassador to Henry VIII, Andrea Trevisano, who in 1497 described the English as 'the greatest epicures'. Then, again, the Dutch merchant Emanuel van Meteren reported after a tour of England in 1575 that they were 'fed well and delicately' and the Swiss Thomas Platter in 1599 described English dishes as 'well prepared, with exquisite sauces'. Only after 1643 and the Puritans where all sauces — except those mixed with bread, mint or onion – were regarded as un-English and therefore wrong. Similarly, after two world wars, British comedians and cartoonists continue to pillory the Germans' goose-stepping, which is now confined to Russians and Chinese.

This links up with changes in Britain's position in the world. The British parliamentary system is no longer widely regarded as a model to emulate. Some 30 years ago Lord Hailsham denounced what he then first called Great Britain's 'prime ministerial elective dictatorship' and many now feel that this has since become a tragic reality. In the course of this development, the parliament at Westminster has lost much of the power it once enjoyed in the politics of this country, bringing it more into line with elected assemblies elsewhere. This has contributed to greater equality between the home-based and foreign media, which, as I mentioned, has long existed abroad; the British government has finally accepted what is convenient and necessary.

In 1957 I joined the staff of a leading German newspaper, *Frankfurter Allgemeine Zeitung.* For a longstanding London resident like me, it was an unusual appointment in the circumstances of the time, but they needed someone who was familiar with British political and cultural affairs. As a foreign correspondent, I was able to make use of the office facilities the Foreign Office and British government had, since 1945, made available in the magnificent Nash building at 11 Carlton House Terrace with great views across The Mall and St James's Park to Big Ben and, of course, of London's royal occasions. The house had been the one-time London residence of W. E. Gladstone, four times prime minister and, from his private diaries, since published in many volumes, we know of his nightly excursions to nearby Haymarket on his private Christian apostolate to rescue prostitutes. At the time, only a few people knew about his pastime and they had reason to fear that a wider public might come to know about it and thus ruin the career of this pillar of Victorian rectitude.

Great scenes in the Commons

One of my journalistic duties was to attend regular parliamentary events like the weekly Prime Minister's Questions and important debates. From the upper gallery of the House of Commons, reserved for the foreign press, I have witnessed many great parliamentary events. One was the appearance of a very ancient Sir Winston Churchill, as though loath to leave the place of his finest hour, totteringly making his way to his honoured seat on the lower front bench while other MPs respectfully made room for him. I heard the resignation speech of the suave minister of war John Profumo over his affair with Christine Keeler, who had also been the Soviet defence attaché's lover. It was considered demeaning that he had 'misled', lied to, the House of Commons and it was the lie that led to his downfall and sacrifice of a promising career. Many, especially from abroad, saw it as typical British hypocrisy. Shamedly and selflessly, he worked his passage back to respectability through social work. There were harsh debates over the Suez crisis, when Eden incongruously compared Egypt's Colonel Nasser with Hitler, not to mention the Falklands war, in which Margaret Thatcher had to prove her mettle. Finally, there was the resignation speech of Thatcher's deputy, the soft-voiced Sir Geoffrey, now Lord Howe, sending, as it were, poisoned arrows across the House, while their target sat stony-faced on the front bench, never once facing her accuser.

I have to admit that I was unable to convey the full drama of Thatcher's fall as the late Alan Clark MP has done in his *Diaries* (1994), a few extracts of which may give their flavour:

> *Tuesday 13 November.* The Party is virtually out of control, mutinous. Apparently the entire text of Geoffrey's speech is the work of Elspeth [Lady Howe].

Later: From the moment he rose to his feet Geoffrey got into it. He was personally wounding, to a far greater extent than mere policy differences would justify. Elspeth's hand [was] in every line. ... Geoffrey ended his speech with an ominous and strange sentence: 'I have done what I believe to be right for my Party and for my Country' (they all say that). The time has come for others to consider *their own response* to the tragic conflict of loyalties, with which I have wrestled for perhaps too long.

Wednesday 14 November 1990. A curious state of limbo. Briefly, and unaccountably, the House has gone quiet. Many are leaving early for their constituencies to take the temperature. The papers are terrible. The Lady is said to be 'foundering'; 'holed below the watering line'; 'stabbed'; 'bowled middle stump'; and similar far from original metaphors. ...

Monday 19 November 1990. The whole House of Commons is in ferment, little groups, conclaves everywhere. ... I went into the members' tearoom. The long table was crowded with Margaret supporters, all nonentities except for Tebbit who was cheering people up. Norman [Lamont] was saying how unthinkable it was to consider dismissing a Prime Minister during a critical international conference. 'Like Potsdam in 1945' I said. Nobody paid any attention. ... I write this very late, and I am very tired. Perhaps I'm just needlessly depressed. I'd ring the Lady if I could, but she's at a Paris banquet. She's not even coming back for the ballot tomorrow. ...

Tuesday 20 November 1990. The afternoon hung interminably. ... As is my style at all counts I went up to the committee floor very late. A huge crowd in the corridor. The entire lobby, TV teams from all over the world. ... There was, inevitably, a balls-up over the figures. ... We, the Tory MPs, packed tight and jumpily joking to each other in the committee room, did not get the figures first, a monstrous error. We heard something between a gasp and a cheer from outside the door, as the journalists digested first the closeness of the result then the killer element —

that there had to be a second ballot. Four votes, that was
all there was in it. ... Later at dinner to my amazement
they were all confident ... 'the abstainers will all come in,
you don't understand, Alan, all those people who wanted
to give her a fright, they'll support her now she's up
again.' How can people get it so wrong? ...

Wednesday 21 November 1990. This is going to be –
politically – the Longest Day ... not only my own prospects, but the whole edifice which we have constructed
around the Lady, are in ruins. It is quite extraordinary.
Fifteen years have gone by and yet those very same people
– Dykes, Charlie Morrison, Tony Grant, Barney Hayhoe –
who have hated her and the values she stood for, are still
around in the lobbies, grinning all over their faces – 'at
last we've got her.'

Later. ... I went down the stairs and rejoined the group
outside her door. Peter said: 'I can just fit you in now – but
only for a split second, mind.' She looked calm, almost
beautiful. 'Ah, Alan ...' – 'You're in a jam' – 'I know that' –
'They're telling you not to stand, aren't they?' – 'I'm going
to stand. ...' – 'That's wonderful. ... But the Party will let
you down' – 'I am a fighter' – 'Fight then. Fight right to the
end, a third ballot, if you need to. But you lose.' – There
was quite a little pause. – 'It'd be so terrible if Michael
[Heseltine] won. He would undo everything I have fought
for.' 'But what a way to go! Unbeaten in three elections,
never rejected by the people. Brought down by nonentities.'
'But Michael ... as Prime Minister' – 'Who the fuck's
Michael? No one. Nothing. He won't last six months'. ...
Afterwards I felt empty. And cross ... sadness envelops me
... of dangers and injustices remaining, of the greed,
timidity and short-sightedness of so many in public life.'

Albany, Thursday 22 November 1990. Very early this
morning the telephone rang, it was Tristan [Garel-Jones].
'She is going. ...' There will be an official anouncement,
after a short Cabinet. Then the race will be on. ...
Apparently John Major is going to stand.

13. Centre of a London correspondent's political world.

Passions and tempers still rise in that chamber, invective still fights against sweet reason or adept ministerial sidestepping. All these great moments are history. Now those green leather benches are rarely full. The increase of the prime minister's powers, not least through nearly a decade of huge majorities of the governing Labour Party led by Tony Blair and the impotence of the opposition parties, has apparently reduced the role of the people's elected representatives. Perhaps their hour will return when the numbers between government and opposition parties are more evenly balanced and what they say may again matter and more decisively affect the balance of power.

To look down from the press gallery inevitably links one to 450 years of parliamentary history under one roof, even though the roof has changed. The voices of Macaulay, Lord John Russell, Bright, Gladstone and Disraeli had been heard in that chamber when, on 10 May 1941, German bombs plucked it out with such neatness that the corridors leading to it were virtually unharmed. The new chamber, now looking more like a television studio, has nevertheless preserved the tradition of the past, with the two red lines that separate the factions still set two sword lengths apart to avoid any unseemly fracas between members. I remember stunning moments, like when Michael Heseltine, the Tory, in an incomprehensible pique, Tarzan-like with his blond mane seized the gilded mace, the symbol of parliamentary rule, and swung it threateningly in the air until fellow MPs managed to restrain him. I also remember the minute young Irish Catholic, Bernadette Devlin, crossing the chamber to inflict tooth and nail retribution on some wretched Conservative.

The chamber's new ceiling, made of wood from the Commonwealth, has now mellowed and invisible lighting gives it an artificial but pleasing daylight effect. From my place in the upper gallery, I could hear but not see the speaker, sitting directly underneath on the high chair raised above the benches and behind the large table separating the two front benches. To the speaker's right are the government and its supporters, to the left the members of the Opposition and the Liberal Democrats. Facing the speaker, beyond the table with its two dispatch boxes and the glittering mace, there is the bar, on the left of which sits the sergeant-at-arms, the only other non-member who is responsible for the management and general maintenance of order of the House of Commons, wearing a sword and knee breeches. He may be required forcibly to restrain some unruly MP and conduct him or her out of the House, as when recently anti-fox hunting demonstrators penetrated the chamber. The House of Commons bar marks the end line on the floor carpet, from which no member may speak.

Outwardly, little seems to have changed since June 1783 when the German pastor Karl Philip Moritz visited the House of Commons. He commented with surprise, as foreigners have done ever since, on the leisurely, relaxed ways of the MPs:

> It was not uncommon to see a member lying stretched out on one of the benches, while others are debating. ... There is no end to their going in and out; and as often as any wishes to go out, he places himself before the speaker, and makes him his bow, as if, like a school-boy, he asked his teacher's permission. Those who speak seem to deliver themselves with but little, perhaps not always with even a decorous, gravity. All that is necessary is to stand up in your place, take off your hat, turn to the speaker (to whom all the speeches are addressed); to hold your hat and stick in one hand, and with the other hand to make any such motions as you fancy necessary to accompany your speech.
>
> The little less than downright open abuse, and the many really rude things, which the members said to each other, struck me much. For example, when one has finished, another rises, and immediately taxes with absurdity all that the right honourable gentleman (for with this title the members of the House of Commons always honour each other) has just advanced.
>
> (Francesca M. Wilson (ed.) *Strange Island*, 1955, p. 113.)

I remember other no less typical parliamentary occasions, not least those moments of almost orgiastic hypocrisy when a member of the Commons died and, as was the custom, colleagues paid tribute to his or her merits. Those were moments of the greatest English rhetoric when MPs outbid each other in sentimental outpourings that bore no relation whatsoever to the late honourable gentleman or lady's real qualities or lack of them.

In my time, most major British diplomatic and foreign jour-nalists attended the daily 12.30 p.m. Foreign Office press briefings, but long since abolished for lack of demand. The outside world is no longer eager to hear about the British foreign secretary's daily engagements, or to know what he might say to whom. The news department's representatives, usually elevated officials due for ambassadorial postings, became our good friends. One was the unforgettable Peter Matthews, popular not least for his *bon mots* and knowledge of drastic expressions in many languages. He once described a newspaper report as worthy only for use in the *Scheisshäusel* (a Bavarian diminutive for shithouse), which he was able to pronounce perfectly. Unfortunately, my German newspaper, with its regard for serious politics and no interest in 'spicy' stories, scorned the use of such language; in fact, leading British dailies, even in their then much more respectable mode, were using far more risqué language than would have been tolerated in Germany.

George Brown, of the 1966 Labour government, was among the British foreign secretaries I remember best, though less for his outstanding qualities than for his likeable if ludicrous behaviour. The clangers he was famous for dropping were increasingly alcohol induced and he often found it difficult even to stand up. What admirable presence of mind the French ambassador's wife once showed when she reacted to his approaches at a dinner by exclaiming: 'Oh, Mr Brown, you are the first man to have proposed this to me before the soup.' A special link connected me with Brown in that I had frequently to collect the keys of the Foreign Press Association, when I wanted to work there after office hours, from his residence at 1 Carlton House Terrace. A doorman invariably opened the door, accompanied by Brown's faithful, sad-eyed, long-eared, tail-wagging basset hound, which was the spitting image of his master.

I covered the British political scene under seven prime ministers, ranging from Winston Churchill to Margaret Thatcher. I came to know Sir Edward Heath because he liked to discuss his prewar memories of Germany and Austria and prided himself on his opposition to appeasement. His tragedy was to have lost out to dictators in their British reincarnation as trade unionists and not to have forgiven the woman he had launched on her career (as he forever reminded one). She was able to answer 'his' question 'Who governs Britain?' more successfully than he could in that awful, strike-plagued February of 1974. For that, he deserved to be judged as curmudgeonly and vain, while she proved big enough, on his death, to acknowledge his undoubted merits. He could be kind, generous and very witty in a deadpan way, as I discovered when I visited his London flat in the Albany and later, at Arundell in the Close, a beautifully peaceful enclave facing Salisbury Cathedral. I remember him recalling some of the great opera singers who were contemporaries of my mother's. Late in the evening, with other guests present, he would improvise on his grand piano, a Steinway, from Richard Strauss operas. He had a marvellous collection of classical records, with several versions of the same work by great conductors, and talked knowingly about their finest points, though I always felt that there was something didactic about his musicality, derived perhaps from a lack of musical culture in his home background.

Lady Margaret Thatcher, by contrast, was more difficult to get to know, distrusting, it seemed, of those she regarded as 'not one of us'. I mentioned this impression once to one of her closest cabinet colleagues, to which he answered: 'Don't worry, old chap, that's how she looks at all of us.' I always disliked those typically male reactions amd thought that many men, confronted by a woman of her indomitable energy and spirit, cowardly feared an argued response, which she of course liked to provoke. They would rather say what they thought of her behind her back.

I had written the first German biography of Thatcher in 1988, in which I tried to resist such 'knocking' postures and when favourable reviews appeared in the British press, she wrote kindly to thank me. My book was not a bestseller, and a few years later the publisher decided to sell the remaindered copies, offering them cheaply to me. I wondered whether she might like to have them for PR purposes, but she politely declined. This was not surprising because her contacts with things German and German politicians were not particulary happy. The German media, for example, evidently taking their cue from hostile British sources, were particularly malicious about her.

The FO blocks Maggie's view

I once stood next to her outside 10 Downing Street while she was waiting for Chancellor Helmut Schmidt to arrive on an official visit. It was a fine day, but as usual darkness fell early in that narrow side street, with the massive Foreign Office opposite blocking out the sun. 'Terrible, that Foreign Office is always in the way,' was her telling comment. That day's visitor was known as a typical 'male chauvinist', a tendency towards which German politicians like the two Helmuts, Schmidt and Kohl, were particularly prone. Schmidt failed to endear himself to the grocer's daughter when they shared a platform at public meetings by blowing his cigarette fumes into her face. Another of his discourteous habits was to lean back in his chair and stare into empty space while she was speaking. These two German politicians clearly underrated the Iron Lady's challenge, or, perhaps buoyed by the anti-Thatcherites in the British media, did not bother to conceal their bad manners.

Britain was becoming a middle-ranking power with many of its previously renowned instititutions such as parliament, the Church of England and the monarchy no longer enjoying universal respect. There was more crime and less civility. The proud old British epithet 'second to none' was becoming a term of sarcastic blame. For me, who owed my survival to this country, it was a painful spectacle to witness, however much the whole of our Western world seemed to be sharing in that politico-cultural process of decline. The losers of the last world war have all overtaken Great Britain in matters of public health, transport, education and, certainly not least, the quality of life they can offer their citizens.

The attitude of foreign correspondents towards this country naturally reflected the changes in Britain's status. All was well so long as the formerly admired institutions and standards functioned properly, but Britain's image was growing visibly more negative. While far-reaching changes have occurred through the security measures introduced since 9/11, even before that the fall of the Berlin Wall and the dismantling of the Iron Curtain had made an impact on the society. Following terrorist attacks by students in the German Federal Republic and in Italy, heavily armed police officers started to guard continental airports, while Britain had to contend with the IRA.

In the face of terrorism on the European continent and at home, the British have been reluctant to forego their trust in the goodness of human nature – unless it spoke English with an Irish accent. It took a long time for British people to accept that some of their fellow men or women might turn out to be sworn enemies. This explains why the security measures that were introduced after every fatal IRA bomb attack proved so ineffective. One needs to be reminded that Downing Street, now heavily fenced off from Whitehall, was once open to pedestrians to stroll through to St James's Park.

I used to park my car opposite Number Ten when attending meetings with the prime minister's press spokesperson. Once I inadvertently locked the front door of my Volvo, with the car keys still dangling from the dashboard. Having no spare key on me, I went to the police officer on duty outside Number Ten to explain my predicament. 'Just a moment, Sir, maybe I can help,' he replied and turned to his colleague with: 'Watch the shop for me, will you, Jack.' He disappeared inside and was soon back with two teaspoons, saying 'Let's have a look'. Like an adroit car thief he then bent one of the spoons, pushed it through under the rubber layer of the front door's quarterlight window, pulling the lever knob towards himself, while using the other spoon to lift the inside lever, and thus opened the small driver's side window. He could then put his hand through and open the door, saying triumphantly: 'There you are. Bob's your uncle!' Thank God for England, I thought to myself, while thanking him. And this was when the Bader Meinhof terrorists were active on the Continent and one could hardly imagine policemen on duty in Paris or Bonn performing such samaritan services.

I was then a regular weekly caller to the PM's press representatives. When the brass knocker in the shape of a heraldic lion was activated, an inside attendant would open the famous door instantly and, according to someone's count, this happened about 700 times a day. George Downing apparently made a packet out of the English civil war by building a few ramshackle houses on that spot near Whitehall. Today, only three are left, 'Number 10', which, according to the plaque on the door, belongs to the 'First Lord of the Treasury', the official title of Britain's first minister. The Chancellor of the Exchequer, who is in charge of the state's finances and expenses, resides at 'Number 11' and a bit further down, near the end of the road, is 'Number 12'. Internal passages, nowadays used mainly for special prime ministerial briefings, link all three houses.

'Number 10' has been the residence of British prime ministers since the time of Sir Robert Walpole. He was the first in the modern sense to have enjoyed both royal confidence and parliamentary support. Lord North, who was an occupant towards the end of the eighteenth century, had to announce the defection of

Great Britain's American colonies. Then came Pitt the Younger who, under threat from Napoleon, spent 17 years there while his debts mounted like the bottles of port he consumed, but who at least had the satisfaction of finally hearing of Nelson's victory at Trafalgar. A later inhabitant, Disraeli, returned from the Congress of Berlin with the historic announcement that 'Peace, I hope, with honour' had been achieved, which, probably because it was so rare, caused Neville Chamberlain in 1938 to repeat it, particularly unfittingly, while additionally waving a piece of paper with Hitler's signature on it.

Less than three decades earlier Lord Asquith had counted the minutes and seconds passing without an answer from Berlin on 4 August 1914 when, according to Sir Edward Grey, the 'lights went out all over Europe'. Asquith then coined the phrase 'wait and see', which was to become so beloved of English pragmatists, though under a later Downing Street resident like Neville Chamberlain, it was customary to add the phrase 'and do nothing'. And so, in 1939 Great Britain and Germany were once again at war. It was left to Winston Churchill to make his famous V-sign in Downing Street six years later. Among all the changes of residents at 10 Downing Street since then, one of the most memorable must surely have been the arrival of Great Britain's first woman prime minister. When she arrived at 10 Downing Street in October 1979, she decided, unusually, to quote St Francis of Assisi: 'Where there is discord, may we bring harmony; where there is error, may we serve truth; where doubt faith; where despair may we strengthen hope.' Rarely had such a pious wish provoked such a strong yell of derision.

When 10 Downing Street was being renovated in the second half of the last century, the idea of a completely new building was rejected in favour of keeping the modest façade, but rebuilding nearly everything inside. Its small frontage belies the depth, comprising about one hundred rooms. The renovation led to some archaeological finds from England's Roman occupation, also of the brewery operated by the monks of Abingdon, when 'White Hall' was the royal residence. Also discovered were the remains of a building Henry VIII had used for cockfights, and the Stuarts had used as a theatre. Under Cromwell, it was used for religious music.

An agreeable, intimate atmosphere characterizes the inside of 10 Downing Street, which differs from the residences of state leaders elsewhere and has the feeling of a private home. There are flowers in the entrance hall and the open fireplace provides a popular backdrop for photographs of handshakes between the PM and foreign visitors. In a corner stands a fine leather-covered Chippendale chair in which the duty door attendant or one of the policemen can take a nap in the early hours of the morning. From the entrance hall, a long passage leads to the cabinet room, which has a window facing out onto St James's Park and Horse Guards Parade. The cabinet table is boat-shaped, so that every minister can see and hear everyone else. In front of each of the 21 seats is a leather folder bearing the name of the particular ministerial department by which people here address one another. On the light-brown tablecloth stand two jugs of water with glasses and three silver candelabras. The chairs are covered in beige and red leather and only the prime minister's one, which is in the middle with his back to the chimney, has arm supports. The offices of the secretariat are next door and reached via steps leading down to a walled garden. About 130 people work there in the daytime.

A staircase with an iron parapet leads from the ground floor to the reception rooms on the first floor. As you ascend the stairs, you pass the portraits of all the previous residents, engravings at first and photographs later. Even in two rows, there is hardly enough room for all 55 of them. The reception rooms contain some fine paintings of landscapes, as well as portraits of Nelson, Pitt, Wellington, Joseph Priestley (the chemist and discoverer of oxygen), Sir Humphrey Davy (who invented the security lamp for miners), and Michael Faraday (who discovered electromagnetism). When French guests are present, it is customary for the host to apologize for the large patriotic paintings celebrating the victory over Napoleon and for the guests to proffer an indulgent smile. Beside the prime minister's elegantly furnished office just above the staircase are three large reception rooms in the style of William Kent, containing paintings by Romney, Van Dyck and Turner. There is some fine English furniture on loan from the Victoria & Albert Museum and old Persian carpets cover the floors. The large dining room, built by Sir Hans Sloane, normally seats 32 guests around a Chippendale table with matching chairs. When there are 60 guests a horseshoe shaped table is used with smaller golden-coloured chairs.

Like other stately homes, 10 Downing Street boasts a ghost, a lady in a scarlet dress who has not made an appearance for a quarter of a century. Residing over 'the shop' has become the practice, somewhat grudgingly accepted by most of the modern tenants. The flat, situated on the second and third floors, is an evident convenience, though rather cramped if there are several children. From the prime minister's official net salary of £165,000, 10 per cent is deducted for rent for this nobly convenient *pied-à-terre* in central London.

Churchill's mouse

There is also a splendid country residence, 'Chequers', of Tudor origins, idyllically situated in a sheltered valley of the Chiltern Hills about 40 miles from London. It was the gift of a benefactor, Lord Lee of Faversham, to the prime ministers for all times and comprises 1500 acres of farmland and woods. There are lovely walks, for instance to 'the PM's quarter-deck' from which, on clear days, one can see the 'dreaming spires' of Oxford's churches and colleges. Among historical souvenirs in the long gallery are a ring worn by Queen Elizabeth I and a standing up writing desk used by Napoleon on St Helena as well as a face mask of Oliver Cromwell, his bible and slippers. The house belonged to one of Cromwell's descendants.

There is a good library and some of the paintings are excellent, not least a Rubens about which the owners keep quiet to avoid cries of 'sacrilege' from the 'politically correct' Establishment. More than half a century ago, another painter, not untalented but amateur in status and a temporary occupant of Chequers, had the effrontery to leave his own mark in a corner of the canvas in the form of a tiny mouse. This was Sir Winston Churchill and whether or not he was in his cups at the time he was excused on account of his fame. Even if not quite equal artistically, it suggested a certain humility, and may even have added something to the value of the painting. Chequers has a swimming pool, a gift from the American ambassador Walter Annenberg in memory of President Nixon's visit there. The atmosphere, both cultivated and simple, of an English country house, which Chequers offers, is naturally much enjoyed, especially by visitors from abroad.

During my time as a foreign correspondent, regular weekly meetings would take place with the prime minister's press people in his office on the ground floor of 10 Downing Street. Of the various ones throughout the years, I remember one especially on account of his blusteringly sympathetic personality. This was Sir

Bernard Ingham, Margaret Thatcher's press chief. No better guide to her government's policies could have existed, whether he lost, or managed to control, his Yorkshire temper. That politically he came from a Labour Party background, yet held out for 11 years as his formidable boss's spokesman, testifies to his qualities: he was the horse's mouth and occasionally also the horse, but always remained, in my experience, a government spokesman and 'civil servant' in the original literal sense of the term.

Anglo–German misunderstandings

Unlike Italy's Risorgimento, German unity was unfortunately not achieved in similarly internationally favourable cicumstances. It was largely the work of the new military monarchy that followed in Europe upon its theological predecessors, such as Henry VIII, Philip II or Louis XIV. Theological monarchy had done its time, as the liberal Catholic historian, Lord Acton has said, Church and state oppressed mankind together. Henceforth, the authoritarian state oppressed for its own sake. The new military monarchs, like Peter the Great and Frederick William I were not particularly attractive, but one has to remember that without one the first Europe might be French, and without the other it might be Russian.

A new form of practical absolutism arose in northern Europe at the time of the settlement of the English revolution. Lecturing at Cambridge in the academic years 1900/1, Regius Professor of Modern History Sir John Acton, who was half English and half German, issued the following warning. He claimed that 'the bayonets of Prussia promoted a new, more rational and economic age, with Berlin becoming more than the capital of a new nation, also its intellectual guide, promoter of wealth, teacher of knowledge, guardian of morality, a mainspring of the ascending movement of man, and the greatest danger that remains to be encountered by the Anglo-Saxon race.' His was not the only warning voice of his age.

Acton's sympathies towards modern Germany clearly leant to the side of Austria as historically and politically better suited than the new German military Sparta to bring national unity to the centre of Europe. As a young man Acton had described himself as an 'Austriacist', but he was also conscious that it was the equivalent of being 'a partisan of sinking ships', with none evidently sinking more quickly in a century of sprouting nationalisms than the multinational Austrian Empire in the century of sprouting European nationalisms. To Acton, the historical thinker, the federal came to appear as the most efficient of all known securities of freedom, for it rests on the idea that liberty depends on the division of powers and that democracy, no less than state absolutism, tends to concentrate and thus unify and corrupt political power. After the disastrous experience of two world wars caused by European nationalisms and the quasi-federal European Union that has emerged from that, one can hardly fault Acton's reasoning.

For its sins, modern Germany had not looked to its medieval roots in the Holy Roman Empire but to Prussia, where state authority and not opinion governed society. In Prussia the state was the master and not the public's servant, as was more the tradition in the German south that had not yet fallen in love with 'blood and iron' as the new nationalist ideal, which was both explosive and self-destructive.

The Austrian Empire had continued to remain among the big powers through the Napoleonic wars, forcing Emperor Francis II to become Napoleon's ally who formally dissolved the Holy Roman Empire in 1806. The emperor became the hereditary Francis I of Austria and was rewarded for his Napoleonic tribulations with Venice and Dalmatia, important new outlets for Austrian foreign trade. Internal discontent, however, grew within his realm among restless Magyars, Italians and Bohemians, though held at bay by the the skills of Metternich and Windischgrätz until 1848, when the revolutions broke out all over Europe, and Metternich had to escape to England.

After that, Austria re-established its absolute rule in Italy and Hungary, but was to lose its former predominance in vying with Prussia in the German unification stakes. These were to be played out on Italian soil and bound up with the movement for Italian unification. The fatal turning point was the summer of 1866, when, on 18 June, Prussia and Italy declared war against Austria and, though the Austrians defeated the Italians at Custozza (Veneto) on 24 June, they were totally defeated a week later at Sadowa (Königgratz). That was the end of Austria's aspirations to lead the German states to national unity. Austria-Hungary, as it became, lost Veneto and Lombardy, but retained its Dalmatian and Istrian (Trieste) naval port until 1918.

14. Lord Acton (1834–1902), historian, Liberal, English Catholic.

Meanwhile, also in July 1867, the Prussians had defeated the Bavarians and occupied Frankfurt am Main. On 23 August, peace was concluded between Prussia and Austria at Prague and it remained for Prussia to beat the French in 1870 in order to gain the German Imperial Crown.

Lord Acton's was not the only voice to warn of the explosive dangers of an extreme German nationalist solution in the heart of Europe. It took two world wars to establish, not least through the phoney Nazi myths of the so-called three Reichs.

The first, or medieval, Reich was of course not nationalist; if anything, it was a supra-national power of which the German territories were merely a part, *deutscher Nation* in the genitive sense. The 'second', Bismarckian nationalist German Empire of 1870, a product of the Franco-Prussian war of 1870, had no historical connection whatsoever with these predecessors. Fortunately, it did not last for 1000 years, as the first Reich had done, and a more democratically fraternal European Union then followed.

There had been other warning voices apart from Acton's, not least that of the great German poet and visionary, Heinrich Heine (1797–1856). Popular though he was, his was perhaps not heard as it ought to have been because of his frivolous and sarcastic modern tone, which upset his serious-minded contemporaries. He combined the great poet's divine gifts with prophetic forebodings of future terrors, instilled in him perhaps by his Jewish heritage and memory. Living in French exile as a German patriot, he foresaw 'a future age when there would be millions of exiles escaping an otherwise certain death'. Condemned by severe spinal disease to spend his last years in his *Matratzengruft* (mattress tomb), he nevertheless retained his high spirits and delighted in all the pleasures of life, telling, for instance a visitor wondering about how things were between himself and his God: 'Don't you worry. God will forgive me. After all, that is his *métier*.' In 1830, however, his mind's eye already saw:

> the threatening monsters which it would need the prophet of a new Apocalypse to invent for the violent times to come, compared to which its Johannine symbolic predecessors would seem like gentle doves and harmless charmers. The very gods would then have to hide their faces from pity with the children of man, their ancient charges, and perhaps also from fear of their own fate. This future smells to me of blood and godlessness and terrible afflictions. And I can only recommend to our grandsons to come into this world with only the toughest of backsides.

And, about the same time, a century before the rise of Hitler, Heine predicted:

a drama to be staged in Germany, compared to which the French Revolution is the merest pastoral idyll. Throughout their history Christianity has tamed but not uprooted the martial brutality of the Germans, but as the wood of the cross, their talisman, crumbles, brittle, the old berserker's frenzy will again break forth, but this time it would not be a francophile revolution, republican and radical. German nationalism is not world-open, aiming at the brotherhood of men, fired by missionary zeal, but negative, hostile, and aggressive.

And elsewhere he wrote:

The Germans need neither freedom nor equality. They are a speculative people, ideologists, thinking only of the future and of the past. For the British and the French there exists also a present time, in which every day has its struggle and counter-stuggle, and past history. The Germans have nothing worth fighting for, and when they think that maybe there are such things nevertheless, their philosophers will tell them to doubt their existence. Nevertheless, it cannot be denied that Germans, too, love freedom, but differently from others. The Englishman loves his freedom like his legitimate spouse, he owns her and though he may treat her with little tenderness, he will defend her if need be like a man, and woe to him that tries to push past him into her sacred chamber, as either paramour or scoundrel. The Frenchman loves his freedom like his bride, he ever longs for her, is aglow for her, throws himself at her feet with all his most extravagant protestations. For this love he goes through life and death, commits a thousand follies. But the German loves his freedom, too, if only like his grandmother.

As London correspondent of *Frankfurter Allgemeine Zeitung* and *Die Presse,* Austria, as well as staff correspondent of leading newspapers in Stuttgart, Cologne and Hanover, I was naturally much involved in the thorny problem of Anglo–German relations. As Theodor Heuss, the German president, aptly described it on his first first postwar state visit, it was 'a chain of firmly forged misunderstandings'. The bad memories go back to

1937 when former champagne salesman Joachim von
Ribbentrop presented his ambassadorial credentials to King
George VI with the Hitler salute. He departed again after hardly
a year's residence and after having embarked on an expensive
programme to renovate the old Nash terrace embassy building at
9 Carlton House Terrace. For this he employed Hitler's architect,
Albert Speer, and the doorknobs are about all that remains of his
design. Outside, in the front garden, there is still the pathetic
little grave and tombstone of 'faithful Giro', the Alsatian dog, of
Leopold von Hoesch, the last ambassador of the Weimar
Republic in London.

Yet Carlton House Terrace had been the embassy's seat also of
the Kaiser's Germany, and before that, of 'dear Prussia', as the
young Queen Victoria called it, to say nothing of Prussia, Great
Britain's glorious ally against Napoleon. In March 1849 the
Prussian minister Christian-Karl Josias Bunsen, the scholar-
diplomat, gave a great ball there to celebrate the marriage of the
queen's eldest daughter, the Princess Royal, with the liberal
Crown Prince Friedrich Wilhelm, later the tragically short-lived
Emperor Friedrich III. They were to be the parents of the
emperor and warlord William II, whose reign was sealed with his
abdication in 1918.

The two eras of Anglo–German relations that ended in the two
world wars were significantly different. While the United States,
then neutral Switzerland, had taken care of the old embassy
during the First World War, after 1918 Great Britain returned it
to the Weimar Republic with everything just as the last imperial
ambassador, Prince Lichnowsky, had left it, including even the
cigarettes in the silver case on his desk. After the 1939 war and
Hitler, however, there was a rift for a decade while the new
democratic Germany made a complete break with the past and
appropriately started a new embassy in London's Belgrave
Square. I wrote and edited a little history of these two London
aspects of Anglo–German relations, which the German Federal
Republic embassy published in 1991.

Three German diplomats who had worked in the Carlton
House Terrace embassy in the 1930s and paid with their lives for
their opposition to Hitler provided one link with the old and
'other' Germany. They were Count Albrecht von Bernstorff,
Herbert Mumm von Schwarzenstein (1898–1945) and Eduard
Brücklmeier (1903–44) and a plaque was unveiled in their

honour in 1961. Count von Bernstorff, who was perhaps the best known of them in London where he served for 11 years, had been a Rhodes scholar at Oxford before the First World War. He was a man large in spirit and stature, six feet tall, dangerously careless about voicing his views of Hitler and the Nazis, yet rejecting the chance of staying in England, where most of his friends were, because of anxiety over his family estate in Mecklenburg.

He gave up his diplomatic career in 1933 and did what was then the most foolhardy thing to do; he joined the board of Wassermann, the official bank of the Jewish community. It was a deliberate and brave move. He sheltered some Jews in his home and aided others to escape abroad. As a member of the anti-Nazi Solf Circle, at the beginning of the Second World War he was inevitably arrested and sent to Ravensbrück concentration camp, where Hanna Solf was also being held, though she survived the war. She told the diplomat and writer Harold Nicholson about Bernstorff's fate, mentioning how he was taken back to his cell after interrogation, and she, looking out through the fanlight of her door, saw him with blood all over his face, supported by two warders, looking at her smiling. She said that she had never seen a like expression of suffering and grim resolve.

Bernstorff was sent to the Berlin Prinz-Albrecht-Strasse prison for trial in the people's court, but it did not come to that because the court building was hit in an air raid and the notorious Nazi judge, Roland Freisler, was among the injured and dying. However, when the Russians liberated the prison in April 1945 Bernstorff was no longer there and, according to fellow prisoners, he had been taken away and presumably shot. It was said that Ribbentrop had ordered his execution because of a report in the Allied press that Bernstorff was thought to be one of the few Germans likely to head a future German government.

The Berlin blockade and airlift, the Federal Republic's membership of NATO and of the Western European Union, and close links between Dr Adenauer, Churchill and Eden were what characterized early postwar Anglo–German relations. In 1951, Adenauer came to London on his first official visit to meet Sir Winston Churchill and Foreign Secretary Anthony Eden. Adenauer was worried about European integration and the 'good neighbour' policy with which the re-elected Conservatives continued the Labour government's old British 'balance of power' line. Their historic conversation is recorded in Weymar's official biography of Adenauer as follows:

Churchill: 'Neighbours of Europe, but not in Europe'.

Adenauer: 'It seems to me that it would be sufficient if Britain were to declare clearly and unmistakably where her sympathies lie.'

Churchill: 'England's task is to maintain a balance. Germany is stronger than France, and France is haunted by fear of a German attack. In such an event we should place ourselves on the side of France, although I do not anticipate that such an event will ever occur.'

Adenauer: 'We must never express such thoughts! I beg you to have confidence in Germany. Germans incline towards extremes, what they support is often too theoretical. But we have paid dearly for our lessons. Today Germany is a shapeless mass that has to be remoulded. What matters is whether this is to be done by good or bad hands.'

Churchill: 'It is not possible completely to eradicate all national sentiments. Germany and France must be friends and walk together. Great Britain will do everything she can to contribute to this German–French friendship. Germany is stronger than France – and the equilibrium is established with the help of England.'

Adenauer then tackled his nightmare of a new 'Yalta', an understanding with Russia at Germany's expense.

Eden: 'Germany need not fear, now or ever, that we shall sell her to the Soviet Union. Britain will only act in accord with the Federal Republic.'

Churchill: 'That is correct. We shall not betray you. If the West is strong enough, the Soviet Union may possibly yield and agree to a unification of Germany. But we would never consider coming to an understanding with the Soviets at the expense of Germany. Only a false friendship could spring from such a betrayal.'

Adenauer: 'We may therefore count on the support of Britain?'

Churchill: 'We stand by our word.'

'No arms for the Nazis' and 'Adenauer go home' were the slogans that demonstrators in London shouted on that occasion. It was the most unfriendly reception he had received in any foreign country, but when he later witnessed similar abuse shouted from the gallery of the House of Commons, but intended for Churchill and Eden, he accepted what he was told by his shoulder-shrugging hosts: 'It's a free country.' Violent attacks by the left-wing *Daily Mirror* (with a circulation then of four million copies) also greeted the first German diplomatic representative in 1950. Though the German Federal Republic was set up in September 1949, it took another six years for the first full German ambassador, Hans von Herwarth, to arrive. The Korean War, followed by an American demand that the Germans should be rearmed for their own defence, caused the delay. This was acceptable to the French only under their proposed European Defence Community, and so had to wait until the Bonn agreements, too, passed the French parliament in 1954. Stalin had died in 1953. To satisfy German opinion, the Western Allies then raised the question of reunification on Germany's behalf in an exchange of notes with the Russians. This established that German reunification was not then a practical possibility and that the divided Germany would be a factor for the time being.

Because of my maternal Austrian descent, I was glad also to represent the old-established Austrian newspaper, *Die Presse*, in London. This, on the whole, was an enjoyable activity if only because Austria managed to preserve its traditional serene image to the outside world, which Germany, despite having done immeasurably more to make up for the past, found so difficult after 1945. Austria also acquired a saving escape clause, both true and convenient, as having been Hitler's first victim. As a pawn in the postwar four-power occupation, Austria was also fortunate in achieving independence through a new kind of 'felix Austria' turn, by becoming neutral. Thus, the Austrians managed somehow to get away with only their own sacrifices and bad memories in the war, and were spared constant reminders of how Hitler, the Austrian, had had his early trial run in anti-Semitic Catholic pre-First World War Vienna. If Germany managed to rise from its past with a new European patriotism, Austria, too, emerged healed from its old attachment to greater-German nationalist dreams, making, somewhat reluctantly at first, what amends it could for its joint responsibility in the crime of the Holocaust. When the Carinthian party leader Jörg Haider recently made a sort of right-wing move, determined resistance showed that times had changed.

Anglo–German problems were less easy to bridge. There were constant signs of distrust on the part of the British mass media, at first over real or exaggerated reports of anti-Semitic outrages in the German Federal Republic and later over the publication of opinion polls. Were the Germans doing enough to face up to their past? Against that, however, the British seemed to cling to their memories of old battles fought and the stereotyped depiction of nasty Germans, which their postwar descendants equally resented as hardly contributing to good relations. In the 1960s and 1970s, the Germans had found it difficult to teach the postwar generation the truth about Hitler. However, the British, for their part, failed to understand why the 'new' Germans did not dream of revenge by uniting with the Russians against the West, but turned their backs decidedly against their past and towards a more hopeful European future.

Thus, decades of mutual Anglo–German incomprehension went by. At the beginning was an understandable German reluctance to face the superhuman task of reconstruction at the same time as having to confront and absorb the issues that Hitler and the Holocaust had raised. The new postwar generation largely took on the latter task, which it then confronted with typical German thoroughness as though nothing mattered more than that *Zeitgeschichte* (contemporary history) and understanding its lessons should take precedence over everything else. Not surprisingly, this phase is also ending and quite a few members of the new generation resent being constantly reminded of their grand- and great-grandfathers' misdeeds.

The new Holocaust memorial in the centre of Berlin between the Brandenburg Gate and Potsdamer Platz, where Dr Goebbels's private residence once stood, is perhaps symptomatic of these changing attitudes. In this case, and for the first time, the German authorities have refrained from their normal practice of telling people how to approach the terrible genocide in their recent past and they gave the American architect, Peter Eisenman, a free hand. His work consists of 2711 upright slabs of dark concrete interspersed with trees. Some basic rules exist to handle the thousands of visitors, but these amount to no more than safeguarding public order. How people interpret the bizarre monument is entirely up to them and this very freedom presents them with the difficult problem of what to think about it. Should they feel sadness or horror? Should it remind them of a Jewish cemetery, which few would ever have seen, of the Warsaw Ghetto? Should they regard it as an incomprehensible labyrinth, or perhaps a large field of wheat, or storm stirring up the waters of a lake? Though their reactions are usually confused, somewhere between wanting to weep and being scandalized, nothing quite captures the horror of the unnerving cold-blooded murders that showed the world of what civilized human beings were capable. One sees young and old alike deriving various vacuous emotions from their strange 'museum-like' outing, which they seem to treat like a kind of picnic at which they munch *bratwurst*, *brezel* and icecream as they skip from stele to stele. That it is impossible to fathom may perhaps merely confirm that some lessons from history can never be learnt.

In Britain, too, people are expressing attitudes that differ from those of the generation brought up on memories of the war against Germany. Partly taking their cue from the German preoccupation with Hitler, they are now tackling old taboo subjects like the indiscriminate bombing of German cities, especially Dresden. However, rancour of some sort continues to dominate half a century of Anglo–German relations.

A typical example of how the government handled such tensions came when there was a threat to sterling as a hard currency in the late 1960s. The question was whether impoverished Britain would have to devalue and, if so, whether it could maintain its profitable financial services sector in London. The Wilson government's strategy was to blackmail Germany, with its infinite reserves, into increasing the value of the Deutschmark, which was the greatest competitor to British goods. Thus, on 20 November 1968, at around midnight, the German ambassador Herbert Blankenhorn received an urgent call from 10 Downing Street that Prime Minister Wilson wished to see him right away about the critical international currency question. Blankenhorn agreed to come over at once and found Wilson, Foreign Secretary Michael Stewart and Chancellor of the Exchequer Roy Jenkins confronting him in the cabinet room like a hostile phalanx.

Most of the participants have since described that historic meeting, with Roy Jenkins feeling almost sorry about the rough treatment the ambassador received. The British government, Wilson said, had done everything appropriate, given the world situation, to build up an effective defence of the Western world, but there could be no efficient defence without an adequate economic base and increasing the value of the Deutschmark would enable Britain to avoid a devaluation of sterling. The alleged threat of 'revalue or we will withdraw our troops' was actually not uttered, but the gist of the message was clearly that. According to the intervention by Jenkins, who was going to Bonn that morning to pursue the matter at a finance ministers' conference, if the Germans refused to revalue and the pound had to float down, the British could not continue the present level of military expenditure in Germany.

The meeting lasted only half an hour, after which Wilson, according to Jenkins, was in 'euphoric mood' while he, Jenkins, felt 'that we had done a bad night's work with Blankenhorn'. The ambassador left and that same night dictated to his economics counsellor, Count Brühl, what had happened. A waiting cipher clerk was to transmit it to Bonn, where members of the Kiesinger/ Brandt government were anxiously waiting for it. Blankenhorn had every reason to resent the way Wilson had treated him, but he took it on the chin, blandly and smilingly, which probably saved Anglo–German relations from further disintegration. The face-saving outcome for everybody was that the Deutschmark was valued upwards, though only later, and that sterling was devalued. Blankenhorn again saved the situation. The British press had described the crisis with glee, though the German papers could not retaliate in that way. Soon afterwards, however, at a reception given by the Queen, the German ambassador was seen walking arm in arm with the British prime minister through the rooms of Buckingham Palace.

Was there a lesson to be learnt from this half century of ups and downs in the two countries' bilateral relations? Did the British just not like Krauts, or Sauerkrauts? After all, they are not particularly keen on Frogs, or I-ties or Americans either. The psychological trouble with the Germans is that, come what may, they want to be loved, or at least liked, and such feelings cannot be enforced, especially since the British media cannot resist exploiting the German desire to be loved. Perhaps in time even bad British comedians might no longer get cheap laughs for being beastly to Germans. It is of course to be regretted that the

British find it so difficult to let bygones be bygones, but in this case it has the wider implication of a reduction of teaching German in British schools, as of foreign language teaching in general. Perhaps it is now time for British and Germans to recall Churchill's magnanimity towards the former Second World War enemy, and for the Germans to follow their ambassador Blankenhorn's example and stoically 'grin and bear it'. In international relations, generosity is a more difficult virtue to practise than charity, but it is worth a try. Ultimately, too, Harold Wilson will be remembered not for 'saving the pound' in British pockets but for cleverly having reminded the world that 'a week is a long time in politics'.

Part of a London foreign correspondent's acivities was meeting the less savoury characters on the international scene. This meant being courted by or involved in the universal public relations machine that is so close to journalism, which overwhelmed one with favours, gifts and invitations. The intention was obvious; it was to appeal to human vanity and to corrupt, however coolly denied that was. If it resulted in a slightly more favourable report of some event than was deserved, its purpose had been achieved. I remember receiving a beautiful leather-bound writing pad at one of my first reporting jobs at the international car race circuit at Monza near Milan when I was not yet 15. Much later, I remember President Richard Nixon beaming all over his face and shaking both my hands at a monstrous London reception, but then after being reintroduced to him, expressing his pleasure at meeting me. Americans are particularly good at observing these social graces and I remember Charlie Chaplin engaging in a lengthy exchange with me that involved holding everybody up in the queue.

Dr Waldheim ingratiates himself

One day, Dr Kurt Waldheim, the controversial Austrian postwar diplomat, politician, ex-secretary general of the United Nations and at that time standing as candidate for the Austrian state presidency, which he won in 1986, unexpectedly called and invited me to lunch. He wanted to talk to me, he said, as the representative of the leading Austrian newspaper *Die Presse*. 'Forgive my surprise attack, but I happen to be in London for my book and your name is of course a household word for me.' Fortunately, by then I was sufficiently jaded to hear the internal alarm bells – hello, hello, what does he want, self-justification? A tall, gaunt figure, he conformed to one's image of the ingratiating Austrian patrician with a touch of humanity, charm and snobbery. Having established common acquaintances – we had after all not met before – like a good Viennese head waiter who is 'able simultanously to bend over backwards and forwards', he went on to plug his book, *The Eye of the Storm.*

This was sometime after Waldheim had left the United Nations to a welter of accusations concerning his, until then, well-hidden wartime activities as a junior officer linked to the deportation of Jews from Salonika, Greece in 1944. His excuse was that he knew nothing about it because he had been on 'home leave' at the time. That summed him up perfectly – through the 'art of amnesia', he was capable of totally reinventing his wartime past.

As a presidential candidate, Waldheim campaigned in measured terms, making his 'bow to history' by telling his electors at one mass meeting that 'great grief has come through the Nazis to the Jews of Europe.' At our luncheon meeting he opened up a little more, regretting how he had always been misunderstood and how that had added to life's difficulties. He tried to enlist my sympathy. 'You are old enough to know what those times were like, that everybody had, for instance, to join some of the Nazi organizations, like the student union or the SA [brownshirts].' He also said that, as a mere *Oberleutnant,* he had to obey his superiors and had no say in policy decisions. He evidently remained true to himself when, much later, as Austrian foreign minister at the time of the Soviet invasion of Czechoslovakia, he succumbed to Soviet pressure by barring Czech asylum seekers from crossing into Austria. His excuse then was that he had simply followed an order from his minister of the interior. He was unsuccessful there because traditional Austrian generosity towards refugees from the East won the day, but he was at the same time able to please the Austrian right-wingers who also opposed the influx. I must admit that after our lunch I felt like shouting 'pass the sick bag'.

A born European Habsburg

How infinitely more agreeable it was on London visits to spend time with that great European, Dr Otto von Habsburg. The last emperor's son, then aged 92, he would eventually preside, in

May 2004, over numerous members of his family and supporters at his father's beatificatio, and to pray to 'Beatus Carolus e Domo Austriae' (1887–1922) 'who accepted the difficult tasks and burdensome challenges that God gave you during your life'. He had remained 'Your Majesty' to his Austrian loyalists, combining his European convictions with a dose of British pragmatism, with which he liked to refresh himself from time to time in London. On that last occasion we were able to avail ourselves of an English friend's membership of most of the leading West End clubs for a veritable 'club crawl'. Arriving at the hidden-away Boodles, we were astonished when the barman, without a word having been exchanged, came with a tray on which were three glasses of port and small change for £20, also 'Good evening, Mr ...'. Our host responded 'Good evening, John' and pocketed the money without further ado. Well-mannered guests as we were, Dr von Habsburg and I made no comment. Only later did it emerge that our host was in the habit of tacitly cashing a cheque on his descent to Boodles. At any rate, he managed to impress an emperor's son that Boodles at least had preserved that magic touch – another relic of greater and imperial times.

The good Herr Karl

Postwar Austrians were understandably eager to forget their disagreeable past. To remind them of it, the Austrian satirist Qualtinger had written an excellent ditty about *der Herr Karl,* a typical Viennese character, the proverbial 'little chap' and time-server who used to lick the boots of the powers that be, fawn over republicans, Jews, socialists and Nazis, but drop them fast when they exhausted their use for him. Qualtinger no doubt exaggerated, but he hit the nail on the head. Fellow travelling 'little men' (and women) are part of human nature, but I was glad also to have discovered one who seemed to match the image and I have treasured his memory.

He was also called Karl, or endearingly Karl Netzl. He was an ordinary Viennese from the Alser suburb, which, as those familiar with Vienna would know, produced a special sort of local toughie, this one being a sturdy little chap belying his muscular strength, ideal for his humble occupation as caretaker of the Austrian Cultural Institute in London, as it was then called. He and his wife, endearingly called 'Rierl' (from Ria)

15. Dr Otto von Habsburg, head of the Imperial Royal House of
Habsburg (b. 1912), an admired European and friend.

lived in an uncomfortable basement flat in Kensington's Rutland
Gate, at one time meant to house the servants.

The Netzls were typically Viennese and might have come straight out of a Nestroy comedy. He was an eternal optimist and was used to taking the blows of life with equanimity. For instance, he comforted Rierl who had burst into tears at the first sight of their miserable London cellar accommodation with a gallant, 'No use crying already now, my little treasure.' However, with their happy nature the Netzls managed their unlikely transition to the British capital and made their mark on it for nearly twenty years. They made friends with everybody, regardless of linguistic problems, and she gave impressive accounts of her idyllic holidays in faraway 'Töörkee', meaning Torquay. Karl was a hairdresser by profession and when an old customer and friend became the first postwar director of the Institute, he begged him to take him and his wife along too. Their children had grown-up and life in Vienna immediately after the war was far from easy. Besides, travelling abroad was still unusual. He soon proved to be a man of many talents, a veritable Figaro. He had shorn the heads of all the prominent Austrian statesmen, pianists and singers then launched in London on their road to fame, entertaining them with stories that sometimes had to be whispered into their ears, or with his culinary skills as a pastry cook and expert maker of lobster salads. One of his devotees was the well-known accompanist Erik Werba who even composed an Austrian song in Netzl's honour – 'from director, deputy, secretary, librarian down to modest little Netzl who nevertheless was the one to mark the whole with its leading tone into what was truly Austrian.' Austrian musicians of future world fame like Alfred Brendel, James King, Gulda, Hans Mejdimorec and Jorg Demus had their early débuts at Rutland Gate. Rudi Buchbinder was 17 years old when he first starred in London, watched over fatherly by Netzl while polishing the crystal chandeliers on his stepladder during their rehearsals. Paul Badura-Skoda invented a new German musical scale for him 'Nett, (nice) netter (nicer), Netzl'.

He was a good magician, and generations of the Vienna Boys Choir claim to have preferred a performance of his tricks in his basement to their successes in the Albert Hall. They then expressed their gratitude by singing their famous *Heitschihum-beithschi*. His boss, the *Herr Direktor*, was allowed to listen from the top of the stairs as Netzl was reduced to tears, but a man with real feelings like his had no need to be ashamed of that. His sparkling temperament alone was worth all the millions spent on advertising Austria's tourist and musical attractions. 'Good morning, my happy Charly', was the response of the English woman next door to his daily greeting. At the great cultural events the institute organized, he was in charge of the cloakroom reception, knowing everybody and greeting them respectfully *'Goot eivening My lady'*, or *'Küss die Hand, gnä, Frau'* or *'Grüssi Gott, Herr Doktor'*, whether or not it was a Doktor. Status, rank and class still mattered in his world of 60 years ago, and he knew that culture, which he too represented, was not just for those clever heads upstairs but had also to do with one's very soul. The British liked it a lot, showing their appreciation through the plate well filled with silver coins before even the first guests had arrived *pour encourager les autres.*

Karl Netzl used to say that people forget sadness, but that goodness remains. This was part of his native nostalgic philosophy of life, reminiscent of the musical lament in Johann Strauss's immortal *Fledermaus*. 'Happy is he who can forget what can no longer be changed.' When the Netzls left London on their retirement he gave me a last haircut, singing once more: *'I bin hat a Weaner, i kann nichts dafür'* (I am Viennese and just can't help it).

John Bull's other island

Because of the terrorism in Northern Ireland, with its thousands of victims, foreign correspondents in Great Britain were accustomed to looking upon that area as part of their agenda, and frequent visits to Northern Ireland became the rule. Tagged onto these visits was usually a more agreeable return to London via Dublin and the Republic of Eire. One could sense a distinct sense of disguised *Schadenfreude* there as people commiserated with the British for having to cope with problems that independent Ireland could pretend more or less to ignore. Invariably, one came back with all sorts of rational solutions that their expert authors, not having to carry them out, were always ready to put forward. In addition, we used to stock up on the latest Irish jokes, whatever the IRA's bloody intent might have been. Similarly, as in old Austria, Irish affairs could consistently be regarded as hopeless but never serious.

In the same way as the benefits of being one of the European Union's major agrarian suppliers has transformed the Irish

Republic, so too has the Irish nation discarded other traditions of its past, not least the religious ones, and basically the image of the drunken and rustic 'Paddy'. Instead of the pubs that once inhabited every street corner, there are now continental type cafés in smoke-free zones. 'Paddy' jokes are now seen as racist, or, what is worse, invented by the British. Like some of the best Jewish or anti-Semitic jokes, they were probably also of Jewish origin.

'Paddy' jokes are both telling and inexhaustible and deserve to be preserved. For example, an Irish labourer turned up at a British building site to ask for a job and when the foreman asked him if he knew the difference between a girder and a joist, he replied, 'Ach, sure, Goethe wrote Faust and Joyce wrote Ulysses.' As Paddy leaves the railway station on his arrival in the British capital for the first time, where he had heard that the streets were paved with gold, he spots a pound coin lying on the pavement. However, just as he is about to pick it up, he changes his mind and says 'No need to start my new life working on a Sunday.'

However, Paddy will forever remain associated with the admirable trait of wanting to please one's fellow men and being unable to disappont them in their expectations. For example, a motorist stopped to ask a local man, 'Am I on the right road here for Athlone?' only to be told, 'If I were you, sir, I would not want to start from here.' All this modern drive and industry must surely lead to the loss of traditional Irish ways, such as the curious Spaniard trying to find out whether there is an Irish equivalent for the Spanish *mañana* and being told, 'sure, but it hasn't got your sense of urgency about it.' Above all, the ways of Catholic Ireland are disappearing. Pretty Brigid, following countless others who went to make their fortune in England, returned not long afterwards with a splendid mink coat. 'How did you get that?' her mother asks suspiciously. 'Mum', she replies, 'I have a confession to make, I have become a prostitute.' At this point, Mum faints, but on coming to again asks, 'what was it you said?' 'I have become a prostitute, Mum.' 'Oh, thank God, I thought you said Protestant.'

The Austrians and Irish have something other than their many attractive qualities in common, for they are both small countries with the misfortune of having a bigger neighbour next door and, as such, are a sort of 'John Bull's other island'. Because of their geography and history, after 1945 both the Austrians and the

Irish felt the need to cultivate the art of charming their conquerors into eventual withdrawal, first the Germans, then the
four powers. Ever since a medieval pope had blessed the English
for beating the Irish, the latter, with later help from the Vikings
and eventually even English and Scottish occupiers, had formed a
new upper class, the so-called 'Protestants on horseback', who
made the struggle for Irish independence their own. The Austrians were also good at forming useful alliances, first through
the peaceful means of dynastic marriages and, after the collapse
of the Austro-Hungarian Empire, by inventing the theory that
race and language were necessary for national unity. The Swiss
had long disproved that theory and after 1945 the Austrians too
were cured of their dream of a 'greater German' unity.

As for Ireland, an interesting question remains. Would the
Romans, had they got that far, have been able to resist the
proverbial Irish 'witchery' and taught them, as they had the other
continentals, discipline and order? Unfortunately for later ages,
the Romans had exhausted their power and will to penetrate
those more northern regions, believing them to be on the edge of
the civilized world and inhabited by evil spirits, given that they
were evidently so close to Orcus near the Orkney islands, their
entrance to hell.

In modern times, according to a joke, an air stewardess
announced before landing at Belfast, 'please fasten your seat
belts and turn your watches back 300 years.' This was supposed
to illustrate what kind of impression an outdated religious war
between Protestant loyalists and Catholic nationalists made on
the outside world. There was no point in the protagonists
denying that it had anything to do with theological issues like,
for example, transsubstantiation or justification by faith. Such
denials, however, appeared to come close to special pleading, as
though religious beliefs had nothing to do with it. Also, the
conflict did not make much sense in purely ethnic/historical
terms like similar ones between Italians and Austrians in
Sudtirol, between Flemings and Walloons in Belgium, or Greeks
and Turks in Cyprus, which have lost their edge through
membership of the European Union.

To make matters more complicated, Protestant Ulster contra-
dicts the traditional Marxist thesis of working-class unity, in that
the sworn enemy is not the capitalist foe but their Irish
nationalist or republican neighbours. It is often also the working

class, with Protestant landowners and industrialists giving their religious support, and all, with their pipes and drums, literally sounding the 'fear of the Lord' into their opponents' hearts on their annual marches, so as literally to drum 'the fear of the Lord' into their opponents' hearts. Nor would the physical separation of these groups be feasible because of the large population movements involved – Belfast alone has 295,000 inhabitants, of whom 77,000 (26 per cent) are Catholics.

The 1921 border, which stretches across Ireland for 450 kilometres, follows a geographical line along the so-called Drumlin Belt. Even to this day, that division separates the rough-sounding northern Irish accents from the southern lilt, and it is interesting to note that archaeologists have found evidence in northern tombs of a sombre puritanical religiosity and of a more life-affirming cheerfulness in the Irish south long before Christianity existed. The latter is confirmed in the great literary tradition, ranging from Jonathan Swift to Seamus Heaney, that has taught the Irish to mix wit and wisdom, and with similarly intoxicating effect, Irish whiskey with Guinness.

'Gay' London attracts the cultural world

A particularly enjoyable part of my professional life was to report regularly on British cultural activities. The musical arts and theatre had always attracted me, and I was glad of the chance to attend the capital's rich fare of events in opera, ballet and drama. Covent Garden then became the home of opera (in its original language) and was where the great Sutherland started and sang her last performance. It was where Domingo and Pavarotti starred, and where the Royal Ballet celebrated its unforgettable triumphs with Margot Fonteyn and Rudolf Nureyev. This was the era when Shakespeare came into his own again with the brilliant Laurence Olivier, John Gielgud and Alec Guinness, and where Peter Brook's unique productions of *King Lear* and *Marat Sade* revolutionized both the ritual and symbolism of the theatrical experience.

In the mid-twentieth century there also began the extraordinary boom in the London art market when the big sales of classical and modern paintings and sculpture at Christie's, Sotheby's and Bonham's became a new part of a London reporter's work. I had an added personal interest in that, though at the lower end of the market, for my future Italian-born wife, under her maiden name Amelia Nathan, ran a small antique and second-hand furniture shop in South Wimbledon, which was appropriately called 'Junkantiques'. She was a very attractive woman and soon became known among the auctioneers for her two tiny, well-trained and well-behaved Yorkshire terriers, a mother and daughter, that always accompanied her and collectively were known as the 'Ninis'. She was also known for her sole interest in the junk end of the market, for she always managed there to find something of small value, but not to be despised on that account and making it worth her while to buy.

Usually, at the very end of a sale when all the professional buyers had gone, she was still there and the auctioneer, knowing her, would call out an encouraging 'Now, what about it, Mrs Nathan, a cardbox of goodies going cheaply for only a pound?' and he would knock the price down for her. These 'goodies' were mostly worthless, but might include an occasional rare book or other item that justified her investment. I, meanwhile, perhaps having been to a sensational Rembrandt sale reaching a million, on which I had to report, would arrive just in time to help her carry her £1 'goodies' to her car. While I did this she would attend to the needs of the 'Ninies' who wanted a little outing after what to them was a boring snooze on a chair next to her. I shall have more to say about Amelia and her animals presently.

The arts in those years seemed to exert an extraordinary new appeal, exaggerated no doubt by the attention they received from the mass media. This was certainly the case in the revival of the postwar English theatre, and its worldwide echo, not necessarily of high quality comedies or drama, but of the vision of a new generation of young writers with less to say that was new, but with a new formless emphasis. Following on from Noel Coward, Christopher Fry and Terence Rattigan, they had come to maturity in the drab British postwar world of nationalization. Great Britain, moreover, exhausted by the war, was then also on the way to becoming a medium power after its imperial greatness. As for relations between Britain and the Continent, the differences between victors and defeated were diminishing with every day.

The prewar depression and scarcities of war had scarred the British younger generation. It had benefited from a liberal education and suddenly found itself in a new world of science, technology and television, in which, however, the old British class system had incongruously survived. Backed by the mass media and the attention of public relations, it took its inspiration from John Osborne's stage success *Look Back in Anger*. When it was first performed at the Royal Court Theatre in London's Sloane Square, I was among its first-night audience in May 1956, but was left unmoved by the furore it was to cause later, as apparently most of the critics and the audience were. It was Kenneth Tynan and Harold Hobson's rave reviews in the Sunday papers that then launched the fantastic éclat.

The differences among these reactions seemed in themselves to indicate an extraordinary phenomenon. The play's hero, Jimmy Porter, is the key to it, described in the stage directions as:

> a disconcerting mixture of sincerity and cheerful malice, of tenderness and freebooting cruelty, restlessness, importunate, full of pride, a combination which alienates the sensitive and insensitive alike. Blistering honesty or apparent honesty like this makes few friends. To many he may seem sensitive to the point of vulgarity. To others, he is simply a loudmouth. To be as vehement as he is is to be almost non-commital.

Jimmy Porter shares a squalid bohemia with his upper-class-born wife. His tantrums and ranting, induced by drink and boredom, which she endures, fill almost two hours, and explain that few were aware that that was to be the pointless point of it and that what they experienced as an empty rage against the contemporary world was itself a new form of theatre. For while the remainder of the European continent was divided between East and West, concentrating on its own economic regeneration and idealist hopes for a united Europe, the British young had been left by their parents who had returned from the war, with nothing left to do but look around their own island and rant discontentedly.

By all accounts, and not necessarily well-informed ones, they could find even less right with the rest of the world, but they ineffectively sermonized against it. There was the failure of the Hungarian anti-communist rebellion, the Anglo–American Suez debacle, South African racism and the atom bomb. Their fathers and mothers' heroics in the war were just one long bore to them. It was only later that they sought an escape in such second-hand thrills. They had nothing worth living for apart from getting into a public welfare society or old Harold Macmillan's uncomforting, 'You never had it so good'. John Osborne's hero thus became an English intellectual named James Bean, a rebel with a high IQ and no cause; Kingsley Amis, the novelist, had also prepared the way for him with that slightly milder-tempered James Dixon in *Lucky Jim* (1954). Countless others were to follow both these authors in novels and on the stage.

Thus, a 'school' of 'angry young men' was born, protesting against nothing in particular, but talking themselves into something meaningful, though really, as Harold Pinter said of John Osborne, just liking 'to take the piss out of everybody, including himself'. What is more, their elders and the media took them seriously. Societies in disintegration and flux and the breakdown of old certainties have always coincided. This happened also to Great Britain after 1945 and, as W. B. Yeats had expressed it half a century earlier, 'Things fall apart, the centre cannot hold; mere anarchy is loosed upon the world. The best lack all conviction, while the worst are full of passionate intensity.' The conventional social stability of the Victorian and Edwardian ages had ended not with the deaths of these two monarchs, but with the social upheavals that followed the Second World War. In the same way, the stable 'Wilhelminian' pre-1914 world had been unable to survive the defeat and revolution of 1918. In the 1920s and 1930s the sons of British middle-class parents, of the Isherwood, Auden and Spender generation, were similarly attracted to the 'gay' Berlin scene of that time, while their German contemporaries were about to create their own very different and dangerous political present. The British 'cultural revolution' of the 1950s and 1960s was, oddly, to exert a similar attraction, happily an apolitical one, to young people abroad, by means of the Beatles, pop music, the capital's Carnaby Street scene and all that became known if only by phoney repute as 'swinging London'.

Nevertheless, the era found its outlet in being 'rebels without cause' in the form of a new satirical show that the BBC, or rather its then director-general Sir Hugh Carleton-Greene, brother of the novelist Graham Greene, started. The BBC of course had good reason to look back to 1922 when its founder and first great general manager, the sternly upright Sir John Reith, derived the concept of a great institution that would become the educator of the nation, through a public corporation funded by the taxpayer's contribution. Then there was that founder's successor, the satirical sexual innovator for whom nothing was apparently sacred anymore. So, on behalf of Sir John Reith, presumably turning in his grave, arrived Mary Whitehouse fearlessly campaiging against pornography, the moral corruption of the times. The wretched Carleton-Greene had to sustain her attacks on behalf of the silent majority, which paid for the BBC as well as its director-general's salary. Being a public servant he had to be beholden to that majority, but he had his revenge, as one learnt, by sticking pins into her picture, kept for that purpose on his desk.

Those were the years when I recall meeting the unforgettable Maria Callas on her concert appearance at the Edinburgh Festival. I also attended the solemn reopening of Coventry Cathedral with the first performance of Benjamin Britten's 'War Requiem', the composer conducting choir and orchestra. This was also the time of annual visits to the Glyndebourne country opera near Lewes in Sussex. It was the grand idea of a rich Englishman and opera lover, John Christie, and built onto his own Tudor family seat in the 1930s. He was then natural science master at Eton, not so much because he needed to work, but to have something to do. His opera house was a wedding present for his wife, the opera singer Audrey Mildmay who was 18 years his junior. It opened in 1934 with Mozart's *Figaro* and Mildmay singing the role of Susanna, just in time to profit from a great artistic and musical partnership with the German conductor Fritz Busch, the producer Carl Ebert and Rudolf Bing as first general manager. The three had just been booted out of Hitler's Germany and Christie was able to give them financial security and complete artistic independence. They repaid that debt by endowing Glyndebourne with international prestige for their Mozart productions of the highest quality in their fine English country house setting. Christie's vision proved uniquely successful, considering what an expensive art form opera was, and that, in England, it was at that time always done on the cheap and badly. Privately financed by a growing loyal opera loving public, Glyndebourne prospered under John Christie's descendants for some 70 years. In the 1950s, the original theatre for 300 was enlarged to take 800 and was recently rebuilt and modernized for an audience of 1300.

Glyndebourne experienced something of a revival in the 1950s. While Fritz Busch still conducted and Carl Ebert still produced most performances, Glyndebourne branched out from Mozart to other classical composers like Cavalli and Monteverdi, usually conducted by Bernard Haitink, produced by Peter Hall and staged by Raymond Leppard, with his empathy for their original scores. There were excellent performances of Verdi's *Falstaff*, Janacek's *The Little Vixen* and the Richard Strauss operas *Capriccio*, *Intermezzo*, *Die Schweigsame Frau* and *Rosenkavalier*, always sung in the operas' original languages. The summer season usually lasted for five weeks with one or two new productions each year.

Glyndebourne's great attraction was its rural seclusion and the possibility of unlimited time for rehearsals. Unfortunately, this did not last into modern times when well-known conductors and established singers had to fly from one engagement to another, and new talent was correspondingly difficult to find and bring over from afar. Being entirely privately financed, Glyndebourne was unique among opera houses of the world, even given its limited season. It managed to cover its expenses from no less than 70 per cent of its box office sales. In the 1930s a stalls seat cost £2, then an unheard of sum to ask, probably more like 40 times the value of the pound at today's inflationary prices, so that the same outing would cost about £80 to £100 today. Glyndebourne's additional attraction was its customary 75-minute interval, and the opportunity it offered of either leisurely dining in the restaurant or, less comfortably but more enjoyably on a fine summer evening, to picnic in the delightful park close to grazing cows and sheep. These, however, according to John Christie anecdotage, apparently reflected his highly cultured, though conservative and classical tastes. The animals were said to flee into the more remote Sussex hills when the Glyndebourne programme included Stravinsky's *The Rake's Progress*, Debussy's *Pelleas and Melisande* or, especially, Henze's *Elegy for Young Lovers*. While the cows and sheep shared the taste of the great Christie, he at least had the sense not to impose his taste on those who did not like what he liked.

Meeting T. S. Eliot
The chance to meet T. S. Eliot was a memorable occasion for me, since I had long admired the author of *The Waste Land*, that

great epic of the early twentieth century. Our encounter took place during the rehearsals for a new production of *Murder in the Cathedral* in the early 1960s – he died in 1965 – in a St John's Wood church where Robert Speaight gave a fine performance of Thomas à Becket. A mutual friend, the New Zealand writer Robert Sencourt, introduced me to the poet and I ventured to bring up what had long puzzled me about him, his early anti-Semitic utterances. He at first seemed irritated to talk about it. It was clearly something that rankled with him, having often been accused of it by Jews and others; they referred to passages from the period of his Prufrock poems and others before the end of the First World War, lasting into the early 1920s. We talked about the differences between Orthodox and freethinking or liberal Judaism. It emerged that the subject of anti-Semitism seemed close to his aversion for all liberal free thought. He accepted that in his mind this was related to the rational humanistic Unitarian faith held by his grandfather, against the domineering influence of which the young Eliot had rebelled.

He agreed with me when I expressed a cultural and religious preference for Orthodox Sephardic or Spanish Judaism. He then mentioned the influence that the Action française had exerted on him, whose leader Charles Maurras he had met in Paris in 1911. Eliot adapted Maurras's description of himself as 'classique, catholique, monarchique' to his own 'classicist in literature, royalist in politics and Anglo-Catholic in religion', though he felt that the later Maurras had become too involved in politics. While rejecting the anti-Semitic ascription to himself, he accepted that there was a certain levity or aggressiveness in his general dis-illusionment with his age at that time that was near nihilism, blasphemy and possibly expressive of aggressiveness and insecurity. He was probably playing dangerously with fire, he granted, and this had found expression in a near physical breakdown. *The Waste Land* (1925) then summed up this malaise on behalf of a whole generation. Eliot felt no regret for his anti-liberal stance, but denied in the light of his previous remarks that it was anti-Semitic. It seemed to me like special pleading of a familiar sort. Knowing that I was a Catholic convert, he said that Catholics of his generation like Hilaire Belloc had shared these views. I was aware of that but did not think that it was therefore justified. It appeared to me as a

certain spiritual shortsightedness in a man of his sensibilities and
stature, but decided, as I took my leave, that it was unbecoming
to say it to his face.

A visit to Henry Moore

Near his seventieth birthday, in July 1965, I was asked to meet
the great sculptor Henry Moore in the old farm house in which
he then lived, at Perry Green, Hertfordshire. His wife and small
daughter, then about 13, joined us for afternoon tea. There was
a large garden behind the house with two studios at the far end
and a wide enough road entrance for cranes to drive in and lift
his heavy plaster casts for shipment to foundries in Berlin or
Paris. They came back as bronzes and, at that point, he and his
assistants would give them their final patina. With his innate
toughness and sense of intellectual independence, Moore was
very much a Yorkshireman. He had been called up in 1917, but
became the victim of a gas attack at Cambrai, which ended the
war for him with three months in hospital. After that, he went to
Leeds art school and resolved to rid himself of the 'arbitrary
influence of decadent late Greek art as the only norm of
excellence'. The standard of art studies at the Royal Academy in
London, which he entered in 1921, was not much better than at
Leeds. He would have preferred to study in Germany, but lacked
the means. However, he found an understanding patron in Sir
William   Rothenstein,   to   whom   he   owed   his   teaching
appointment at the Royal College of Art in London.

It was about this time that he discovered the cultic forms of
the archaic cultures of Mexico, Sumeria, Africa and Greece,
which related to eleventh-century finds in Yorkshire churches.
They seemed to him to have the formal values he found lacking
in the European sculptures of the humanist tradition. Another
turning point for him was a visit to Maillol in Paris where he saw
Cézanne's 'Les Grandes Baigneuses'. These naked figures lying
on the ground, seemingly as hewn from rock, had impressed him
as much as Chartres Cathedral, he said. A trip to Italy on a
stipend and seeing the works of Michelangelo, Masaccio and
Donatello shook his belief in the transcending importance of
non-European art. He then tried to reconcile the two traditions
in his 'Lying Figures' of 1929, especially the concept of the
female figures as a symbol of a hilly landscape. He spoke of
having searched for a 'spiritual life force' that 'as far as I was

concerned was more moving and went deeper than the senses'. This was when the art historian, Nicholaus Pevsner, wrote a controversial book about the importance of national character in the arts entitled *The Englishness of English Art* (1955). Pevsner had to admit defeat when he came to discuss great painters of world stature that England had produced like Turner, Constable, Gainsborough and Hogarth as equals of the greatest Italian, French and German masters, but which seemed then to disappear again. However, the emergence of great modern English sculptures and painters, then already in their third generation like Henry Moore or the younger but no less gifted Reg Butler, whom I got to know well, seemed to show that individual artists would always break through these national patterns, the exceptions proving the rule.

Sir Karl Popper: happiest of philosophers

'I am, I can only assume, the happiest philosopher whom I have ever been able to meet.' Or, so said Sir Karl Popper, whom I went to see close to his eightieth birthday in July 1982 in the village of Penn in the Chiltern Hills half way between London and Oxford. He and his wife had lived there in great simplicity since 1950 after returning from Christchurch in New Zealand, which had offered him a refuge from the Nazis and a professorship in philosophy. Though he would have preferred Oxford, the London School of Economics became his next and happy British home until his retirement in 1975, when he received an English knighthood. A grand piano in the room in which we talked was a reminder that he had once toyed with the idea of becoming a musician. He had grown up in an academic and musical family, related on his mother's side to Bruno Walter under whom he sang in the choir during Bach's St Matthew's Passion. My own cherished memory of singing St Matthew's Passion in my school choir provided a lively link. He spent two years in close contact with Arnold Schönberg, which confirmed his aversion to modern music. He then studied church music for two years before deciding that he was insufficiently gifted for musical studies, as previously he had discovered for mathematics, physics and indeed starting on a joiner's apprenticeship. He was also a communist for a few months after the end of the First World War, which at any rate produced its decided rejection: 'The most dangerous of all political ideas is perhaps the desire to achieve man's perfection and happiness. The attempt of creating heaven on earth has ever only produced hell.'

All this probably had to do with his being a perfectionist, though this is not at all a bad thing to want to be. It all probably started with Aristotle who wrote that an educated young man should learn to play the flute, but not too well, lest he might be confused with a professional. Popper has always been critical of Aristotle, though he says now that he was a bit unfair on him in his *The Open Society and Its Enemies* (1945) because he had not then sufficiently studied Aristotle's biological writings. Being a perfectionist, he has long made good this omission. Indeed, what was most astounding in this astonishing man was the range of his work. He has worked his way into the Greek classical texts of Plato to such an extent that great classicists have come to respect his interpretations of certain obscure passages in the Timeaus. At times his favourite readings were the fragments of the pre-Socratic philosophers, that is when he was not reading his favourite English novelists Jane Austen, Trollope and Dickens. What would be quite sufficient for any hard working scholar was never much more than a sideline for him. His life's work has been devoted to the philosophy of science, which he has revolutionized. Referring to Einstein's predilection for theological parables, he said to him after their first meeting at Princeton:

> If God had wanted a world that contained everything from the beginning, he would have created a universe without change, without organisms, evolution and without men and their capacity to bring about changes. But God seemed to have thought that even for him a living universe with sometimes unexpected happenings would be more interesting than a deadlocked universe like that of Parmenides.

He did not mention Einstein's response to his objection. *Unended Quest* was the title of Popper's autobiography, indicating his belief, like that of Democritus, the founder of 'atomism', who was one of his models, having reconciled the monism of Parmenides and Zeno with the pluralism of Empedocles and Anaxagoras. Popper's way of formulating his theses seemed to border on arrogance, and yet there was the humility of the genius about him. He said of Einstein: 'One simply had to trust him, surrender unconditionally to his kindness, goodness, wisdom, his openness and almost childlike simplicity.' That also seems to apply to Sir Karl Popper, who once said from the amoeba to Einstein was only a brief step.

Dylan and Caitlin Thomas as parents

Children of great men often have difficult lives. Aeronwy, the daughter of the poet Dylan Thomas was no exception to this rule. She came to be a close friend of my late wife, who played the role almost of a substitute mother to the half-orphaned Aeronwy. Her famous father died half a century ago from the effects of excessive alcohol and narcotic drugs. Now entering her sixties, she seems finally to have freed herself of this burdensome inheritance. Not since Byron has any poet claimed such public interest for himself, and as with Byron this is not linked merely to his creative achievement. A veritable Dylan Thomas industry has grown up over the years. The public's need for ever new and revealing biographies was insatiable, and doctoral theses about him and his work have accumulated in the universities, especially in the USA. The house of his birth on Cwmdonkin Drive, Swansea, and the boathouse at Laugharne, acquired by friends for the poet who all his life suffered from penury, have become much frequented places of pilgrimage. The picturesque view from Laugharne (pronounced Larn) on the mouth of the river Towy with its flocks of herons has found expression in some of his finest poems. Members of the family have since died – the famous or infamous widow, Caitlin, who died not long after the publication of her biography illustrating her chaotic marriage, and Aeronwy's brother Llewellyn who grew up in America and died in Ireland. Two children remain, her elder brother, Colm, who was a taxi driver in Australia and now lives in a house owned by the family in the Italian Abruzi hills, and Aeronwy. Whether they like it or not, they have become part of the industry. While the sons had little interest in their father, Aeronwy cherishes his life and work, and defends him against his detractors.

Dylan Thomas used to call her Aeron, but realized only later that it was a male Christian name. The confusion shows how alienated Dylan Thomas had been from his Welsh roots because, though remaining emotionally attached to Wales, he grew up in an English cultural environment. Both his middle-class parents spoke Welsh, but never encouraged him to learn it. Actually, Aeronwy, like her brothers, had little cause to bask in their

father's fame. Their mother, for example, was not at all sure who
Aeronwy's father was, although these doubts were dispelled
when the baby's face showed unmistakable traits of the father,
and today their resemblance is quite uncanny. Her childhood
memories recall sitting on his knees while he read Grimm's
fairytales to her and him imitating the voices of all their two- or
four-legged characters. In the poem 'Country Heaven', which he
dedicated to her, appears the fairy wolf in a sheep's skin, which
Thomas called the 'bleating wolf.'

However, she has never forgotten how the drunken Caitlin
attacked her father and any child who came between them. As a
child, she feared that the mother's constant violent slaps might
cause her concussion of the brain. Her brother Llewellyn, whom
one of Caitlin's sisters brought up, was very different in
character from her and enjoyed a relatively idyllic childhood. If
ever two people were destined to make each other's life a hell on
earth, it was Dylan and Caitlin. The fateful meeting between 22
year-old Caitlin Macnamara, a mixture of charm and wildness,
and the poet with the baby face and curly hair took place in a
Soho pub in 1936. They got married the following year. The
baby face became bloated like a pudding and one of Caitlin's
sisters said of them: 'The great difference between Dylan and my
sister is that he was naturally unspoiled.'

Caitlin's special tragedy was her huge and brutal openness
towards other people (a very Irish trait), while his negative Welsh
characteristics found expression in lies and deceit. He was
incapable of Caitlin's brutal, selfish and lacerating frankness.
'My God', says his daughter today, 'how much I prefer that
Welsh deceit to the cruel honesty we had to suffer from our
mother.' Aeronwy regards Caitlin's alleged nymphomania as part
of the exaggerated myths that grew up between her parents. 'Sex
had not really that significance for my mother. She needed her
lovers only to confirm her own attraction.' That Dylan Thomas
was unable to satisfy her, she denies as part of the 'legends'.

Aeronwy's marriage to Trefor was like entering a calming
harbour after a stormy voyage. He was a former miner, now
employed by an oil firm, also a member of the London Welsh
Chorale, an excellent mixed voice choir of 75 members. Aeronwy
performs occasionally, reciting her own poems and her father's.
Her star turn is undoubtedly her father's enchanting celebration
of childhood A Child's Christmas in Wales. It begins:

One Christmas was so much like another, in those years around the sea-town corner and out of all sound except the distant speaking of the voices I sometimes hear a moment before sleep, that I can never remember whether it snowed for six days and six nights when I was twelve or whether it snowed for twelve days and twelve nights when I was six.

But here a small boy says: 'It snowed last year, too. I made a snow man and my brother knocked it down and I knocked my brother down and then we had tea.' 'But that was not the same snow', I say, 'Our snow was shaken from whitewash buckets down the sky, it came shawling out of the ground and swam and drifted out of the arms and hands and bodies of the trees; snow grew overnight on the roofs of the houses like a pure and grandfather moss, minutely white ivied the walls and settled on the postman, opening the gate, like a dumb, numb thunderstorm of white, torn Christmas cards.' ...

And then the Presents, the Useful Presents: engulfing mufflers of the old coach days, and mittens made for giants sloths; zebra scarfs of a substance like silky gum that could be tug-o'-warred down to the galoshes; blinding tam-o'-shanters like patchwork tea cosies and bunny-suited busbies and balaclavas for victims of head-shrinking tribes, from aunts who always wore wool next to the skin there were moustached and rasping vests that made you wonder why the aunts had any skin left at all. ...

'Go on to the Useless Presents.' Bags of moist and many-coloured jelly babies and a folded flag and a false nose and a tram conductor's cap and a machine that punched tickets and rang a bell; never a catapult; once, by mistake that no one could explain, a little hatchet; and a celluloid duck that made, when you pressed it, a most unducklike sound, a mewing moo that an ambitious cat might make who wishes to be a cow; and a painting book in which I could make the grass, the trees, the sea and the animals any colour I pleased. ... Hardboiled, toffee, fudge and allsorts, crunches, cracknels, humbugs, glaciers, marzipan, and butterwelsh for the Welsh. ... And a whistle to make the dogs bark to wake up the old man next door to make him beat on the wall with his stick to shake our picture off the wall. ... And a packet of cigarettes; and you put one in your mouth and you stood at the corner of the street and you waited for hours, in vain, for an old lady to scold you for smoking a cigarette, and then, with a smirk you ate it. And then it was breakfast under the balloons.

There were always Uncles at Christmas. Some few large men sat in the front parlours, without their collars, uncles almost certainly, trying their new cigars, holding them out judiciously at arms' length, returning them to their mouths, coughing, then holding them out again as though waiting for an explosion; and some few small Aunts, not wanted in the kitchen, nor anywhere for that matter, sat on the very edges of their chairs, posed and brittle, afraid to break, like faded cups and saucers. ... For dinner we had turkey and blazing pudding, and after dinner the Uncles sat in front of the fire, loosened all buttons, put their last moist hands over their watch chains, groaned a little and slept. Mothers, aunts, and sisters scuttled to and fro, bearing tureens. Auntie Bessie, who had already been frightened twice, by a clockwork mouse, whimpered at the sideboard and had some elderberry wine. The dog was sick. Auntie Dosie had to have three aspirins, but Auntie Hannah, who liked port, stood in the middle of the snowbound backyard, singing like a big-bosomed thrush. I would blow up balloons to see how big they would blow up to; and, when they burst, which they all did, the Uncles jumped and rumbled. ...

Auntie Hannah, who had got on to the parsnip wine, sang a song about bleeding hearts and Death, and then another, in which she said that her heart was like a Bird's Nest; and then everybody laughed again; and then I went to bed. Looking through my bedroom window, out into the moonlight and the unending smoke-coloured snow, I could see the lights in the windows of all the houses on our hill and hear the music rising from them up the long, steadily falling night. I turned the gas down, I got into bed. I said some words to the close and holy darkness and then I slept.

Meeting England's 'Queen of Romance'

A woman of a very different type was Barbara Cartland, the late

'Queen' of an unlikely modern Romantic age, best-selling author of 723 novels, the common bond of which is that their heroes and heroines proudly practise chastity until they sink into their wedding night bed on the last page. The titles of these stories, of which she produced 14 a year, dictating them, curled up on a sofa, to a bunch of secretaries, were listed singly in *Who's Who*, making Cartland's entry the longest in that volume.

Lord Beaverbrook, the Canadian newspaper king, who was one of her many admirers, taught her how to write with short sentences and paragraphs. Lord Mountbatten, another devotee, uncle of the queen and victim of a terrorist attack, used to greet her with a peck on the cheek, which gave her lasting frissons, she says. She had two or three rich husbands of well-born Scottish ancestry, who died early and left her with growing wealth. She lived into her late nineties on about eighty vitamin tablets a day, honey, Gelée Royale and other health-giving foods, with her sons running what became an impressive enterprise and industry.

Her colour, Cartland pink, was a characteristic feature of much of her life, down to the heavy make-up she wore, along with the longest imaginable eyelashes. Her Rolls Royce was pink, as was the fence of her house, Camfield Place in Hertfordshire, recognizable from afar and naturally ever so smart. All this was, of course, sheer affectation, but impressive in the way she played the part. I have always had great admiration for women of her sort who are fundamentally tough but able to carry it off with the sheer guts of their spirits and ability. There was nothing phoney about that. 'This is a present for you', she said when she came into the sitting room in which I had been waiting, an apparition in pink, right down to the feather boa. 'I only wear false pearls and jewels nowadays,' she said later, 'it is much too risky to take the things out of the bank safe.' Her present for me, normally only given on leaving, was clearly intended to disarm any doubting Thomas of a journalist. However, I had no difficulty succumbing to what was clearly a very talented lady, seemingly no older than in her bewitching sixties. The present, incidentally, was a paperweight, beautifully wrapped in pink, containing a gold leaf 'from the tree in my garden in which Queen Elisabeth I hunted her first stag'.

In the dining room, in which pictures of her late husbands adorned the walls, tea was served on beautiful old silver and fine hand-painted china cups and plates. There were meringues with

whipped-cream, to which I was very partial. 'They are a
speciality of the house, have another one,' she said. I needed no
encouragement. 'Did you make them yourself?' What a thing to
ask! 'No, my chef makes them,' she answered grandly. We talked
about her great fight for the preservation of virginity in young
girls and her hope for its general return to our modern society.
She was all for the equality of the sexes and had certainly done
her bit for vindicating women's rights. 'But in the bedroom one
of the partners has to dominate', she said. 'I can't help feeling
sorry for those poor men faced with those bitches with their sex
handbooks and insistence on 15 orgasms every five minutes. No
wonder men lose their self-confidence.' I could not but agree and
helped myself to the last of the meringues. 'My daughter is now
mistress of 53 bathrooms, 40 more than we have here,' she
informed me. Her daughter was then married to, but then
divorced from, the Earl of Spencer, and thus a stepmother of the
late Diana, Princess of Wales. When I met her, I could only
conclude that Raine had evidently inherited her mother's grand
airs, but none of her abilities or charm.

An Englishwoman among the Arabs
The famous traveller in Arab lands, Dame Freya Stark, was
another impressive English lady. I called on her at Asolo, a
charming mountain village at the foot of the Dolomites, where
she lived in a little cottage near the old castle residence of
Caterina Cornaro (1454–1510), the tragic queen of Cyprus who
had been forced to abdicate and then died surrounded by poets
and artists. Dame Freya lived similarly, but more modestly, in a
gatehouse Robert Browning had once inhabited.

At one time Freya Stark's house was a centre for friends,
Arabists and diplomats, with many good-looking young men
among them who were her willing slaves. She served drinks in
silver cups and food on coloured Italian ceramic plates, but
would immediately put guests who tried to help and make
themselves useful in their place: 'Leave that', she told one, 'that
is what the girl is there for, you only confuse her.' Arab,
Persian, Kurdistan and Turkish souvenirs were all over the
house. She used to ride a Vespa into her late old age, which
frightened the villagers. She would arrive at parties on it with
disarranged hair, in a caftan-like tunic and girdle, and covered
in diamonds – she was the English female eccentric personified.

Having been born in Paris of well-to-do English parents who lived mainly apart, Freya spent most of her rather unhappy childhood in Italy with her mother and sisters, so spoke English with an Italian accent.

She was 34 years old and unmarried when she went on her first journey to Beirut in 1927 'to explore the Near East'. A Capuchin priest in San Remo had taught her Arabic and her first book, *Baghdad Sketches*, published in 1932, was an immediate success. Later she went on more strenuous, adventurous trips through Persia, to the yet undiscovered fortresses of the Assassini. Following the old incense trade route, she went to villages on the Persian western border, including the disappeared city of Shabwa in south Arabia. Other explorers had preceded her, but she was the first European woman in many of these unknown parts. Later she learnt to speak Persian and Kurdish in addition to her French, German and Italian. She travelled mostly alone, accompanied only by a servant or someone who knew the area; sometimes she also went with armed escorts if some concerned sultan had sent them out to her. Her fearlessness impressed everybody. She rode ponies, donkeys and camels, and she took her time, for she was ever open to and ready to identify with the landscape, inhabitants and old cultures.

Freya Stark was not used to putting up her own camp bed, lighting a fire, making her own coffee in the morning or loading her luggage onto packhorses, but she was quite prepared to pass the night in a primitive nomad tent or under the open desert sky. 'This is to confirm', read a certificate from Sayid Arabs who had pleased her, 'that Miss Freya Stark, an Englishwoman of noble birth, traveller, familiar with foreign laws, led by her religion, is the first woman to travel alone from England to Hradhamout, used fearlessly to put up with hardships, fears, suffering and danger.' Being familiar with Arab hospitality, 'in which every service is a kind of sacrament', she was generally well received. She would spend the day discussing with the men, the nights in harems, which she found as boring as life in the west English villages of her youth. Someone said of her that she was a pagan in church, but a Christian in the mountains or desert.

She liked men, but was unlucky with them; they were probably not up to a woman with her domineering ways. The Italian, to whom she was engaged as a nurse in the First World War, left her and the scholarly W. P. Ker of London's Bedford

College, under whom she had read history and with whom she climbed mountains, 'suddenly uttered a little cry and fell down dead'. After the Second World War, she worked for the British propaganda department in Aden, Cairo and Baghdad. She then married Stewart Perowne, a British colonial official who was 12 years younger than she was, but the marriage did not survive the Christmas holiday they spent together. She put together some volumes of her collected letters and wrote about twenty books about her travels. What raised her books above those of other travel writers and made them popular was a gift for intellectual objectivity and emotional restraint. She acquired the recognition of the Royal Geographical Society and received the Royal Asiatic Society's Burton Memorial Medal. Above the entrance to her cottage she nailed the inscription, 'We are all pilgrims like you'. She once wrote to a friend that she had felt as a traveller like a passing visitor and pilgrim. Behind her urge for distant travel 'was a wish for overcoming my human fears and my mortal weakness'.

An unusual nuncio
I like to recall my friendship with Archbishop Bruno Bernhard Heim (1911–2003), the first pro-nuncio in Great Britain. A nuncio's function is to act as his papal master's listening post, and Heim had the good fortune to have had the charismatic Roncalli groom him for the job. Roncalli's great achievement was to call the Second Vatican Council and thereby to see to the first and long overdue ventilation of the dusty Vatican corridors – whether or not this was always good for the Church. Though a divine institution, the Church consists, after all, of the most fragile and fallible human elements. One of the nuncio's tasks is to select the names of episcopal candidates. This process had for far too long been a purely clerical prerogative, as though the flock need have no say in who was to guard them. This could no longer be tolerated in modern times and, being Swiss with some democrat blood in his veins, Heim almost started the process of consultation, though at that time it seemed a pioneering venture in the Church. Among the 40 appointments he made during his 12-year tenure in London, there was certainly one for which he earned unstinted praise. This was to propose the charismatic George Basil Hume (1923–99), the former Benedictine abbot, for the See of Westminster; he proved a great success as priest and pastor.

During Heim's stay in Britain, he had his status upgraded from that of a mere apostolic delegate. As a belated punishment for Henry VIII's act of having made himself Pope, his predecessors had humbly had to get by without the emoluments of the job, the diplomatic privilege of getting their smokes and drinks duty free. In Heim's case, this was of tangible consequence. He had, when he first arrived, entertained the late Queen Mother among his royal dinner guests and discovered her liking for a particular brand of Swiss chocolates. Little did he realize how much of a hole this would, over an extended period, burn in his meagre Roman income, for he had to go on providing replacements on his visits home. The change of title was therefore of inestimable personal benefit, since he could now indulge Her Majesty's sweet tooth without blinking a diplomatic eyelid.

Bruno Heim was unusual in many ways. He was an excellent cook and home gardener who in his greenhouse cultivated all sorts of wild herbs and rare flowers. The religious sisters paid to look after the nunciature did not always appreciate his domestic gifts, for they sometimes felt done out of their jobs when he took charge of the pots and pans. They also had to put up with his biblical adage: 'It is better to be invited to herbs with love than to a fattened calf with hatred' (Proverbs, 15, 17). Inevitably, the puritanical media nominated him 'THE GOURMET ARCHBISHOP', and one female reporter even maliciously scented 'the odour less of sanctity than of something delicious being prepared in the kitchen'.

He was a stationmaster's son from Olten, that most Catholic of all Swiss parts. He was also truly Swiss in his mixture of spiritual, worldly and simple burgher characteristics. As a devotee of St Thomas More, he had even troubled to Anglicize his Swiss sense of humour. He also had good taste, a rare quality among his predecessors, which he demonstrated when he moved to his Wimbledon residence by stripping its walls of various pictures of saints and martyrs writhing in sacred ecstasies, seen as fitting for conveying a Vatican-like atmosphere. His own artistic formation had been part of his studies in canon law. His doctoral thesis at the Roman Gregoriana was on the subject of heraldry in the Church, and being sent to London was an enhanced delight for coming home to the seat of heraldry, the College of Arms and the Lyon Court.

He had become the official designer of the coat of arms for

four popes (John XXIII, Paul VI, John Paul I and John Paul II).
Since no pope can exercise his authority without this emblem, it
has to be provided at great speed, especially when the result of a
papal election is not foreseen, as in the case of John Paul II. It
also proved the most difficult. Monsignor Heim sat at his
Wimbledon telephone, ready with paintbrush and pen, waiting
for the news from Rome. Eventually the Polish pope wanted to
retain his coat of arms as archbishop of Cracow, which had,
however, been drawn up by someone with little knowledge of
heraldry. There was some dispute about the colouring and the
letter 'M' for Mary, which was quite unheraldic, and for which,
Heim suggested, an artistic symbol for the Virgin Mary should
be substituted. The Pope would not give way on the letter 'M',
which he had long used, and his wish naturally prevailed. In the
case of John XXIII, whose personal secretary Heim had been
when Roncalli was nuncio in Paris, matters were easier, and all
the designer had to do was to give a more human smile to the
lion of St Mark, which the Pope, as former patriarch of Venice,
wanted to have as well.

Comparatively simpler were the designs for some of Monsignor
Heim's dinner guests, a useful addition for his guestbooks. He
would suggest an apt theme to them if they lacked such personal
arms. For instance, for Margaret Thatcher, then just the 'iron
lady' and depicted in Soviet cartoons as a witch, he proposed a
sword cutting through a witch's broom. It is unclear whether
Lady Thatcher retained the emblem when she was raised to the
Upper House. For Dame Agatha Christie, Heim invented an axe
dripping with blood. He had high regard for her, having
improved his English through her books. His mixture of
German-Swiss simplicity and robustness contradicted those who
regard heraldry as only of interest to snobs and pedants. He was
able to enliven the subject with a creative and historical imagination. One flattering compliment paid to him on leaving London
was by the illustrious Somerset Herald of Arms who said that he
would be assured of a job there if the Vatican closed down.

Honouring W. H. Auden

I always regarded it as fortunate that my admiration for Wystan
Hugh Auden as one of the greatest English poets of the twentieth
century enabled me also to play a small part in the public
recognition accorded to him in Austria, which became his

country for the last 16 years of his life (1907–73). Having prematurely died in a Vienna hotel, his house at Kirchstetten on the edge of the Wienerwald in the province of lower Austria has become a small museum, where the centenary of his birth was duly commemorated on 21 February 2007.

Perhaps it was his mocking, frivolous, roguish, disarmingly simple, unexpected poetic tone and his tremendous honesty that attracted me to his large following. He was held to be the voice of his generation but later rejected that claim since that generation had also made Hitler and Stalin possible, and probably also because of the sexual chaos of his own life. In Kirchstetten's Catholic parish church, he attended Sunday Mass regularly, recalling the high Anglicanism of his Yorkshire ancestors. I always felt that he was nastily, if understandably, attacked by men like Evelyn Waugh for literally 'buggering off' to New York in January 1939. He was not the traitor they alleged him to be and not a pacifist like Isherwood, his companion.

He showed that in his patriotic poem '1st September 1939', by volunteering to serve in the British army, and, after obtaining American citizenship, by later joining the US forces. Moreover, the winter of 1938/9 was still part of the British appeasement of the dictators, abhorrent to Auden. That appeasement had made him feel guilty for some of the things he had written in the 1930s, as he told the *Sun* in an interview in 1966: 'nothing I wrote against Hitler then saved a single Jew from being murdered; nothing I later wrote ended the war a minute earlier.'

His dislike of being regarded as an intellectual leader of his generation was undoubtedly influenced by the infamy in which the term *Führer*, regardless of right or left, came to be held in the years in which Auden reached intellectual maturity.

The beginning of Auden's poem, entitled 'Words': 'Words have no words for words that are not true' may be said to illustrate the basic principle of Auden's spiritual and intellectual integrity. But, as Rüdiger Görner has reminded us when considering the mastery of Auden's poems, one could never be sure that they had not been written for the sake of their rhymes, although that cannot exclude the fact that they happened also to make exactly the right judgement on his fellow intellectuals, as for example in:

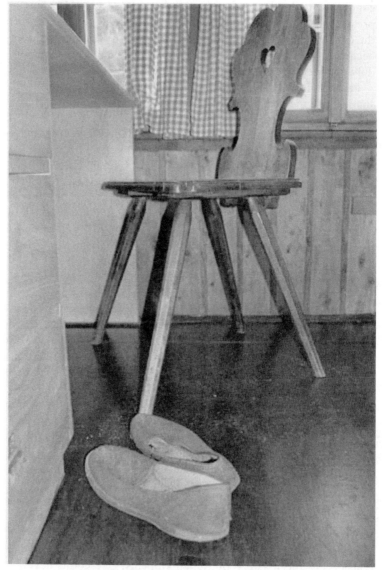

16. W. H. Auden's last home in Kirchstetten, Austria.

Intellectual disgrace
stares from every human face,

and the seas of pity lie
locked and frozen in each eye.

Or as in another poem:

More than ever
life out there is goodly, miraculous, lovable,
but we shan't, not since Stalin and Hitler,
trust ourselves ever again.
For we are conscripts to our age,
Simply by being born; we wage
the war we are.

Early in 1980 friends of the Austrian *Gesellschaft für Literatur*
asked me to visit Kirchstetten in lower Austria where Auden had
bought an ordinary peasant's house with the 120,000 Austrian
Schillings he had been awarded by way of the Italian Feltrinelli
prize. I also went to see his grave at the local cemetery. An
Anglican clergyman, Montefiore, had conducted his funeral and
Stephen Spender, his lifelong friend, had been among those
present while a Vienna Philharmonic Orchestra recording of
'Siegfried's Tod' from Wagner's *Gotterdammerung* was played,
as Auden had wished.

Why Auden and his companion, Chester Kallman, had chosen
the obscure village of Kirchstetten remains unclear, but they
wanted to be off the beaten tourist track. It had to be a German-
speaking country, as Auden loving and knowing Goethe had
stipulated, but not Germany, though with a temperate climate
and in a wine-growing part, and not too far from an opera house
like Vienna's. Kirchstetten happened to be ideal for that, for it
also reflected a typical Austrian mentality in its good and bad
ways; it had been the home of Josef Weinheber, the eminent
Austrian poet who had joined the Nazis and then, disillusioned,
committed suicide in 1945. He was thus not allowed into the
hallowed ground of the official cemetery, but, as Auden put it,
living among the ghosts of fascism, 'they buried you like a
loved/old family dog'.

In his last poem, Auden had looked forward to his own death
as a release:

He still loves life

But O O O O how he wishes
The Good Lord would take him.

But in a poem the original German title 'Stark bewölkt', 1971,
(Much clouded over) Auden expressed that he had no illusions
about the nature of his Austrian surroundings:

The Beamterei, it's true,
is as awful as ever,
the drivers are dangerous,
standards at the Staatsoper
steadily decline each year,
and Wien's become provincial,
compared to the pride she was.

Still it's a cosy country,
unracked by riots or strikes
and backward at drugtaking.

At the time of my visit, Auden's affairs were still in the chaotic
legal mess into which his sudden death had thrown them.
Kallman, heir to the property, had died soon afterwards, also
prematurely, in Greece. He had allowed their former housekeeper to stay on living there with an annual gratuity to look
after the house. However, she had no other interest in cultivating
the poet's memory, so this was an unsatisfactory solution. After
her death, the house eventually came under official Austrian
care, as I had also suggested in my report at the time. A suitable
caretaker couple in the form of the Weinheber's son, Christian
Weinheber-Janota, and his wife, was then found.

They are keeping it as a small Auden museum where visitors,
by previous appointment, can see those of Auden's personal
belongings that remain. These comprise some of his English
books, his typewriter, as well as some documents and photographs. Auden kept his study and bedroom separate from
Kallman's living quarters, which were in the former main part of
the house. An outside staircase leads to Auden's upper storey.
Some of his furniture is there, including his wooden armchairs
and a bookcase of his English books. There his shabby soft
slippers, which he always wore because of his corns, even it is
said when going to the *Staatssoper*, still lie, along with his electric

kettle for making tea. There are some portraits of his unforgettable face, so deeply furrowed from the anxieties of the life he vicariously lived, a face compared with a tortoise's or, by Auden himself, with 'a wedding-cake left for three days in the rain'.

Busybodies in the media

I was finally elected president of the Foreign Press Association in Britain, an honorary office, for which colleagues used to applaud one for being public spirited in taking it on. They preferred to have nothing to do with such voluntary chores, pleading the old excuse that they had too much to do and/or 'you rather than me'. It was the age-old reaction, which caused Edmund Burke (1729–97) long ago to observe: 'It is necessary for good men to do nothing for evil to triumph.' I had learnt early, I hope, not to overestimate my 'goodness' in that respect or the damage that others could do that I might be able to prevent.

International organizations seem to attract all kinds of dubious 'fellow travellers', and our association was no exception in this regard. Some were claiming to represent newspapers or media organizations, but were really acting as agents for their governments. They seemed to spend much time at the bar, trying to get into the ruling committee. Being elected to such a body in London would sometimes add to their prestige in their own countries. Some were even able to secure pensions or other state awards for such spurious fame. Fortunately, the harm these people were able to do in our association was limited. As for Soviet spies, for whom journalism served as a well-known disguise, this could be left to the attention of the British security services and, from time to time, these types had their British visitor permits withdrawn and went back home. I remember in those days of the cold war receiving the persistent attention of the press attaché of one of the Iron Curtain countries. He always wanted me to write articles for him on aspects of British politics, which would be highly paid. I refused, knowing the entanglements to which this could lead and the subsequent difficulties of extricating oneself. Then, one day, a dozen bottles of wine arrived on what happened to be my birthday. I was in a quandary over whether to return or keep them. I kept them on the grounds that, as a diplomat entitled to duty-free alcohol, it would not have cost him much and not wanting to make too much fuss by returning a possibly well-meant gift.

One of my duties was to chair functions to which we had invited British ministers or other personalities. I remember an animated luncheon conversation with Indian Prime Minister Desai about the health benefits of drinking regular doses of one's urine, and being surprised by the vanity of Sir Edward Heath, who was unable to resist the temptation to read under the table an article about him that I had just published. Innocently, I thought at the time that a prime minister of his stature would be above wanting to know 'what's in the papers' about him, but far from it.

We naturally also received members of the royal family as occasional guests. It fell to me, for instance, to present the Prince of Wales with an honorary membership of our organization. The late Princess Margaret's marital affairs were matters of international interest in their day, high on the list of a London correspondent's watching brief. When she married the Earl of Snowden, as he became, I had to go and see him to select some photographs he had taken to illustrate an article of mine. I spent nearly two hours picking out suitable ones with him in his office at Kensington Palace. He had photographed nearly everybody who was anybody in the country. He was not unfriendly but irritating in his self-importance and rudeness displayed towards inferiors like his secretary, for whom I could not help feeling sorry, marvelling at the deference with which he expected to be treated.

Wearing unusually tight trousers, perhaps a corset, he seemed to fit the arty world he and the princess cultivated, with her cast in the fairytale role of the queen's wicked sister. They lived surrounded by sycophants. Princess Margaret enjoyed much public sympathy because of the sacrifices she had apparently made in not marrying the divorced Group Captain Townsend, though she was also very keen to observe the privileges of her position wherever she went.

I hosted a lunch for Princess Anne who, similarly, because of her haughty attitude had long had a tense relationship with the press. She was just then returning to favour because of her charitable work for children, about which she was going to speak at our invitation. I was taken aback by her frank avowal 'You know, I really can't stand children,' an observation that, since it was not meant to be funny, seemed to me to be remarkably jejune.

17. As president of the Foreign Press Association in Great Britain, hosting a lunch for the Princess Royal.

On the occasions of state visits by German presidents Heuss, Heinemann and Weizsäcker, I attended the gala dinners the Queen gave for the guests of honour. These were grand occasions and perfectly organized by long practice; the mixture of stiff formality and apparent ease, for which the British have a special knack, was always impressive. On one occasion, for instance, the Guards' officer in charge of the welcoming detachment for the Austrian president on his first postwar state visit had to do some quick thinking.

The honoured visitor, an ex-print worker and socialist, endured the ordeal well of walking along the ranks presenting arms, accompanied by the officer with his drawn sword held high. After that, he was supposed to salute smartly and make his about turn, but not on this occasion, however. Amiably *gemütlich*, as the Viennese are, the civilian president stretched out a thank you hand to the officer still presenting his sword in his own right hand. This was not foreseen by protocol, but the officer proved up to the unforeseen gesture. He quickly restored the sword in its scabbard and thus shook the President's hand in the hearty spirit in which it was offered.

The Queen has a natural gift, no doubt due to long practice, of overcoming a visitor's awkwardness and making him or her feel at ease. German President Heuss's visit in 1958, being the first German one since the war, was particularly sensitive, with all sides nervous about everything going as smoothly as possible.

This was also when the changes in social manners of the 1960s were beginning to take place. German reporters who had come over for the occasion but were unaware of British habits felt that the venerable president might have had a warmer reception, that Oxford undergraduates should not have been standing about with their hands in their pockets (which they normally do) and that the London crowds did not cheer enough. The guest of honour, aware of how much of a breakthrough the occasion was, found these objections childish – '80 per cent of the cheers were naturally meant for the young Queen, 10 per cent for the horses and 10 per cent for me', he said humorously.

When Prince Philip finally asked him whether he had any special wishes, Heuss said that he would have liked to see the famous Holbein drawings. These were at Windsor, however, which was not included in his programme. On the final evening the Queen had prepared a special treat for him: the priceless drawings had been put on an army van, with a corporal sitting on top of them, and brought to London. Heuss was of course delighted and really appreciated the gesture. At the gala dinner, the Queen referred to her German ancestry, which upset the British press, but it was done at the behest of the Macmillan government, which had decided that it was time for a change in Anglo–German relations.

My wife and I were invited to the gala dinner for President Richard von Weizsäcker in 1986, but being severely allergic, she was unable to touch any of the dishes, except for a peach at the dessert stage. However, having long been used to it, she held out bravely. I was seated elsewhere, next to the Duke of Northumberland, and the people near us – altogether there were about 170 guests – were heartened when the duke set a good example by turning his hand-painted Sèvre dessert plate around to study closer its famous numbered origin. We felt obliged to follow the good-mannered ducal example and there was an unusual general turning around of dessert plates at our end of the table. Afterwards, excellent coffee was served in the long room, which enabled my wife to restore her spirits after her evening of fasting. The custom is then for individual guests to be asked to talk to the Queen and the guest of honour in an adjoining little room.

We both enjoyed our conversation with Her Majesty. She has a refreshing sense of humour and is excellent at small talk, as I knew from social occasions at recent Commonwealth conferences. Something about her made one proud to be one of her subjects. 'Have you come far?' she addressed us on that occasion. 'From Wimbledon, Ma'am,' my wife replied. 'Ah, in the suburbs,' Her Majesty commiserated with us. The conversation touched on a recent garden party at Buckingham Palace where I mentioned how much a Franciscan friar with a bishop's pectoral cross, who was among the guests presented to her, had intrigued me. He was a bishop, she told us, who on his retirement had become a missionary. 'Isn't it marvellous to be able to do that?' she added. This was bound to cause the journalist in me to anticipate the headline 'Queen Thinks of Abdication', but it was clearly only a case of royal dreaming, and she went on: 'You know I couldn't take my eyes off his feet.' This seemed a frivolous observation to me, clearly caused by the holy man's naked hairy legs and sandals among all those dressed-up other guests, so I felt emboldened to give tit for tat and said to the Supreme Governor of the Church of England: 'He might at least have painted his toe nails for the occasion.' However, I sensed I had gone too far, that a royal eyebrow had invisibly risen, though my cheeky remark was graciously passed over. My previous history was then touched upon, with the internment camp on the Isle of Man and my wartime experiences in the Highland Light Infantry. We were then nicely dismissed with Her Majesty saying: 'Oh, you must go and talk

18. Off to see the Queen and her welcoming us 'from the suburbs'.

to my sister over there, she is an honorary colonel of the
Highlanders', which we did.

Looking back on my life as a journalist, I always had a
gnawing feeling that, despite my outward success, I lacked an
important ingredient for the job. My discontent was probably
due to my lack of enthusiasm for all the trivia, as it seemed to
me, that newspapers print, though I knew that such trivia is what
makes the world go round and what most people care to read

about. My great interest had always been to delve beneath the surface and find things out for myself. I dislike what happens in daily affairs and politics when you depend too much on people who know and, for some reason, do not want you to know and try to stop you finding out. Alternatively, they do not know themselves, yet are unaware of the extent of their ignorance.

I dislike having to speculate, especially when it seems not to matter, and not having the bricks needed to build whatever little house one is building. At the same time I knew of course that this is a general human dilemma; we all want 'to know' the 'pourquoi du pourquoi', the core of truth.

In view of these limitations placed on journalists, their findings are, of course, what eventually become the bricks of history. However, it is tiresome to discover that political events, like fashions, repeat themselves and, in only a slightly varied form, seem to come round at regular intervals. One does not have to be a Marxist, as someone aptly said, to see that history repeats itself, first as tragedy, then as farce.

What my profession may also teach those willing to learn is that one needs to get over the difficulty of not seeing the wood for the trees. The historian A. J. P. Taylor, who said that the aim of a journalist is to interest and of a historian to instruct, was able to do that, but then he also had a brilliant memory, which helped the historian in him. The best history combines scholarship and art, which brings me back to the divine spark, which, as I had learnt from my musical mother, defines all the highest human achievements. Ultimately, it comes to having to accept the wisdom of the sage who, with Hamlet, says 'the rest is silence', or, with Wittgenstein, 'whereof one cannot speak, thereon one must be silent'.

10

Tracing the Footsteps of a 'Flawed Archangel'

My retirement from journalism gave me the welcome chance to take up an old historical interest. This concerned the personality and ideas of the great English historian Lord Acton (1834–1902), who had long fascinated me. I also had a closer link. His granddaughter was the wife of Douglas Woodruff, then editor of the English Catholic weekly, the *Tablet*. Both of them had kindly taken me under their wings when I first arrived in this country. Although born too late to know her grandfather, Mia Woodruff did more than any other of his numerous modern descendants to keep his memory alive through her empathy with him and by getting to know most of his close family or associates in this country and abroad. She eventually asked me to write his full-length biography. While David Mathew and the American historian Gertrude Himmelfarb covered most aspects of his life and ideas, around the same time more knowledge about him became available with the publication and scholarly editing of his copious correspondence. Although this was mainly with his Munich teacher, the church historian Ignaz von Döllinger, he also exchanged letters with Richard Simpson, his younger literary associate, and many others. They provided keys to his understanding and virtually led to a rediscovery of the 'historian of liberty' who had foreseen how power relations in church and state would work out in the late twentieth century.

Acton, an English baronet born in Naples, was a Catholic European before his time; his ancestors had gone abroad because their religion blocked their professional advance in their own country. His father died early when he was just three. His mother, the last of the Rhineland Dalbergs, soon remarried, this time to the future second Earl of Granville, which added another tradition to Acton's already diverse heritage. That second marriage to a younger man took precedence in her life and led to strained relations between her only son and his stepfather. The boy, a precocious child, was unhappy in his early English boarding school and, at the age of 16, he was sent to Munich to study under Ignaz von Döllinger, the prominent church historian. This had an emancipating effect on him, for Bavaria was also the home of his maternal relatives, the Arco-Valleys, whose daughter he later married. Acton's Anglo–German development became decisive for him and presented some linguistic difficulties to the British–American public to which his historical ideas had primary appeal. When he inherited his in-laws' residence at Lake Tegernsee, where he eventually died and is buried, the German world became more than a country of adoption.

He spoke and wrote German, French, Italian and English well and was familiar with these countries, particularly Italy. When later, to crown his life's achievements he was appointed Regius professor of modern history at Cambridge, one of his students bragged that he managed quite well without knowing Italian, he rebuked him by saying: 'Not to know Italian is a severe handicap.' Having lived in these countries and experienced comparable situations, has added to the pleasure of embarking on Acton's biography. Apart from the linguistic advantages, I was also fortunate in having the support of Amelia, my Italian friend who later became my wife. She had a rare gift for reading old hand-written letters and documents in French and Italian, then of course the only means of communication. Acton's handwriting, from his teens onwards, was unusually balanced and legible, reflecting his even character. Sometimes these letters, particularly in the neo-Gothic German style and manifesting the enfuriating custom of criss-cross writing to save weight and postage, could prove trying.

I felt a personal debt to the family because of the kindness the Woodruffs, who had no children, showed me, along with other homeless refugees, when we arrived on these shores. To know them opened doors to other British Catholics, who at that time were visibly on the move from their formerly shunned ghetto status to one of wider social acceptabilty and equality. Early on Woodruff encouraged me to contribute articles to his journal, which, after the war and my own university years, led to my joining his editorial staff.

It was then that I became more closely acquainted with that strange genius, Mia Woodruff's grandfather. His fame lay in the fact that, though he had written widely, he never wrote an actual book. It was as if he wanted to save the world from adding to all those books that gathered dust on shelves, even those of the other great historians of his time like Burkhardt and Michelet, or Gibbon and Ranke who eclipsed him in range and achievement. To Ranke he felt particularly indebted later in his life. As Cambridge Regius professor of modern history, he was instrumental in transforming the British writing of history from a form of *belles-lettres* to a rigorously scientific discipline on Ranke's model.

Acton's handicap was that, while gifted with a phenomenally brilliant mind and memory, he knew too much. Perhaps because of his restless early upbringing, or because his Munich teacher, Döllinger, himself an industrious author of many historical works, allowed Acton's mind too much freedom to roam unhindered through the ages, he never acquired the discipline needed for great scholarship. That, rather than lacking the ability, was his problem and Döllinger was convinced that, having reached the age of 40 without having written a book, Acton would never write one. Instead, he became a great historical thinker who cast his ideas widely like pearls, which related minds such as Owen Chadwick or Herbert Butterfield's would then link together. Ultimately, he seemed to have done little else than impoverish himself on accumulaing books for the *History of Liberty* that remained a dream. The 60,000 volumes he collected, then the biggest private library in the country, are now honourably stored in the basement of the Cambridge University Library, which also houses many hundreds of large boxes of Acton's notes and letters, as I know so well from working through them.

A single writer could perhaps never have accomplished what he aimed to achieve with his *History of Liberty*, namely an original analysis of the nature of individual and political freedom through the ages and of the forces that foster and threaten that freedom. For Acton, 'the idea of liberty is the unity, the only unity of the history of the world, and the one principle of a philosophy of history.' 'It is the reign of conscience.' Its definition covers a vast field of human history:

Security for minorities; Reason reigning over reason, not over will; Duty to God unhindered by man; Reason before will; Right before might. It is not a gift but an acquisition; not a state of rest but of effort and growth, not a starting point, but a result of government, of advanced civilization, not of nature. The idea of freedom is right does not loom for a thousand years, until slavery is wrong. For thousand of years man's history is the growth not of freedom but of enslavement. Liberty has not only enemies which it conquers, but perfidious friends, who rob the fruits of its victories: Absolute democracy, socialism. Political atheism – End justifies the means. This is still the most widespread of all the opinions inimical to liberty.

In the early 1950s these Acton notes and papers (now properly ordered and preserved by the Cambridge University Library manuscript department), were kept untidily in an old medieval barn that adjoined the Woodruffs' house in Abingdon near Oxford. I then assisted Woodruff in editing a volume of Acton's *Essays on Church and State* (published in 1952). They were written by the young Sir John Acton, as he then was, after his return from Munich, and originally published in the *Rambler,* the Catholic review of liberal progressive views, which he edited. Feeling obliged to follow in the footsteps of his stepfather, Lord Granville, who held leading offices in different nineteenth-century Liberal governments, he entered the House of Commons as a Liberal MP for an Irish constituency. Acton's political career, however, lasted only seven years and was unremarkable. Party politics were too narrow-minded to appeal to him, though they led to his friendship with the Liberal leader, W. E. Gladstone, to whom he owed his peerage in 1869. Their links and his status as the Anglican Gladstone's *éminence grise* were important for his whole life, not least his Catholicism.

Acton's journalism led also to his collaboration with John Henry Newman, the great convert who co-edited some issues of the *Rambler* (after renamed the *Home and Foreign Review*). The review's circulation never rose above 1000, but it attained a high reputation among non-Catholics at a time of British literary and political reviews of great distinction. Its readers were largely university-educated former Anglican clergymen who had followed Newman into the Catholic Church. The bishops of the

new Catholic hierarchy, restored in 1850, were hostile to Acton
and Newman's endeavours to raise the Catholic intellectual level.
As products of Catholic seminaries, remote from universities,
they opposed Catholic higher education and feared that
Anglican-dominated Oxford and Cambridge might endanger
their Catholic faith. They respected the laity as providers of
church funds, but jealously guarded the Church's lead as their
own preserve.

Newman's classic *The Idea of a University* was alien to their
mentality, as was Acton's German training in the new non-
partisan pursuit of historical knowledge, irrespective of any
supposed political interests of the Church likely to suffer through
that. United in the common endeavours of their review, Rome
inevitably denounced Acton and Newman for not toeing the
Catholic party line, particularly when Newman published his
famous essay 'On Consulting the Laity in matter of Doctrine' in
July 1859. Using the Arian conflict of the fourth century, he
showed how the 'teaching Church' of the bishops was let down
and how the ordinary faithful had to rescue it from error. It was
this idea, unheard of at the time, and Newman's vision of a
Church that united the pope, bishops and laity in a collegiate
association, that caused more than a century later, the Second
Vatican Council to become known also as 'Newman's Council'.

On the issue of the dogma of papal infallibility, passed at the
First Vatican Council, Newman was among those moderately
opposed to it as not then 'opportune', whereas Acton and
Döllinger played a prominent and active role in combating it on
behalf of the so-called 'minority bishops' among the Church
Fathers. This opposition was substantial, numbering more than a
hundred then forming the intellectual elite in the Catholic
Church and representing France, Austro-Hungary and Germany.
However, the way in which the opposition had completely
melted away by the time of the final vote remains a shameful fact
of its history. At the time, it was said that the minority was
reluctant to oppose the Pope because he had set his mind on the
dogma, or that it was upholding the spurious principle of *Roma
locuta, causa finita est.* Newman showed his unhappiness by
keeping a telling silence, though he afterwards provided a
lukewarm theological apology for infallibility by saying that
Catholics would of course always honour the Pope by 'drinking
a toast to his health, though to Conscience first'. It showed his

order of values, as also the Church's today, but it also led to the
speculation that, had he known that infallibility would be on the
Pope's agenda 30 years later, the famous conversion would not
perhaps have happened at all in 1845.

The problem behind the debate over papal infallibility was
that it had become politically loaded and confused with the
unification of Italy and the threat to the pope's survival in the
Vatican. It also raised the question of the temporal power the
Church had exercised ever since the fall of the Roman Empire,
and which had almost become part of the Catholic truth. With
the existence of the papal states then threatened, Catholics all
over the world rallied in his 'Ultramontanist' defence of the pope
in the future secular capital of Italy. In this struggle between the
political interests of the Church and its theological verities, the
latter were sometimes dangerously compromised until the final
accord in the form of the internationally agreed Vatican State
was reached under Mussolini in 1929.

While the temporal power of the Church had originated at a
time when no other power existed to exercise governmental
functions, it inevitably came to distract the Catholic Church
from its primary spiritual office, not least through the alliances
forced upon it with worldly rulers. This was irrespective of
whether they were 'Catholic', 'most Catholic' or mere 'Defenders
of the Faith' like Henry VIII. Then suddenly, by 1870, they had
to dispense with all this worldly encumbrance of centuries and
this naturally constituted a tremendous historical upheaval.
Acton's mentor, Döllinger, was actually the first to advocate an
internationally agreed future settlement in a famous Munich
lecture of 1861. It became notorious, not for its truth, generally
accepted all over the world today, but for the fact that the papal
nuncio left the lecture hall in angry protest. The idea that the
Church could exist at all without its worldly powers was
unthinkable then and could only have sprung from an enemy
mind. So, when Döllinger actively opposed the dogma of papal
infallibility a few years later, this was remembered against him
and his rejection of infallibility was punished by the most severe
form of public excommunication, while Acton escaped a similar
fate only as a highly placed Catholic layman under the protection
of the British prime minister.

Newman, honoured belatedly for his loyalty to Rome with the
cardinalate, and Acton were thus frequently companions in arms

in many of their aims as well as trials, which the Church in its human form tends to inflict, particularly on those serving it most loyally. The age of Enlightenment and French Revolution had brought the Catholic Church to almost the lowest point in its long history, but in the early nineteenth century, an unexpected turn occurred in the Church's fortunes when it found itself among the victors over Napoleon. Remaining opposed to the modern secular state, as it had emerged from the revolution, the Church nevertheless adopted the state's centralized structures to strengthen its own institutions. After the failed revolutions of 1848, Pope Pius IX, who began his pontificate with Italian liberal ideas, was forced to join the reactionary majority of the Church. Driven into exile from Rome, he famously greeted a visitor, his former protégé Antonio Rosmini and the saintly founder of the 'Institute of Charity', with the words: *'Mio caro Abbate, non siamo piu costitutionali.'* (My dear Father, we are no longer supporters of liberal democratic ideas.) Rosmini was one of many, like Newman, Döllinger and Acton, temporarily victimized for not following the authoritarian pope's line.

Under the new 'Ultramontanist' politics, the Church saw itself as a bastion of the faith surrounded by a hostile secular and materialist world. This attitude produced the famous syllabus of 1864, by which Pius IX condemned the 80 leading ideas of the time, including those concerning liberal democracy; there was even a suggestion that the syllabus might be considered infallible. It could certainly be seen as preparing the way for the proclamation of infallibility, though again there were worlds of difference between its actual theological meaning and the political implications of the time as believed to affect the Church.

Thus, the restrictive theological definition of infallibility, tied strictly to papal *ex cathedra* pronouncements, sank under the occasional triumphalist interpretations in which it came to have been accepted. Cardinal Manning, a convert like Newman but his great antagonist and the leading advocate of infallibility in its widest sense, could not disguise his disappointment that the actual definition had fallen so short of what he, with the council's majority, had aimed to achieve – a restoration of papal powers to their medieval heights, as exercised for example by Innocent III. Political consequences followed this mis-understanding of infallibility as actually defined. For this the

Church must bear some share of the responsibity, for it frightened the world's governments over what an infallible pope could do in future, say, in interfering in the educational field. In the *Kulturkampf* in Bismarck's Germany, Catholics were made to bear the brunt of expulsions from Protestant parts for their alleged loyalty to Rome rather than to their country. Indirectly, this served to encourage German Catholics from the centre party, albeit unconsciously, to over-emphasize the nationalist feelings they were said to lack; and this at the critical time of Hitler's rise to power.

The apparent triumphalist ending of the Vatican Council also negatively affected ecumenical contacts that were still in an early phase. The largest of the churches was thus condemning itself to 'cultivate its own garden', and at a time of great danger for the survival of Christianity under the dictators and the Holocaust, when there should have been no doubt that God's call to be 'my brother's keeper' was meant for the New Testament as well as the Old. It needed the charismatic John XXIII to convoke Vatican Two with the justification of an overdue *aggiornamento*, namely bringing the Church into conformity with modern times. This vision Acton had expressed, evidently 100 years too early, when writing in his review in 1863:

> The Church must always put herself in harmony with existing ideas, and speak to each age and nation, in its own language. A kind of amalgam between the eternal faith and temporal opinion is thus in constant process of generation and by it Christians explain to themselves the bearings of their religion, so far as their knowledge allowed. ... But as opinion changes, as principles become developed, and as habits alter, one element of the amalgam is constantly losing its vitality, and the true dogma is left in an unnatural union with exploded opinion. From time to time a very extensive revision is required, hateful to conservative habits and feelings, a crisis occurs, a new alliance has to be formed between religion and knowledge, between the Church and society.

Finding himself denounced in Rome for this attitude, he decided, out of loyalty to the Church, voluntarily to cease publication rather than face condemnation. In his last number, in

1864, he wrote: 'A direct controversy with Rome holds out the prospect of great evils, and at the best a barren and unprofitable victory.' He concluded: 'I will sacrifice the existence of this *Review* to the defence of its principles, in order that I may combine the obedience that is due to legitimate ecclesiastical authority with an equally conscientious maintenance of the rightful and necessary liberty of thought.' He took leave of his readers with the thought that:

> From the beginning of the Church it has been a law of her nature, that the truths which eventually proved themselves the legitimate products of her doctrine, have had to make their slow way upwards through a phalanx of hostile habits and traditions, and to be rescued, not only from open enemies, but also from friendly hands that were not worthy to defend them.

He closed by humbly anticipating a time when the development of ideas would be too powerful to be arrested or repressed, and relegating his *Home and Foreign Review* to history; he saluted it as 'the partial and temporary embodiment of an imperishable idea'.

Acton was able to express himself concisely and aphoristically, rather like Pascal in his *Pensées*, which explains their similarly lasting impact. Best known probably is his: 'Power tends to corrupt, and absolute power corrupts absolutely. Great men are almost always bad men, even when they exercise influence, and not authority; still more when you superadd the tendency or the certainty of corruption by authority.' The maxim has lent itself to easy misquotation, since the exercise of power in human affairs is an evident necessity – therefore Acton's emphasis on 'tends to'. This seemed to point to his posthumous totalitarian century as well as to an earlier age and comparable abuse of absolute power.

In an exchange of letters with his friend, Mandell Creighton, the historian of the sixteenth-century papacy, and, with some sarcasm, Acton rebuked Creighton, later an eminent Bishop of London, for his lenient 'Anglican' ways. He did not even suspect a Borgia Pope Alexander VI as a poisoner, likely to get rid of enemies by putting 'verdigris in the saucepan or a toadstool in the mushrooms'.

Another of that historian's attractively timeless dicta is: 'Resist your time — take a foothold outside it.' It recalls his own personal experience, when, aged 16, he arrived in Munich, 'stuffed with Macaulay and raw Whiggery', and had to have his mind first to be cleansed, especially of Macaulay's bewitching skills. In 1895 Acton ended his inaugural lecture as Cambridge Regius professor on a combined note of Victorian confidence and humility:

> The historians of former ages, unapproachable for us in knowledge and in talent, cannot be our limit. We have the power to be more rigidly impersonal, disinterested and just than they; and to learn from undisguised and genuine records to look with remorse upon the past, and to the future with assured hope of better things; bearing in mind that, if we lower our standard in history, we cannot uphold it in Church and State.

Regarding himself as an honest historian, he took good care in defining him 'as one who pleads no cause, who keeps no shelter for a friend, no pillory for a foe – who does the same justice to that which he loathes and to that which he loves.'

Historians have theorized about the rights and duties of majorities in the context of democracy. Acton never tires to point out that 'democracy tends to despotism because the old system of liberty did so little for the masses. ... Happiness of the people [does] not [lie] in Liberty for the masses, [that is of] no benefit. [The masses want] progress, comfort. Liberty [is an] obstacle to progress.' In 1881, he wrote in a letter to Mary Gladstone that 'the true test of liberty is the position and security of minorities, particularly unpopular ones.' That was peculiarly the problem of future democratic governments. He also notes 'Democracy tends to destroy representative government: Plebiscite, Referendum, Extinction of minorities. [The remedy is] a strong second chamber. This was the American plan' (CUL Add MSS 4862/64). 'Democracy: Elsewhere institutions protect the mass from the supreme power. But what institution is there that protects the individual from the government when the government represents the whole people and acts in conformity with the will of the vast majority? Therefore the great problem of freedom becomes more difficult' (CUL Add Mss 8570/34). 'The essence of democracy: to esteem the rights of others as one's own. This was not only Stoic. It received a glorious sanction from Christianity' (CUL Add Mss 4939/39). 'Democracy has been known to cherish slavery, imperialism, wars of conquest, religious intolerance, equality in ignorance' (CUL Add Mss 5684). With many reservations with regard to democracy, Acton would perhaps have been close to Sir Winston Churchill's 'Democracy is the worst form of government except all those other forms that have been tried from time to time' (November 1947).

What is the best time to write about someone's life? Sigmund Freud, in a letter to Arnold Zweig who had offered to write his biography, thought, pessimist that he was, that it cannot be done at all because of all the lies, concealments, hypocrisy and flattery involved, or because of the writer's lack of understanding. According to Paul Valery, however much one learnt about Racine, for instance, one could never convey the art of his verse. Acton, moreover, having died in 1902, had clearly passed the best phase for a biography because those who knew him and his ideas were no longer alive. One could argue also that it was only in the century after his death that much of what he had anticipated in Church and state relations actually happened. Then again, it is only in our own time that we have become more sceptical about finding the absolute truth in archives. Having been one of the first to use the newly opened ones, he was also at first more optimistic about their private revelations, and towards the end of his life he had no doubt that the archives, too, could lie.

Rounding the archives

I replicated Acton's journeys in my work on his biography, first to Italy and Bologna, the home of his maternal Marecalchi relations, and then to Rome and to the *Archivio Segreto*, the Vatican's secret archive. These Italian stages, however, were more agreeable in themselves than in yielding many archival discoveries.

The Vatican archivists tended to make up for their badly paid jobs by not overworking. They delivered only one or two files to one's desk that contained only one or two documents for perusal. Soon the enforced two-hour luncheon interval would come and the reading room would close – again delightful because of the excellent cheap trattorias outside the Vatican walls, but not conducive for work. With the help of many cups of strong espresso coffee in the little cafeteria high up on the archive terrace, one managed to get through the working day. Thinking perhaps of the archives as places of 'heavenly revelations', Acton called them the *Himmelsleiter* – Jacob's or the heavenly ladder. His friend, Augustin Theiner, the prefect of the archives, also lived there, in a papal grace-and-favour apartment high up in the tower in which Galileo had been imprisoned, overlooking the Vatican gardens and Rome, and with his own private door and key to the archives. It was another typical Italian compensation for a badly paid job, which at least contributed to the enjoyment of life. The unfortunate Theiner, too, got into trouble with Pius IX who falsely accused him of having supplied some of these secret heavenly documents to Acton who, as Pius IX said of him, 'licks my feet, and at the same time works with my enemies'. In retribution, the wretched Theiner one day found his private door to the secret archives walled up, and himself given the sack.

Sometimes, heavenly anger also seemed the more fitting reaction for me up there. For example, when the Holy Office still, 100 years later, insisted on holding back a file on Döllinger's excommunication, I was told that I could probably get it if I knew Cardinal Ratzinger, now Pope Benedict XVI. I did know him though common links with my Catholic publishers Herder of Freiburg, but by then my eagerness to see the ancient document, which had surely lost whatever urgency it may have once had, had also vanished. Using such annoying, tortuous, typically Roman by-ways to get round the authorities was not my 'cup of tea' (or espresso).

Then I proceeded on to Naples where Acton was born on the Riviera di Chiaja, the promenade by the sea. The villa still stands, much dilapidated, behind an entrance portico containing a little chapel, with a lovely rising garden with palm trees behind it. Concerts and art exhibitions are still held there and I saw the first-floor bedroom of Acton's father and mother, with its large terrace where the future 'historian of liberty' had slept peacefully in his cradle while his playboy father gave a grand and noisy carnival ball below. Hundreds attended it, led by King Ferdinand VII of the two Sicilies (King Bomba) and his queen, scourge of the Liberals of Europe, like young Acton's later friend, Gladstone. Naples is still the residence of Acton's Italian relative, the Barone Leporano di Acton, whose ancestors rose to high office in naval commands or as ministers of marine.

Florence was not strictly on the biographer's itinerary, but, knowing Sir Harold Acton (1900–94) well, I wanted to see his magnificent villa, La Pietra, on the road out to Fiesole and Bologna. He was a descendant of the Italian Actons, brother of his direct great-great-grandather, the prime minister of the two Sicilies. Sir Harold Acton was a wealthy grand-seigneur and aesthete, poet and author of a history of the Sicilian Bourbons, whom he exonerated from their bad reputation among Liberals. Educated at Eton and Oxford's Christ Church, he was much maligned for his homosexuality as a character in Evelyn Waugh's *Brideshead Revisited*. His Renaissance villa, left on his death to the American University of New York, was built by Franceso di Tommaso Sassetti. The illustrious Capponis lived there for three centuries. I got to it after a storm had caused havoc in the cypress trees lining the long drive to his house. In the great heat of that summer, we sat in the cool central courtyard, now roofed over, and afterwards had lunch in the lofty dining room. I regret having been unable to take in many of the splendid paintings on the walls, or to having done justice to the excellent meal and service in the grand Italian manner, since I had little time and wanted to talk family history with my host. Harold Acton's American father had established a connoisseur's collection of great pictures and sculptures, which extended to the terraced garden sloping down behind the house and ended with a lovely view over the roofs of Florence below. The garden was full of seventeenth-century statues of naked figures, among them Bacchus and Apollo embracing Daphne who turns into a tree. Harold remembered his Irish nurse forbidding him to look at so much naughty art. His earliest memories were of the great world of Russian exiles who had established themselves in Florence, and of precursors of Italian fascism like that extraordinary fraud, Gabriele d'Annunzuio whom he knew well as a child. When, on leaving, I thought of revealing to him a closely guarded family secret, one of my archival 'finds' that he was really an illegiti-mate son, he disappointed me by being already aware of it!

More productive was the 'Döllingeriana' section in Munich's state archives. Acton's maternal Arco descendants still live in the scenically lovely Bavarian lakes region, some as brewers of Bavarian beer and mineral waters. A private clinic now stands on the grounds of his former Tegernsee lakeside villa, where the Gladstones and Tennysons were frequent visitors, and where he died, laid out in his crimson Cambridge professorial robes, and then buried in the little village lakeside cemetery. Since the descendants failed to maintain the grave through two world wars, it was let go, but the place is known even though the grave has been abandoned. I went there on the 100th anniversary of his death, when a memorial mass was said in the nearby village church hall on 19 June 2002. Ludmilla Countess Arco, a descendant of his wife's family, was among the small congregation. The Tegernsee city authorities recently placed a plaque on the cemetery wall and the German inscription reads: 'Lord Acton (1834–1902) international scholar and first Catholic member of the English Upper House since the Reformation.' This is not strictly correct, since he was not the first Catholic since the Reformation in the Commons or House of Lords, though he was the first Catholic to get the Regius chair at Cambridge. He would certainly have cherished this German civic recognition with his favourite Italian quotation: '*Se bon e vero, e ben trovato*' (If not true, it is at least well intended).

I also went to Zagreb in Croatia to trace Acton's close associate Bishop Josef Strossmayer. He was then among the most popular liberal-minded of contemporary bishops and an opponent of papal infallibility, although he submitted to it later. He was also a leading pan-Slavist, though this eastern European church movement practically disintegrated through the dissolution of Yugoslavia and the demise of the Soviet Union. British archives were more productive. St Andrew's University in Scotland yielded some unexpected Acton–Newman letters, though the bulk of these are part of the major collection of Newman's *Diaries and Letters,* annotated by the Birmingham Oratorian Fathers and now covering more than 30 large volumes. Oxford's Bodleian Library and Pembroke College preserve the papers of Acton's close friends, James Bryce, the Liberal politician and historian, and Peter Le Page Renouf, the Catholic writer. The Shropshire County Council Record Office, close to the Actons' former residence at Aldenham, near Bridgnorth, yielded previously unknown family letters.

The royal archives at Windsor Castle were a rich source on Acton's function as lord-in-waiting to Queen Victoria, who appreciated his social graces as a table companion with whom she could exchange family gossip in German. It was a political appointment and Acton combined it with a minor spokesman's office in the House of Lords, which brought him, aged 58, his first very small, but official salary. 'Waiting', however, involved wasting time, which he disliked. He would spend it 'cajoling' the Queen's various ladies and frequenting the Windsor library, which he regarded as 'not an intellectual place' because it failed to produce some German classics he needed.

The richest source of Acton material was undoubtedly the windswept, sometimes icy Tower manuscript room in the Cambridge University library building. I came to feel quite at home there, enjoying my retirement researches as a second kind of childhood, with necessary breaks in the tearoom and involuntarily listening to the concerns of a new generation of graduates lucky enough to be part of the Cambridge atmosphere while I came by train from London on weekly visits. I had the good fortune to stay with university friends in an enjoyable mix of squalor and heartfelt hospitality.

Yale University Press published my biography in 2000, with introductions by two Actonian links, Mia Woodruff and Sir Owen Chadwick. I was able to follow it up two years later with a German version published by my old German Catholic friends, Herder of Freiburg. It carried the subtitle 'A Protagonist for Religious and Political Freedom', which was thought necessary because his name is strangely less widely known there than in the English-speaking world. This may seem surprising in view of his Anglo–German origins, but is perhaps also due to the contortions involved over more than a century of Anglo–German relations dominated by nationalist antagonisms including two world wars, and Acton's hostility towards its nationalist trends. Happily, this is now past history and, with Lord Acton resting in his unmarked Tegernsee grave, people might one day recognize him as the main protagonist of two centuries of Anglo–German historical relations. Who else deserves the honour of having prophetically predicted the catastrophes to which the corruption of absolute power can lead?

A positive reception
The biography had a gratifyingly positive international reception, particularly among those historically a little more familiar with its background. In my own old journal the *Tablet*, Cambridge's Eamon Duffy found it 'a splendid and gripping biography, tirelessly researched, densely documented yet

consistently and racily readable, offering a memorable and believable account of one of the most intriguing and influential of Victorian Catholic lives.' Niall Ferguson in the *New Republic* found that 'it explains how the extraordinary wheeling and dealing of the Vatican Council could become a more important event for a liberal Catholic than the contemporary Franco–German War'. According to John T. Noonan Jr in the *New York Times*, 'Hill does not sit in judgment, is sympathetic as a good biographer should be, but not sycophantic. ... The mystery of the man endures, safe from any final judgment on earth.' Gertrude Himmelfarb, whose Acton biography was published 50 years earlier, found it:

> although blander than mine, essentially the same Acton, 'out of sorts' with his age, and even more, with ours, but a generation that has experienced the horrors of the Holocaust can appreciate as his contemporaries could not, the principles of liberty and morality. And we may well marvel at his extraordinary presience in warning us against evils that have become all too real.

Michael Bentley in the *Times Literary Supplement* wrote that:

> Acton followed two horses pulling in different directions. One of them headed in the direction of Ranke's historical science and the possibility of a record of the past disinfected from the intrusion of present perspectives. The other wanted to find a domain in which the historian could be Right as well as right ... his considerable intellectual powers inclined towards the first horse, but his heart was harnessed by the second. The difficulty of writing history that goes in both directions simultaneously may well have proved insuperable; at least it is hard to see how he could have gone about it.

According to Simon Heffer in *Country Life*, Acton, as one of the essential figures of Victorian intellectual life, comes across in this weighty book as rather unsympathetic. 'I suspect that is because, as a result of his diligence in the vast Acton archive, the author has given us rather an accurate picture of his subject.' According to Noel Malcolm in the *Sunday Telegraph*, 'Acton left an ideal of

scientific history, which was so ideal and so scientific that no one
human being could ever have written such a thing, as his own
failure to do so amply proved.' In *Theologie und Philosophie*,
Klaus Schatz SJ, the author of a magisterial history of Vatican
One, wonders whether Acton's 'basically ahistorical rigorism
does not also anticipate a political correctness which judges,
from the high pedestal of Western human rights notions, and
without being conscious of the relativity of its own point of view,
both the Christian past and other civilizations with other ideas of
values'. He suggests that Döllinger had a greater understanding
of the grey zones of historical conditioning that contradict any
subjectivist 'absolutism'.

Looking back on my long preoccupation with Acton, while
left admiring his range of brilliant ideas, I also found him
strangely unlikeable in his later years, due perhaps to the many
trials in his life and consequent desire to have his moral right-
eousness confirmed. This emerges especially in comparing him
with the tragic figure of Döllinger, whose humanity and saintly
acceptance of his shameful treatment by the Church has
contributed to his modern rehabilitation. This is largely due to
the editor of Döllinger's life and letters, a work of major scholarship by my Luxemburg friend, Professor Victor Conzemius.
There is something remote about Acton's moral intransigence,
which adds a mysterious lack of clarity to his personality despite
its brainpower. There was something of the 'flawed archangel'
about Acton, as Eamon Duffy has called him. Significantly, his
emphasis on moral judgements in history lay behind his
estrangement from Döllinger after a lifetime of close friendship
and alliance. Was that perhaps because he felt that Döllinger was
right and he wrong in submitting, Christ-like, to his
condemnation of the relativity of all historical judgements? In his
recognition of a grey borderline of all human conditionality, he
recognizes that Döllinger has 'grown on me', as he has on many
who, after his condemnation by the Church, were inclined to
write him off as a failure.

Döllinger's last word

Döllinger was probably not the creative thinker that Acton was.
He never produced a historical work of overriding importance,
though Acton of course had none to show at all. About his own
scholarly life, Döllinger said once: 'I have been digging,

diligently, indefatigably, for treasure in the vineyard of knowledge, and always came up with something, too, though admittedly quite different, things from what I had expected to find.' Among these was certainly his lecture on 'The Jews in Europe', delivered to the Bavarian Academy of Sciences in July 1881. At a time of dominant anti-Semitic views, particularly among Catholics, Döllinger's theme was the blindness the Church had shown to the Jews, 'whose destiny is perhaps the most unnerving drama of the history of the world'. The Christians, he said, have made the Jews into what they are, through their explicit oppressions, degrading torments, persecutions and massive slaughter, followed by a vicissitude of expulsions and resettlements. 'It is as though the European nations had vied with one another to realize the madness that, according to the decree of heaven, the hardest slavery of all is destined for the Jews, and that the sons of the Gentiles were called to perform jailers' and hangmen's services.' It was as though he foresaw that worse was to come in his own country.

He showed empathy with Israel's suffering. Contrary to the basic attitude of the New Testament, particularly Romans 9–11, Christians had acted against God's irrevocable promises to his people. The Jews should not be blamed for the Crucifixion or stigmatized for it. Döllinger criticized the prevalent misunderstanding of the role of the Pharisees as no more than an arrogant elite among the Jews, 'partly professionally appointed, partly putting themselves forward as guardians of the Jewish faith'. Probably thinking of his own condemnation, he referred to the high priests of the Roman era as the 'Jewish Church'. The 'commandment of the love of God', he said, was 'not a mechanical abstraction but Israel's closest links with God, a basic truth, which even later alienation cannot change.'

Considering the various causes, particularly the economic ones, of the persecution of the Jews, Döllinger held Christians and Jews equally to blame for them, but with the final balance favouring the Jews, since in pre-Christian as in Christian times, 'It is always the dominant forces in society that have imposed their stamp, including their behaviour pattern on the Jews.' As though in anticipation of Hitler, he referred darkly to 'the destructive power of chaos, with one abyss opening upon and destroying another'. While the historian in him could only deplore how few lessons mankind learns from history, Christians must additionally plead guilty that the humiliations they have heaped upon the Jews have been one ever renewed Crucifixion of Jesus the Jew.

11

Commemorating Amelia

Having lost my heart to Italy at an early age, I longed to be able to give it some more permanent expression. Eventually that came about through my adopted country, England. Returning to 'Blighty' was not for me what it was for most. I had become doubly homeless. No members of my family remained in either Germany or Austria, and there seemed no immediate opening for me in either country. In addition, I could not expect to continue being a burden to my London friends, though they had always welcomed me on army leave.

After the luxuries of a victor's life in Germany, I plunged into a student existence in London's bed-sitter land, Hampstead, in furnished rooms, sometimes with the use of a kitchen and bathroom. An annual government grant, which included a cost of living allowance, just adequately covered my living expenses. Though food rationing continued in Britain after the end of the war, I was just about able to manage financially on my own. By the time I had finished my studies at King's College, London University, and with an income from freelance journalism and work as a publisher's editor, I even rose to the householder's status of an unfurnished first-floor flat in West Kensington. This consisted of a living room and attached bedroom, bathroom and tiny kitchen. The rent was about £3 a week. I gradually acquired some furniture and various girlfriends helped with sewing curtains and other chores for which I could plead male incompetence.

The exception was always cooking, for which I had acquired an early taste, inherited I like to think from my multi-talented, artistic Austrian mother. To her I owed many early kitchen tips and recipes, invaluable for anyone wanting to rise above his normal ignorance in these matters. I advanced from primitive beginnings, having to make do with a small gas ring on the floor near the fireplace. However, in those student days – I was after all in my late twenties – I had learnt to produce quite good one-pot dishes for a party of three or four friends, such as *spaghetti al aglio e olio* or *risotto alla Milanese* to satisfy even fastidious Italian tastes, or, as far as my Hungarian goulash was concerned, central European ones. Later on, having acquired a tiny kitchen and a gas cooker, four-course meals were *de rigueur*, concluding with the *pièce de résistance*, a 'real' Viennese *Apfeltorte* (apple tart), with the qualification 'real' implying that many aberrations may be committed by the ignorant. I was faithfully and almost always successfully following precise maternal postal instructions.

What I had not learnt from her, I am afraid, was tidiness and leaving the kitchen working area spotlessly clean, as she would have done, proving her true mastery of the art, and not like the scene of a battlefield. I must admit to not putting up much resistance when kind women guests offered afterwards to clear up the mess I had left behind.

Not having my own home at first also meant that after my father's death in 1945 my mother and I were forced by circumstances to go on living apart. She remained in Rome, able even with advancing age to earn her own living either as a teacher of bel canto or as a housekeeper. The Italian families who engaged her services much appreciated her musical talent, her open-hearted Viennese temperament and her innate cooking and baking skills. Thus, into her late fifties, she was fortunate to manage on her own, lonely though her life often was. However, she was well able, as a foreigner to integrate into Italian life, helped no doubt by the humanity and courtesy of the Italians, their blessed climate, and her own adaptability and knack for making the most of things.

The mother–son link continued by post and by my occasional visits to Rome during the holidays. Many years passed before I was able to afford a home for both of us. In the meantime, she accepted an invitation to go to Vancouver, British Columbia, where her widowed sister had remarried. My mother would naturally have preferred to be near me, but I think we both realized that living together after years of separation would be difficult. I had early on become used to my independence, for better or for worse, and acquired corresponding habits.

Symptomatic, perhaps, was an incident involving my future Italian wife Amelia, to whom I was long close before we finally married in 1972. That incident was to all appearances of minor importance. When Amelia happened to brush some crumb or speck of dust from my lapel, I reacted instinctively, as it were, by drawing back as though resenting the implied proprietary gesture suggesting possibly: 'You belong to me, you are mine.' I did not of course consciously intend this, but it was bound to hurt her. After years of independence and living on my own, I had to relearn the tenderness of a loving attachment as from the beginning.

One of my mother's domestic jobs had been as housekeeper to a young woman separated from her husband and living in an apartment near the Piazza Navona in Rome with her small daughter. The young woman was Amelia. The snag about my mother's job, however, was another, four-legged inhabitant in that flat, a tame cheetah. With all her fondness for pets, my mother was not used to living with, even tamed, wild animals. But this being Rome and the era of *la dolce vita*, the elegant world promenading in the Villa Borghese thought nothing of anyone taking a cheetah or even *gattopardo* (leopard) on a lead on their outings, or sharing their home with them. After all, seeing and being seen was part of the Italian way of life, but not so for my mother who protested: 'Either that monster leaves or I go.' She prevailed. The 'monster' had anyhow fallen ill, probably because, quite apart from the mess it caused in the flat, it had developed a craving for chocolate and had to be put to death.

Afterwards, Amelia and my mother became good friends, so I owed, as it were, Amelia to her. In the old days, of course, parents often used to choose their children's spouses and, over the years, I too came to think that the gains and losses of that arrangement were probably not too bad. Naturally, my mother never mentioned her intention – that would have been counter-productive – but she gave Amelia my address. Having grown up in prewar London, where her father was director of the Banca d'Italia, Amelia wanted her daughter to go to an English school. Our meeting came about when I had a nasty cold. Having not written to my mother, she got worried, wrote to Amelia enclosing a pound note, and asked her to cook me a chicken because I was unwell. That chicken played as providential a role in my falling in love as the motorcycle had done in my religious conversion when Fritz took me into the Vienna woods to talk about God. It remained unclear whether the one or the other was the decisive factor. While it was some years before we married, my mother thus acquired a daughter-in-law of whom she fully approved.

Amelia did not have an easy life in London at first, for she had to work hard to be able to afford the high fees of Vasani's, the ballet school in Notting Hill to which she sent her daughter Dawn. Amelia's life strangely resembled my mother's life in Rome, living in cramped conditions, working as a housekeeper, or cooking for other people's dinner parties. She was often late and exhausted on coming home, having had to do all the cleaning and washing-up, taking her well-earned fee and, usually, also a bag of leftovers that would come in useful for the two of them over the next few days, but she managed cheerfully with her innate resolve and good spirits. Her flat at that time became a meeting ground for her friends – Italians and, through her mother's relations, Australians, usually a young and lively crowd, and Italian journalists working in London, some in the Italian section of the BBC World Service. Everybody would help her make a quickly improvised *Spaghettone* with cheese and wine. It was a gay lot, both in the old and new sense of that word, not without a few 'lame ducks' whom Amelia always seemed to attract. She was a kind of Anglo–Italian (Brechtian) *Mother Courage,* caring for those whose troubles in life needed solving, indeed 'ameliorating'. Undoubtedly, something in her character and life of physical suffering fitted her to be a healer, though she had had to give up her medical studies because of illness and the circumstances of the time.

In London she eventually found her 'niche', as I have mentioned, in a growing general interest in antiques and running her own little shop, 'Junkantiques', in West Kensington. She supplied it from acquisitions in the newly flourishing auction sales and, sensibly, began by concentrating on cheaper items – undoubtedly helped by the good taste she had acquired through her upbringing and environment.

I had immediately felt drawn to Amelia. She was slim, graceful, very attractive, with long black hair, brown eyes, a dark voice, and she resembled, indeed was often mistaken for, the film star Hedy Lamarr. She was serious, much more practical than I was, intuitively sensible and artistic. Everything about her reflected style and good taste. She had a religious sense that seemed to complement my own, with a serene disposition and she could be very jolly. Though Roman born she spoke English well, without an accent, having been brought up in an English school in London's Swiss Cottage, and with all the nursery rhymes, songs and love of the English environment that gave her a natural feel for it. My own 'school of English', namely the British army, London University and a journalistic apprenticeship could not compete with that.

She was the eldest of the three daughters of Giuseppe Nathan. Her family was important to her, not least because it had played a part in recent Italian history. Her grandfather Ernesto Nathan (1845–1921), a popular Roman *sindaco* (lord mayor) from 1907 to 1914, was well known in the Italian independence movement. He made his mark by acquiring a reputation for scrupulous honesty, rare in Italian public life, and is still remembered on that account. For example, he dispensed with the use of his expensive carriages, even on official occasions, to cut down the city's expenses. When an annual account of a few hundred liras appeared in the books, he asked, 'What is that for?' 'It is for feeding the cats in the Coliseum, which deal with the rats and mice with which the place is infested.' 'If they feed on these, why spend money on feeding them as well?' So that extravagance was done away with.

He deserves less renown for the Victor Emmanuel II memorial, the marble monstrosity for which he was responsible during his tenure of office. Also known as the 'Typewriter' or the 'Wedding Cake', it became quite a Roman symbol, opposing, as it were, St Peter's, in the new secular and materialist stance of the modern Italian state. Mayor Nathan represented its democratic, republican, largely anti-clerical character; he was also a freemason.

This was mainly because he had grown up close to Giuseppe Mazzini (1805–72), the principal theorist and ideologue in the struggle for Italian national independence. Mazzini was a gentle and moderate revolutionary, not the anarchist, terrorist and Che Guevara of his age that he was made out to be. He looked forward to a united Europe into which the nationalist and independent movements of his age would, he hoped, lead. However, he affronted Pope Pius IX and the Church by demanding religious reform, upset Marxists by criticizing communism, and his contemporaries by campaigning for social justice, universal suffrage and women's rights. He was romantically convinced that the Christian religion, although not the Catholic Church, was the highest expression of the progressive human spirit, yet he deplored the Reformation for shattering the unity of Christendom and opposed the materialism of his age and its emphasis on science as a substitute for religion. He stood for the liberty of conscience for all, and thought of bigotry as misguided. According to the nineteenth-century historian Lord Bryce, of all the Europeans of their generation Mazzini and Gladstone were the two with the greatest faith in liberty and in the power for good (Denis Mack Smith, *Mazzini*, 1994, p. 195).

After 1837, Mazzini spent 25 years in English exile where other *émigrés*, the Nathans and their Rosselli relatives, were among the closest friends and financial supporters of 'George Brown', as he called himself. In London, the Frankfurt-born stockbroker Meyer Nathan (1799–1859) married an Italian, Sarina Levi (1819–82), who had seven children. Mazzini never married but felt a particular attachment to their daughter Janet (who married Pellegrino Rosselli) and to the last-born, Ernesto. Being Mazzini's protégé later helped Ernesto to become chief mayor, especially since his mother, Sarina, as a rich widow was Mazzini's close political supporter and secretary. In his last years, Mazzini stayed at her house La Tanzina, at Lugano, Switzerland, and died at Livorno in Janet Rosselli's arms. Mazzini's close relationship with Sarina caused the Jesuits of *Civiltà Cattolica,* the papal organ, to spread salacious rumours about his being the father of some of her children (*La Civiltà Cattolica,* 26 April 1872, quoted in Denis Mack Smith, *Mazzini,* London 1994, p. 182). Ernesto's alleged likeness to Mazzini caused speculation in the Nathan family, but Sarina always denied the imputation.

When Amelia, who was Catholic, received a papal medal in the early 1980s for her charitable work on behalf of allergies – she was also named 'Catholic woman of the year' in Britain and Italy – it seemed that the Vatican might have intended a belated gesture of reconciliation. She was, after all, the granddaughter of the Roman mayor and freemason whom the Vatican hated for what he represented, but the time for such 'ecumenical' gestures had not yet come.

Amelia's mother, Dorothy or 'Peggy' Whiting, was an Australian actress from Melbourne of Portuguese and Danish–English descent. To her were probably due some of the distinct eccentricities that characterized her children. In later life 'Peggy' specialized in playing minor parts of old ladies in Fellini films, less because she needed the money than because she enjoyed acting. The director, often feeling sorry for her after a long day's filming because of her age, used to offer to take her home late at night, but she enjoyed declining by grandly saying: 'No, thanks, I have my chauffeur waiting.' She acquired some notoriety for bossiness, being quite capable at the parties she threw for actors and Roman bohemians suddenly to turn out of her house one or other of her guests who had displeased her, but for no apparent reason. Everybody, especially her children, if not her husband, was correspondingly in awe of her.

Three inseparable sisters

Amelia had first come to England aged three months, disappointing her parents in their expectation that their first-born would be a boy. She was educated at Bedford House School, Swiss Cottage. The family then decided, inauspiciously, in the early 1930s, to sell their fine Hampstead house for a pittance and return to Italy. They could not foresee that a few years later Mussolini would so fatally ally himself with Hitler.

Their three girls attended high school at the Convitto Nazionale at Tivoli, near Rome, but when under German pressure Italy passed racist laws in 1938, they were expelled from their school. They never forgot being called to see the school secretary who embarrassedly informed them of the decision. A few letters followed from school friends saying how sorry they were. They then left Italy with their mother to stay with her relations in Australia. Their father remained behind to settle their affairs, but within a few months they had to return to Europe to look after him because he had fallen ill. It was another decision of those times they wished not to have made. While they were still on board ship, Italy entered the war on Germany's side and they arrived back in Rome only to have their passports confiscated. They found a refuge in the mountainous countryside near Rome, but lived in constant fear of being arrested, or even deported. With rare courage, Amelia walked three miles a day to bring food to partisans and escaped Allied prisoners of war. She also went round the Roman ghetto helping to collect the eight kilogrammes of gold the Germans demanded in return for the lives of ransomed Jewish hostages in Rome. They handed over the gold, but the Jews were not saved. During this period, in 1943, she married a young medical student, but her marriage broke down, leaving her with a baby daughter.

It is said that '*les extrèmes se touchent*' and this applied to us. Amelia and I came from different backgrounds and had different interests. Mine were more intellectual; I liked ideas, history and literature; she had a good mind, was able to write well and spoke publicly with great poise. Despite our basic differences, we felt a common bond, perhaps influenced by Catholic ideas. As a child, she had wanted to become a nursing nun, probably because she was prone to illness and allergies. Our common experiences were a link, for we had both lived through some awful times, she in Italy and I in Germany and Austria. We both felt a deep debt to Great Britain for its solitary stance against Hitler and for the freedom it upheld. Moreover, her resilience and style, her panache for coping with the unexpected and making the best of it, though actually having an introverted and shy temperament, fascinated me. I clearly fell for her good looks and sensed how attuned she was to me both in mind and spirit. These became common bonds. She had probably inherited some acting talent from her mother, had a refreshing gift for seeing the world as a stage, but never lost her simplicity of heart and feelings.

Two little incidents may illustrate that. We were invited to a party one evening for which I had already dressed but she had not. Earlier we had been together with a friend, a Jesuit priest, and decided to drop him off on our way. He was sitting next to me in front of the car, but when we arrived at his place and Amelia got out of the back seat to change places, his face showed utter amazement, for a quite different person from the one he had last seen had emerged. She had used the time, sitting behind us, while continuing our conversation, to change into her evening dress and make-up. She matched his surprise by coolly pretending that it was the most normal thing in the world for her to have done. For a time she also acted as my secretary, with her thick glasses adding conviction to the role. I was expecting a visitor, an ex-army officer who had not met her before and who had to wait a little because I was delayed. When he left later, he said to me, referring to her dark and sunburned looks, 'I hope I have been nice to your secretary. You can never tell with these darkies.'

The three 'Nathan sisters', as they were known even in later life always retained their close and intimate links despite occasional exasperation with one another. Their bonds of shared memories and fun were always stronger. When once all three were in London they decided to give a fancy dress party, sending out invitations in the name of the 'Nathan Sisters' and assuming that, as in Rome, every one would know who they were. Some of my friends, attached to embassies and anxious to do the right thing, rang back before accepting to enquire to what religious order these party-loving sisters belonged. One of them, tempestuous, fair-haired Georgina, was married to Winston Burdett, a well-known American Middle East and Rome CBS correspondent and they had a grown-up son and daughter. The youngest, Virginia, had an Italian husband and one son. Amelia, the most reserved of the three, was either full of determination or like a frightened bird. Like her sister Virginia, she had trembling hands that made one anxious when watching her pouring tea from a dangerously shaking pot. Her two saintly models were Teresa of Avila and Teresa of Lisieux, also known as the eagle and the dove, and, like them, she enjoyed soaring the heights. Above all, she seemed to have something in common with St Francis of Assisi, especially in identifying with the lot of the poor, suffering and sick, having also come from a well-to-do background and in her attitude to animals she was likely to talk if not to preach to them. The Franciscan spirit was quite natural to her, as her sister Virginia remembered from the example of the valuable fur coat, which she had hanging in her entrance lobby of her Kensington flat before we were married, and which was always available for the first person needing it in a sudden cold spell.

Nevertheless, our getting together was beset by many obstacles that reminded me always of the old legend of the two royal children in love but unable to cross the deep gulf keeping them apart. Amelia and I were often together, but for a long time we had separate households and led separate lives, she at first living with her daughter until she got married, Amelia living partly in London, partly in Rome, waiting for her divorce to come through. Her first husband had become a Roman society doctor with the fads of a playboy, which included a private zoo. Although he also married again and had a new family, he remained a friendly, if uncertain figure in his first wife's background, because their daughter continued to work for him managing his private clinic.

'Glamour is when a man knows a woman is a woman.' Surprisingly, this accurate observation is ascribed to an intelligent and beautiful Italian woman, the famous film star Gina Lollobrigida. When I said that my love for Amelia covered an all-inclusive attachment to Italy, I did not mean a starry-eyed tourist's madness over Italian wine, women and songs. My love, I hope, had been tried over the years and was part of a long experience. It included all the physical beauties of the country, its people, looks, colours, tastes and smells. Stendhal summed it up when he said that 'the charm of Italy is that of being in love', which merely confirms what so many others, similarly seduced, have said. The sensitive romantic Heinrich Heine noted in his *Reisebilder* that 'simply letting yourself live is beautiful in Italy ... in the shades of laurel bushes it is more pleasant to weep than under fir trees: and it is sweeter to daydream following the shapes of Italian clouds than under our ash-grey skies.'

I knew Lollobrigida slightly in Rome long ago. This, I hasten to add, came about through Amelia and indeed in her presence throughout. Amelia was working at the time for her brother-in-law, Winston Burdett, the American CBS correspondent in Rome, and was busy making a television film of Luigi Barzini's excellent book *The Italians*. In it Barzini presented the private virtues and public vices of his countrymen in their chosen role, happily cloaking despair against a backdrop of sun and history, and instinctively coupling charm, talent and intelligence with flattery, corruption and a rugged contempt for law. The glamorous Gina was asked to portray and explain the significance of some of those silent Italian gesticulations and the full day of filming took place in Barzini's house in Rome. My part was more or less confined to *stare zitto* (shutting up), namely playing the role of a silent, admiring onlooker, though I did join the crew in occasional loud applause for La Lollo's gestures of the common Italian man or woman with so much inward fun and evident talent. Born at Ciociaria in the Arno valley near Subiaco, she had risen to fame and riches without ever denying her humble origins, which evidently helped her art.

It is said that Italy is full of natural actors, more than fifty million of them, and that only the worst are sometimes encountered as professionals on the stage. That did not apply to

Lollobrigida, for she was perfectly natural. The whole point about her unique gestures was that she performed them silently, which made them even more telling and funny. For example, in folding her hands and fingers except for the forefinger and little fingers she was conveying that her opposite number should, or will shortly, wear horns, namely be cuckolded. Very slowly raising her chin meant, 'I don't know', or 'I do know, but I won't tell you.' This, of course, is the response foreigners encounter from diffident peasants when they ask for the way. Moving an extended finger of one hand slowly back and forth under a raised chin is clearly and everywhere understood to convey: 'Nothing to do with me old chap; count me out; it is none of my business.' It has a real historical origin because a young man made the gesture in Garibaldi's face when he had just conquered Sicily in 1860. He had been sitting dozing on a low stone wall when the great general reined in his horse and called out to him, 'Will you not join us in our fight to free our brothers from the bloody tyranny of the Bourbon kings?' Garibaldi's response to the gesture was apparently to spur his horse on.

La Lollo was particularly good at closing both eyes in an otherwise immobile and expressionless face. This signifies resignation in front of the inevitable, acceptance of a difficult and unpleasant duty, as for instance in 'Haven't I told him again and again? But he is just stubborn and won't listen to reason.' Or, when apparently listening to someone's long argument, lifting one hand perpendicularly in a straight line as far as it will go and uttering merely one sound, a prolonged 'eeeeeeeeh'. Everybody in Italy knows that this means no less and no more than: 'How quickly you rush to conclusions, my friend, how complicated your reasoning, how unreasonable your hopes, when we all know the world has always been the same and all such bright solutions to our problems as yours have in turn just produced more and different probems.' It was an unforgettable Italian experience for me.

My life in London as a foreign correspondent was very different. I had my own circle with other women friends and Amelia had her set. Because she suffered severely from allergy and migraine attacks, things got very complicated for both of us. We loved each other, but all the obstacles that seemed constantly to be in our way upset us. When you have to deal with unusual situations in an Italian context, the British equivalents seem

comparatively easier to cope with, but while English 'eccentricities' used to be more or less confined to a particular social
set, in Italy they seemed to be universally spread.

Would anyone in Britain think of inflicting a leopard on his or
her teenage daughter? Such an animal, not fully grown but full of
mange and growling so loudly that it seemed to want to swallow
you up, suddenly arrived one Saturday, as a gift from her ex-
husband, at the Roman flat Amelia shared temporarily with her
daughter. Even if these animals are quite harmless, that is no
consolation if you had never come across one before. All
attempts to get the donor to take it back were in vain, for he had
disconnected his telephone. Other friends approached for help
naturally thought they were having their leg pulled. Finally,
Amelia managed to find a vet who, for a vast fee, came in the
middle of the night and told her what to do, anyhow until
Monday. People were afraid to touch the animal when she
jumped on a bed or chair and all that time Amelia had to hold
her own terrified and trembling Yorkshire terrier in her arms.
However, the leopard was only a small and typical illustration of
what could suddenly emerge out of the blue just to complicate
matters.

Animals were not really an obstacle, though as a city dweller I
was less used to them. Amelia, however, had grown up in the
country so had always been surrounded by them. As a young girl
in Italy, capable of extraordinary devotion and patience, she used
to sit up many nights with her sick horse, Bebe; she also
cherished a little lamb called Anita that she took with her and
placed in the saddle in front of her when riding her favourite
horse Stella. There was also a tame pig called Garibaldi.

All three girls had their favourites. Virginia, for instance, had
a small horse called Fiorello when she was ten, known for his
uncanny sense of time. Every morning at ten o'clock, he would
come out of his stable and cross the yard to the kitchen, where
he would be given some spaghetti and beer. One could tell the
time from his regular habits. The family had a farm called 'I
Galli' (The Cockerels) near Tivoli and the river Aniene, and
bordering Hadrian's villa among cypress and olive trees.

After all our ups and downs Amelia and I were finally married
on 21 December 1972 at the register office of the southwest
London district of Merton. Afterwards there was a brief blessing
by a priest friend in a nearby Catholic church and a celebration

19. Signing the register at our wedding in 1972.

lunch with 30 close friends at an Italian restaurant in Wimbledon.

We spent our honeymoon in Monte Carlo, where Amelia's mother then lived in a penthouse apartment with wonderful views over the Mediterranean and of the French hillside behind us. Our luggage going astray slightly marred our stay, though it turned up later. That added to my reputation as a pessimist because, on dispatching it before our departure at Heathrow, I had flippantly asked: 'I wonder whether we'll see that again?' I had not been to Monte Carlo to stay before. It seemed to be full of elegantly dressed elderly people, rather like walking ruins, but offering a spectacle of mode and demi-monde. We spent enjoyable days at the swimming pool behind the Casino and on trips to Beaulieu and Menton.

Back in London, we were able to move into our new Wimbledon home, an old cottage, the former gatehouse of a now built-up estate that Amelia had discovered and that we were able to acquire cheaply. We stayed there happily for 30 years, had many improvements made, like adding a top floor and laying out the ground floor with ceramic tiles, which gave us both Italianate feelings. There was a fine, half-wild garden at the back. The only snag was its name, 'Little Mynde', which, we had to explain to friends, was no reference to our brains but stood in Middle English for 'memory', and proving the best one as far as we were concerned.

Amelia helped to find and furnish a small house near us for my mother who had become increasingly unhappy in Vancouver. There were strained relations with her sister's second husband, causing jealousies between the two sisters and there were inevitable signs of ageing. At first, she thought that cars passing her block of flats at night were targeting their light beams on her as though to annoy her. Was this a delayed fear of persecution from her Italian war years, we wondered? We then brought her over to London to stay in a ground-floor apartment with a nice person living upstairs to look after her. We had hoped that she would be happy there listening to radio music, but the arrangement worked only for a year or two before her mental condition deteriorated. Eventually, she had to go to a clinic in our area where her dementia, as it was diagnosed, got rapidly worse. It was terribly sad to witness her decline: first, her piano playing, once so accomplished gradually became like a child's tinkling, and then her speech was affected. She forgot her English words, the language she had learnt last, but still knew Italian and German. Then these too went and there were only almost inaudible sounds and words. Her treatment in the clinic seemed fine; she ate well and the nurses were good at their difficult job, but we often went away crying, wondering what went on within her. Her eyes and smile still showed that she recognized us for a further three years.

However, the costs were rising steeply. We had to look for another place, eventually for a home for her but outside London, near Guildford, where we could visit her only sporadically. Once we found her sitting in a room with other patients, tied to her armchair, so that she would not fall out. It was pathetic to see her. We felt awful to have moved her. Then a few months later, we received the dreaded phone call that she had died in her sleep that night. She was born on 7 August 1898 and died, aged almost 85, on 2 July 1983. A mother's death is terrible. 'Do not stand at my grave and cry, I am not there. I did not die', we comforted ourselves, as with the psalm 'The Lord is my shepherd, I shall not want; He makes me lie down in green pastures.' There was an appropriate 'Farewell to the World', Schubert's *Abschied von der Erde:* 'Goodbye beautiful world! Only now do I know you and see how joy and pain are sent to us. Goodbye, all pervading pain! I thank you with moist eyes – I take joy with me, but leave you behind.'

Pets galore

Over the years our 'Little Mynde' developed not least into a gallery of animals, Amelia's friends in the first place who became mine too – dogs, cats, a white rat, tortoises, a duck, birds, pigeons, squirrels and beetles rescued from someone's paws. 'Animal gallery' was a fitting description in that nearly all of them were, after their death, immortalized by a friendly taxidermist and master of his craft. He was able to make them extraordinarily lifelike, stuffing them into polyurethane foam form and tailoring the skin to fit. He made the body parts he could not preserve, such as ears, eyes, noses, lips and tongues, by hand. In fact, these former darlings did not really seem dead at all, which was a good reason why 'Amelia's Valhalla', as we called it, had to be kept hidden away, out of sight, high up on a shelf in her downstairs office. She did not want to offend those likely to be discomfited by what to them might seem a black art, close to witchcraft and voodoo.

Amelia had not acquired many of these pets in normal ways at all. They somehow 'just happened' to her, either by literally appearing on our doorstep, it evidently having got around that

'Little Mynde' was a suitable shelter, or Amelia might have come across them in the street and they had followed her, waiting patiently outside until they were admitted, if found acceptable. There was nothing sentimental about her love of animals; it was more like a commonsense brother- or sisterhood, as would have been recognized at Assisi. She was naturally a valued and popular client of various vets in our neighbourhood, sometimes making history by going there with both murderer and victim, a cat for instance, and the bird it had nearly swallowed. Overall, the animals in her care came to respect the 'live and let live' principle she insisted on under our roof.

Some of the more unusual members of her clan probably reflected Amelia's character. One was Donna, brought to us as a wet bundle of beak and feathers, picked up by my wife's nephew, or rather the large mouth of Milton, his bulldog, on nearby Wimbledon Common. Milton had obediently spat her out, but the park warden was not interested; the little duck had possibly lost its family or been rejected by it. That happens all the time, he said. If you put them back in the water, they only perish, so it came to her. The local papers had recently reported Amelia as being behind a similar rescue operation. She had some of our neighbours, nuns from an Ursuline convent, climbing all over their roof to rescue an ailing pigeon and bringing it to us for further care.

Donna was actually no duckling at all, and thus originally wrongly named Donald. She did not have the male blue and yellow feathers but brown ones and seemed always to have an urge to lay eggs. She slowly recovered, bedded on a hot water bottle and scarf in an egg chest under Amelia's writing desk, whence she nevertheless exercised a dominant influence over the whole household. While used to a whole range of creatures, a duck had not been among them before. What was surprising, as we learnt more about ducks, was Donna's aversion to her own element. The little goldfish pond in our garden, the bathtub and the kitchen sink were all anathema to her. When my wife wanted to put her out into her natural environment, a big pond on the common, and some ducklings already seemed to show an interest, she escaped anxiously back to *terra firma*. Nonetheless, a daily bath was required, if only to keep her feathers in a supple condition. This took place behind the closed bathroom door and with a great deal of nervous splashing. Gradually, we found that to put up with her daily ordeal she had to have the bathtub filled with water no higher than ten centimetres. This enabled her to keep one foot firmly on the bathtub bottom and adopt a wading posture.

Donna loved going for walks inside and outside our house. We considered her needs in making the expensive decision to have our ground-floor area laid out with tiles, for no amount of training would get her to control her bowel movements. Ceramic tiles proved ideal, for all the maintenance they needed was watchfulness and a large supply of paper handkerchiefs. She resisted our attempts to make her wear waterproof baby panties; only when our nephew, her saviour, got married, she relented and put up with that ordeal, as well as with wearing a large white festive bow tie. She joined with all the other guests in a toast to the happy couple; naturally and inevitably, she briefly stole the show.

Normally Donna passed the day in my wife's office – my own study on the first floor and carpeted from wall to wall was happily out of her reach. Alternatively, she liked sitting on someone's lap or on some papers or books, especially just when these were constantly in use. This was a habit she had probably picked up from Amelia's two Ninis, the mother and daughter Yorkshire dogs with which Donna lived, more or less, in harmony. The dogs at least knew that she was *persona grata* and had to be left in peace, which made them eye her askance. As time went by they accepted her, especially as she had adopted dog manners, uttering her 'quack-quack' in a barking tone and rushing with them on a sudden cat hunt impulse into the garden. The animals had their meals in common. Donna seemed to like what the dogs got twice a day, but also sunflower seeds and vegetables, though they had to be watery and allowing her to slobber. Food did not seem to be as important in her life as it was for the dogs who would have given their soul for any titbits.

Donna clearly had a fixation on Amelia, following her wherever she went. Travelling by car, she had to sit in the back, although she would have preferred the driver's lap. She liked children and being patted by them. She left her eggs generously to Wendy, the recuperating pigeon, who made vain attempts to sit on them, but always fell off because they were too big for her.

The highlight of the day was the evening walk preceding Donna's bath with my wife, the two dogs and Ercolino, the cat.

Donna would bring up the rear, smelling lantern posts, garden fences and occasionally trying to embark on a little flight, but quickly and clumsily landing again on the pavement, which, as her instinct though not her experience told her, was unlike water. There was less of a traffic danger in the late evening, but the strange procession nevertheless caused passing motorists to stare, particularly those on their way home from the pub at the top of our road. 'Look, a duck', they would say, and maybe wonder how much they had had to drink, and if the duck had become something of a pink elephant.

Having reached the end of our road, the procession would obediently stop, sit down and wait while my wife crossed over to the opposite road to drop her letters into the postbox. When she returned they would greet her with a general joyous wagging of tails, as after a long absence, and would then start on the journey back. It happened on one of these trips that Donna took off and managed to fly into a big garden. There was a long search, but we could not find her in the darkness, and the notices we put up the next day 'Duck lost – reward offered' brought no result. Then we received the sad phone call that she had been found, the victim of a fox, but her attacker may have been frightened off because he had left her with a broken neck. She was two and a half years old. Our taxidermist then recreated her so that the deadly wound could not be seen, and she joined the others on the Valhalla shelf.

For us, too, life returned to normality, with the procession to the postbox taking on something of a memorial walk for some time. Mother and daughter Nini seemed not too sorry, since they had returned, with Ercolino the cat, to being sole centres of attention and affection. The Ninis were particularly happy examples of Amelia's training skills, small as they were, having learnt to follow her legs without a lead even in the densest crowd of a nearby Woolworth store or at Harrods, with the daughter Nini always running behind her mother. There was always a stampede into the garden through the cat flap in the kitchen door, when a strange cat or fox was scented. First, the cat rushed through in silence, followed by the two little barking dogs. Inevitably, daughter Nini would be hit on the nose by the flap's reverting movement. So, by way of an early Pavlovian lesson, we watched her learning to hesitate a second, so as to catch the flap without hurt on its next outward swing. We took the Ninis

everywhere, even on various summer opera visits to Glyndebourne where they stayed in the car through the acts, but joined
us for the customary picnic in the long interval. They enjoyed
these cultural outings, even once falling into the pond in the park
but being good swimmers got over it by only getting wet. Amelia
was, as usual, by long practice, prepared for all eventualities (in
addition, of course, to providing for our guests and us a three-
course dinner – the drinks were my responsibility). She had even
thought of towels so that, when dried, we could take the Ninis
back to the car to sleep while we returned to Mozart.

Discovering allergies

Amelia's love of nature and animals had something to do with
the various food and environmental allergies from which she
suffered throughout her life. Her illnesses had started during her
first pregnancy, and forced her to give up her medical studies.
This was long before the medical profession took allergies
seriously. Unsuccessfully, she sought professional help for what
to her were physical ills or addictive symptoms caused by
particles in the physical-chemical environment. Undoubtedly,
these affected a higher percentage of people in developed
countries than was admitted at the time, but doctors repeatedly
told her that her troubles were 'all in the mind', were mere
products of her imagination, and were probably related to some
psychic or sexual disorder. In other words, she was behaving like
a 'hysterical woman'. She resisted these explanations, which
undoubtedly applied to many people, but for her they were
definite physical, not imaginary, ailments like chronic pains,
migraines, real stomach upsets, and aching limbs and joints.
Occasionally, they caused her to be bedridden for days, until she
came across a revolutionary diet programme, pioneered by Dr
Richard Maccarness at his allergy clinic in Basingstoke, Surrey,
and later in Australia where he died in 1996. The diet helped her.
She became Maccarness's loyal chief disciple and propagator.

Maccarness was then drawing attention to what, in the later
twentieth century, was a new trend in medicine, developed in the
United States, and called 'clinical ecology'. It was a movement
away from the psychiatrist's couch, as well as from the ever-
increasing and self-defeating demand for pills. It saw man more
as a product of his environment and foods, the victim of all sorts
of culprits, sometimes cunningly disguised ones, that caused

allergic reactions to tobacco, dust, animal hair, foods, alcoholic spirits, cleaning materials, medicaments, aromatic fragrances, like chemical gases from coal and petrol, smoke from open fires, or an environment insufficiently understood by scientists. Until then, what they could not explain or had not been part of their medical studies, they tended to deny as existing at all or as having to be taken seriously. The reaction was typical of the medical profession, as it is of other academics, particularly, it seems to me, also of theologians.

Maccarness had developed a simple 'elimination diet' that gradually got to the root of what patients could tolerate and what they must always avoid. Although it was a restrictive diet, it improved Amelia's condition to a level of near normality, which she had not enjoyed for many years. In 1978, she founded 'Action Against Allergy', a registered charity based in Richmond, Surrey, now with many branches also in other countries. The aim was to spread greater awareness of the physical nature of allergies among a then still largely sceptical medical profession, press for its recognition by the National Health Service, and help fellow sufferers. Amelia was aided in this work by her friend Aeronwy Thomas-Ellis, daughter of Dylan Thomas, the poet, and herself an allergy sufferer. The campaign for better public understanding of the problem of allergies has made great progress in recent decades, not least through Amelia's contribution and the work of her organization, though the root cause of allergies remains yet to be discovered. In this sense, she was a true pioneer and in the vanguard of a movement that has since been taken up by others, individuals and voluntary organizations.

In 1980, she wrote *The Unsuspected Enemy*, a moving account of her life and medical history, and the book was translated into many languages, including even Finnish. That unknown 'enemy' affects people in different ways, she wrote, and described how she had originally and ignorantly tried to stick to what she had considered 'harmless foods'. What could have been less dangerous, she thought, than boiled chicken? Then she discovered that the innocuous chicken had been reared on wheat products and that it was these to which Amelia happened to be wholly allergic. Another danger proved to be a gas leak, long denied by the Gas Board, which we remedied eventually by changing over to an electric cooker. Slowly her condition improved, at least to the extent that she had learnt what to do without.

Amelia was born with many gifts, chief of which were an inner fortitude and a deep religious faith that enabled her to confront the many adversities in her life. She was admirably selfless and never complained. In that she owed much to the example of St Teresa of Lisieux, whose autobiography she particularly liked and to whom she had a special devotion. She had a strong dose of common sense, which I, like many males, lacked. She was at home both in Italian and English ways, which complemented my own German–Austrian background.

Amelia's English schooling also made her an invaluable collaborator and critic in judging my work. She often helped me, in the course of my historical research among the Cambridge Acton papers, to decipher private letters in early nineteenth-century French or Italian handwriting.

Her many illnesses undoubtedly blighted our marriage, especially in the last two years of her life. She had to spend these in a private clinic that could cope both with her continuing basic allergies and, independently, a worsening osteoporosis from which she became bedridden, so it became impossible for her to remain at home. Fortunately, it happened in the course of my own retirement and freelance activities, so it was not difficult to cope with for me. We certainly became closer in a life of half separation in her clinic, watching TV programmes together in the daytime, which normally we would not have done. Reading became impossible because of her difficulties in merely holding a book.

Thus, Manchester United, Amelia's heroes, the Wimbledon tennis and annual ice-skating championships had a bonding effect on both of us, which they would ordinarily not have had. Cilla Black, Esther Rantzen and some other TV personalities, with their off-putting stances, one would otherwise gladly have missed. For my sake, Amelia put up with Colombo or even police series like The Bill. In her physical helplessness, much of the outside world seemed like a breath of fresh air. It was interesting that in the environment of the clinic, where we occasionally saw such pitifully handicapped human beings, we became more closely united and appreciated each other more through our common memories and, luckily, active minds. We suddenly needed so very little to make us value our togetherness for what little time that lasted. As far as we were concerned, we could have done without some of the entertainments the clinic organized, although others enjoyed them. Nevertheless, she loved the occasional visits by a man who brought his tame animals – a monkey that at once became attached to Amelia, or a blind owl that radiated enormous dignity by an ability to turn its head right round. We also relived some of our common Italian memories. Amelia was surprisingly thoughtful in the understanding she showed for Pope Pius XII who had done much privately to help endangered Jews in the Hitler years, though his diplomatic silences pained her greatly. She may also have come close to a right diagnosis of his well-known bad temper as being due to allergies. Suffering all his life from stomach troubles, his doctors put him on a milk diet, which probably merely exacerbated his condition. Unfortunately, we were unable to prove her thesis because, for that, a postmortem operation of his stomach would have been necessary.

Amelia and I also had happy and joyful memories of our times in Italy, of holidays in Tuscany, the Etruscan hills, Sardinia, Naples or Capri, in the mountains or at the seaside. There were also warm Roman summer nights to remember of being enthralled by *Cavalleria Rusticana* in the Thermae of Caracalla or Verdi's *Simon Boccanegra* in Milan's Castello Sforzesco. Scarcely any part of Italy had been left untouched by the history of our love, and this charm remained for her until her death and continues for me who am left behind.

Given Amelia's weakened physical condition, her death, a few weeks after her eighty-second birthday, was not unexpected, though its impact on me is still fresh. On that Friday in September 2001, I had left her as usual in the early evening, but some time later, I had a telephone call from one of the nurses to say that she wanted to see me. I found her pleased that I had come but unable to speak. I sat by her bed, holding her hand but with her back turned to me because this was a more comfortable position. Her breathing was hardly audible; from time to time, the nurse came in to feel her pulse. Then, past midnight on Saturday 27 September 2001, the nurse confirmed that in her sleep life had quietly left her.

Only an emaciated face with an open mouth remained of Amelia's once strong and beautiful features. I did not cry as I might easily when moved by music when Mimi dies in Rodolfo's arms in *La Bohème* or similar moments in literature. This was a very different rupture; it made me feel dried out, empty, alone. It was the sudden break of a real attachment. All vision, sound, touch and smell were off. Gradually letting go of her lifeless hand, I felt terribly sad, of course, as I had felt after my mother's death, merely remotely aware that life had gone where I would follow as billions before and after us.

According to my faith, these loved ones had been taken up in the arms of Christ and the Communion of Saints and Angels, and all was just a physical separation. Faced with the mystery of death, I also knew that for countless others there was just no survival after death, just nothing but our sentimental wishful thinking, as Alfred Ayer, the philosopher and atheist, had found when he returned from supposed death and was merely confronted by a blinding light. However, Amelia and I had lately prayed together, not nearly enough as it seemed afterwards, the Our Father and Hail Mary, which, by mere repetition, has a soothing, almost hypnotic effect, not to induce sleep but a sense that somehow our prayers are heard, and not just in our imagination or as a self-deceiving hoax.

Kind people in the clinic told me to go home and get some sleep. There were things to do in the morning, register the death, prepare the funeral and Requiem Mass, and notify many people. There was fortunately help to pack her belongings. Then I left the little third-floor room for the last time. For more than two years it had been hers, looking out now on the autumnal misty Richmond Park, though, from her bed she would only have seen the sky. She knew to the last moment that the earth was there and beautiful, not all sad, full of illness or evil. I also knew that she would now be at peace, to the last moment with her God-given spirit, courage, mind, humanity and resignation unimpaired.

Amelia was a great inspiration and not only to those close to her. She was also a delightful person and companion, kind and caring and always thinking of helping other people in spite of her own disabilities. In fact, it was these that had caused her to achieve her life's aim, as it were, to put allergies 'on the map'. Having herself been let down again and again by alleged medical experts, she proceeded to demonstrate to them and to the world the lessons of her own experience, namely that there were significant health problems that the profession was failing to

20. My late wife Amelia had the rare distinction of being nominated
'Woman of the Year' in both London and Rome for her work on
behalf of those with allergies.

address. In word and deed she persuasively showed a public
overfed on psychological jargon that, as often as not, it is simply
'not all in the mind'.

Thousands of those like herself suffering acute physical ills
that were not taken sufficiently seriously by doctors, have thus
come to bless her for founding Action Against Allergy, both as a
pressure group for publicizing the need for medical help that was
so slow in coming, and for converting a few pioneer doctors who
were willing to listen and learn. Their number, however, has
grown considerably in this country and abroad within very few
years, so she was still able to feel satisfaction at having reached
her aim. The medical profession and the National Health Service
now take allergies seriously.

I am happy to think that one woman's determination and
efforts are largely behind that achievement, even though science
has yet to discover the real cause of these wide-ranging physical
illnesses and why they affect some people and not others. Faith,

hope and love are summed up in the message of Amelia's life, and what more fitting ending could I wish for an account of my own life.

Index